Wines of South America

Wines of South America

Monty Waldin

MITCHELL BEAZLEY

Wines of South America
by Monty Waldin

First published in Great Britain in 2003 by Mitchell Beazley, an imprint of Octopus Publishing Group Limited, 2–4 Heron Quays, London E14 4JP.

ISBN 1 84000 609 9

Photographs by Jason Lowe

Commissioning Editor: Hilary Lumsden
Executive Art Editor: Yasia Williams-Leedham
Managing Editor: Emma Rice
Editors: Susan Low, Wink Lorch
Indexer: Hilary Bird
Production: Alexis Coogan
Maps: Encompass Graphics Ltd, Brighton, UK

Typeset in Univers and Jansen
Printed and bound by Toppan Printing Company in China

Mitchell Beazley would like to thank **Catena Zapata**, **Valdivieso**, and **Bibendum Wine Ltd.**, London, for their support in sponsoring the photoshoot for this book in South America. We also extend our thanks to everyone at Catena Zapata in Argentina and Valdivieso in Chile for the generosity, hospitality and assistance offered to the photographer, Jason Lowe.

The Publisher acknowledges that the photography contained throughout this book will not always correspond to the text contained in the section in which the photograph appears.

Acknowledgments

I'd like to thank the following people, listed in alphabetical order, for their assistance during the writing of this book:

Marina Ashton, expatriate, for sheltering me during severe floods in Chile's Maipo Valley, and for ensuring that even as the waters threatened her own house both I and my writing equipment remained dry.
John Atkinson Master of Wine (MW), of Adnams, Southwold, for allowing me access to his uncensored written critical observations of various South American wines.
Gérard Basset MW, sommelier, of the Hotel du Vin, England, for giving me the chance to taste South American wines I might otherwise have missed.
Iván Bluske, wine writer, for introducing me to Tarija, Bolivia, and for facilitating my debut on Bolivian TV.
Tom Coulson, and Martin Darlison, cartographers of Encompass Graphics, for creating the maps for this book.
Stefan Dorst, winemaker, for accompanying me on my first winery visits in Chile in 1994, and for answering technical questions on grape-growing and winemaking.
Christopher Fielden, wine writer, who unstintingly provided contact details of wine people I sought to interview, having just completed his own book.
Andrew and Emma Graham-Brown, friends, for giving me a peaceful place to write when my personal circumstances meant that to do this at home was impossible.
Karine Guillemin, of Westbury Communications, London, for her patience, indefatigable support and supreme organization during visits to Argentina and Uruguay.
Andrew Jefford, wine writer, for leading by example.
Richard Kershaw, winemaker, for helping make this and other books more entertaining to write.
Santiago Laugero, businessman, for finding me a quiet but centrally located abode during an unexpectedly extended stay in Mendoza, Argentina.
Wink Lorch, writer/editor, for her necessarily robust but constructive editing of the first draft of this book.
Susan Low, writer/editor, for editing the final draft of this book with typical sensitivity.
Jason Lowe, for his sensational photography.

Hilary Lumsden, of Mitchell Beazley, for overseeing every aspect of this book's gestation with efficiency, humour, and flair.
Marcelo Marasco, of ProMendoza, for effortlessly organizing at short notice visits to dozens of Argentine wineries against a backdrop of intense political, social, and economic turmoil.
Josimar Melo, wine writer, for generously helping me access Brazil's wine scene.
Heinrich Neisskenwirth, of Switzerland's *Institut für Marktökologie*, for helping me locate the men and women behind Chile's increasingly abundant organic vineyards.
Laure Pagès, partner, for enduring with equanimity my highs and lows while writing this book, and for coming to Peru when fatigue and illness threatened to engulf me.
Emma Rice, of Mitchell Beazley, for coordinating all things editorial.
Cliff Roberson, wine merchant, for pulling many corks and for organizing my first winemaking job in Chile.
Jancis Robinson MW, wine writer, for helping me target my Brazil research more effectively.
Dominic Shiach, director, for taking me to Chile's Atacama desert in 1994 to film a total solar eclipse, ensuring I thought of Chile as something other than a wine producer.
Duncan & Victoria Simpson, entrepreneurs, for driving me around Uruguay without losing their temper or bearings, despite the absence of road signs and, in many cases, roads.
Rebecca Spry of Mitchell Beazley, for asking me to write this book.
Tom Stevenson, wine writer, for sharing South American facts I should have known but didn't.
Prof. Tim Unwin, of the Royal Holloway College, Surrey, for sharing his knowledge of South America's historical wine geography.
Yasia Williams-Leedham, of Mitchell Beazley who, with Design Revolution, developed a design structure for this book to compliment my idiosyncracies as a writer.
Graham Wynde, bon vivant, for giving me food, advice, wine and information (in that order) when I needed them most.
Dr Marc Zeise, of *Universidad de Santiago de Chile*, for providing a sanctuary for me in Santiago de Chile on more than one occasion.
And to the hundreds of taxi, bus and private car drivers who enabled both me and my equipment to travel around South America and return in one piece.

introduction

As a wine writer, I am often asked to name my favourite wine. Because I've been fortunate enough to taste so many great wines, I usually warn the questioner that a truthful answer may take several hours. Naming the most influential wine I've ever tasted, on the other hand, is easier: it was a Chilean Cabernet Sauvignon. It was the first South American wine I had tried, and that bottle was to have a profound effect on my career as a wine writer. In fact, it eventually led to the writing of this book. I had first encountered Cabernet Sauvignon in its Bordeaux homeland some years before, while working as a trainee winemaker at a family-owned château during the 1989 harvest. What struck me most about this Chilean wine was not just its incredibly deep colour, or its bold, ripe, fruit flavours, but the clarity, the richness, and the smooth, silky insistency of its texture.

I'd not tasted anything in Bordeaux with such comparable "naturalness" of texture, even though I had managed to visit some of Bordeaux's top châteaux during my days off from winemaking. And no one in my local wine shop back in Britain, where I'd bought that Chilean bottle, could tell me why I might find Chilean Cabernet Sauvignon to be so utterly different from its Bordeaux counterpart.

After conducting some research, it occurred to me that one possible reason why that Chilean bottle had so impressed my young taste-buds was the fact that Chile's vines grow on their own roots. Vines in Europe must first be grafted onto the rootstocks of other vine types in order to make them resistant to a pernicious soil louse called phylloxera, which attacks vine roots.

This conjured up an image in my mind of Chilean vines running wild across the landscape, like barefoot children, in contrast to the Bordeaux vines, which were not allowed outside without first putting on their shoes and tying their laces tightly. The Chilean vines seemed to me more vivacious, more in tune with their surroundings, and less inhibited – wilder at heart.

When I discovered that most vines in Argentina were ungrafted, too, I pulled the cork on an Argentine wine made from Malbec, another grape variety that, like Cabernet Sauvignon, originates from southwest France.

below The Andes, formed over seventy million years ago, divide Chile and Argentina, two important wine-producing nations.

It, too, had the vibrancy and energy the Chilean wine had possessed.

I resolved to work in a South American winery as soon as possible, and, in 1994, landed a job as part of a winemaking team in Chile – ironically, helping a leading winemaker from Bordeaux, one of the first "flying winemakers" to work in South America. Around this time, I began to write about my winemaking experiences and – more by luck than judgment – became a wine writer, while still doing the odd bit of winemaking, too.

But I could see straight away that flying winemakers such as the one I worked with were to going to influence significantly first Chile, and then Argentina. Under their influence, South American wines would change from the musty, oxidized styles favoured by South American wine drinkers to the bolder, cleaner "fruit-driven" wines favoured by wine drinkers in Europe and North America.

Part of the process was to correct the basic winemaking faults that had become engrained in wineries isolated for generations by political dictatorships and economic embargoes. But as dictatorships turned to democracies (all the countries featured in this book are now run by democratically elected governments) local winemakers caught the new mood, and became more confident of their own abilities – and the potential quality of their grapes.

above Winter prunings lie ready to be mulched into the soil in Central Mendoza. Decomposing prunings return nutrients to the soil.

The result was a new wave of South American wines, that offered excellent quality and value. Chile, to which the largest chapter in this book is devoted, still produces arguably the world's finest value-for-money reds; and while not all critics are convinced that Chile's most expensive, top-rank wines justify their high prices, the country's offerings remain unbeatable for attainable, everyday enjoyment.

Argentina is emerging, too, after many false starts, as a producer of quality wine. Although Argentina's current economic turmoil is indeed a bitter experience for the country's long-suffering people, the dark cloud does has a silver lining: the economic crisis means that Argentine wines are better able to compete with Chilean wines on the international market. What's more, Argentina now offers the best value in South America for wine tourism. The currency is cheap and the vineyards are simply some of the most beautifully and dramatically sited in South America – or indeed the world.

Of South America's smaller wine nations, both Uruguay and Bolivia boast governments that are keen to support their wine producers. Of the two countries, Uruguay is farther down the road to maximizing its winemaking potential; its most serious red wines are based on the undervalued and relatively unknown Tannat grape. I hope the space this book gives to Uruguay will go some way towards encouraging this often-ignored country's efforts, for, at its best, Uruguayan Tannat is well adapted to modern tastes, offering a full, rich, deeply coloured mouthful of red wine. And while Brazil, the world's fifteenth largest wine producer, largely continues to style its wines for the thirsty home market, a number of producers capable of producing wines of export quality are emerging. But Brazil remains peripheral on the global wine stage, as does Peru (South America's oldest wine-producing country) and Venezuela, although they do feature in these pages.

Not all wine-producing countries in South America are covered in this book, however, for several reasons. In Ecuador and Colombia, the wines are essentially made from lesser-quality grape varieties, or from imported grape juice. Paraguay's small winemaking community is mainly made up of German expatriates, who consume most of the wine produced locally. Consequently, none of these countries are important from an export point of view.

Each country featured in this book has its own introduction, covering wine regions and wine styles, organized by wine colour, then by grape variety. Wine producers and the names of their specific wines are listed in alphabetical order after grape variety or wine style entries. Longer entries, with detailed descriptions of individual producers, can be found in the "Notable Producers" sections, which follow the chapters on each main wine-producing country.

To help potential visitors to South America's wine regions, contact details for each producer are provided, either telephone numbers, email addresses, or website addresses. Where there are no such details listed or producers do not appear on the maps it is because no permament address was forthcoming at the time of writing. Increasingly, South American wineries, particularly in Chile, Argentina, and Brazil, are becoming part of organized wine routes. A growing number have visitor facilities, such as tasting rooms, souvenir shops, restaurants and accommodation. However you'll save time and potential disappointment by calling ahead to arrange a visit with a named individual, rather than just turning up with no prior appointment. That said, some wineries, particularly the larger ones, are open to receive drop-in visitors during the summer months (November to April).

It's also worth bearing in mind that South Americans enjoy frequent public and religious holidays, when wineries and their offices are closed. Also, religious festivals specific to individual towns or villages are still quite common – another reason to call ahead before finalizing an itinerary.

South America is the world's second-largest wine-producing region, just behind Europe. Yet, there is still much to discover about South American wine. South America's wine industry is different from that of other "New World" countries. Being a nation of recent European immigrants, wine was drunk, rather than exported. But, as wine becomes increasingly global, South American wines are being discovered and acclaimed by drinkers outside their homeland for the first time. I hope this book will inspire you to discover more about them, as they inspired me.

CHILE

chile

Chile produces the perfect modern wine style: smooth, elegant, fruity wines that are fresh enough to drink with food and affordable enough to please budget-conscious consumers. Chile owes its success to natural conditions, which are sometimes (justifiably) described as a "wine-growing paradise". To this can be added a fairly stable economy, which makes Chile's wines among the world's most competitively priced. Throw in Chilean winemakers' proven ability to supply just the style of wine that consumers want, and you have the most successful wine industry in South America – and one of Planet Wine's most coveted.

Chile's reputation for being a wine-growing paradise rests on a number of factors. The climate is sunny enough to ripen any grape variety you care to plant. The growing season is long enough for grapes to ripen into late autumn, allowing for complex wines. Low humidity levels and high luminosity (bright skies) mean vine fungal diseases are rare, making organic vineyard management as easy as anywhere in the world. Cool nights, a product of coastal breezes off the Pacific or downdraughts from the Andes, keep the grapes from overheating, allowing them to retain their intense flavours and colours, and providing Chilean wines with their characteristic vivacity. Grape-growers can relax, knowing that if it gets too dry or too hot, plentiful irrigation is provided by snow-melt and rainfall from the Andes. Chilean winemakers can relax, too, knowing that the best grapes will almost certainly have enough colour, sugar and acidity without too much interference from them in the winery.

key facts about chile

Bordeaux-style Cabernet Sauvignon and Merlot offer **unbeatable quality** and value for money; **remarkable Rhône-style** Syrah (Shiraz) reds starting to appear; more refined white wines as vineyards shift to **cooler areas**; Carmenère remains **unique**; modernization and **versatility** produce styles suited to current tastes; new hillside vineyard sites mean better wines; **ungrafted vines** and a dry sunny climate create perfect conditions for **organic viticulture**.

Wine-growers from California's mountain vineyards or from around the Mediterranean could claim to enjoy many of the conditions that make Chile almost perfect, too. Yet Chile is unique in one respect: most of the country's vineyards are ungrafted. Phylloxera, the parasitic louse to which *Vitis vinifera* – wine grapevines – are intolerant (a phylloxera infestation in the mid- to late nineteenth century devastated Europe's vines), was for many years prevented from entering Chile by natural physical barriers – the Andes, the Pacific Ocean and the Atacama Desert. It seems likely that phylloxera has been brought to Chile from Europe on infected vine cuttings since then, yet the louse has not survived here; no one knows why.

This means that most Chilean vines (*see* Casablanca Valley, p.25) can grow on their own roots. In most parts of the world, vines must first be grafted onto phylloxera-resistant roots. Ungrafted vines enjoy better sap flow, live much longer, and are inherently more resistant to pests, diseases, and bad weather than their grafted counterparts are.

Vines were brought to Chile from Bordeaux and other European regions by wealthy entrepreneurs, just before the phylloxera outbreak hit Europe in the mid-nineteenth century. Neither these vines, nor cuttings taken from them, have ever been grafted. Some Chilean producers claim that ungrafted vines are the reason why Chile's red wines are alleged to contain the

N

BOLIVIA

Arica

Iquique

Calama

Antofagasta

San Salvador
de Jujuy

OCÉANO PACÍFICO

Andes

San Miguel
de Tucuman

Copiapó

CHILE

ARGENTINA

La Serena
Coquimbo

San Juan

Cordoba

Viña del Mar
Valparaíso

Mendoza

Rosario

■ **Santiago**

Rancagua

San Rafael

Buenos Aires

Talca

Chillán

Talcahuano
Concepción

Río Bio Bio

Temuco

Andes

Neuquen

Bahía Blanca

Valdivia

Puerto Montt

Patagonia

Coihaique

Cochrane

El Calafate

Río Gallegos

Punta Arenas

0–500 ft/0–152 m

500–1,000 ft/152–304 m

1,000–2,000 ft/304–608 m

2,000+ ft/608+ m

0 km   400

0 miles   400

highest levels of "heart-friendly" compounds compared to wines from any other country. No truly independent research exists to substantiate this link, however.

But temptation exists in every Garden of Eden. Chile's beneficial growing conditions, plentiful irrigation and the rather too-fertile soils of the Central Valley, where most vineyards are planted, encourage overcropping. The result can be cheap, bland wine. Lazy grape-growing also means that most Chilean wines are boosted with acidification in the winery; this process shouldn't be necessary – even if the levels used are are generally lower than in Argentina. Complacency means that when tougher harvests do occur, usually caused by the El Niño weather phenomenon (last seen in 1998), Chile's lazier winemakers are unprepared. Partly to blame is the fact that conglomerates, rather than more hands-on

family producers, dominate Chile's wine industry. For these bigger companies, wine is currently a more profitable commodity than fruit crops, spirits, beer, processed foods, and mining. But often wine is just that: a commodity. It is no coincidence that along with its value-for-money wines Chile also produces South America's most overpriced wines. The conglomerates sometimes think they can blend a Reserva-level Merlot with a Reserva-level Cabernet Sauvignon to make an "icon" red wine and charge quadruple the price for it, without anyone either noticing or objecting.

What's more, few of the largest employers provide insurance and health-care cover for the vineyard workers, the bedrock of any wine operation. As these workers must switch between the wine and fruit industries according to the seasons (they work under

temporary contracts), they must pay health and insurance cover from their minimal hourly wage. This means that field-workers have no realistic means of challenging employers when health problems occur, often years later. It is true that field-workers in other parts of the world endure similar working conditions to those in Chile, but human rights activists claim that five per cent of children born to agricultural workers in Chile suffer from deformities; no Chilean winery has yet categorically proved that pesticides used in their vineyards are not the cause. Wineries now provide protective clothing, and educate workers about the safe handling of dangerous chemicals.

Investment in wine from within Chile and by foreigners such as Miguel Torres and Franciscan

Vineyards (*see* Caliterra and Veramonte in the following section) brought in the foreign winemaking expertise that Chile lacked until the early 1990s. The key was convincing Chile to burn its old beech (*rauli*) vats and adopt the more hygienic stainless steel or epoxy-lined concrete ones. Almost overnight the intense, vibrant fruit flavours in Chile's wines were revealed to an appreciative world audience. Chile became the world's fifth largest wine exporter in the late 1990s.

Chile's export success has sparked a wave of planting. Between 1995 and 2001, the vineyard area doubled to more than 106,000 hectares (ha) (260,000 acres), which is about the same size as Bordeaux, or half the size of California's or Argentina's vineyard hectarage. The challenge for Chile is to continue to make fruit-driven everyday wines from its young vineyards and, at the same time, to prove conclusively that it can produce world-class wines to rival the best of Bordeaux, the Rhône, or California.

The way to do this is to resist the temptation of high grape yields, and to take more risks in the winery. Chilean wineries, inspired by Australia, New Zealand, and California, have gone from being among the world's dirtiest to being the most oversanitized – places where, for example, wild yeasts present on the grape-skins are sterilized in favour of laboratory yeasts giving predictable, standardized flavours. (Errázuriz's Wild Ferment wines are among the exceptions.)

Also, almost all Chilean wines made without barrel-fermentation or barrel-ageing are protected from oxidation by inert gas during winemaking. Although the inert gas does mean oxidized, vinegar-like smells and flavours are largely a thing of the past, it also means that the wines fail to develop their full personality in bottle – and age rather quickly, too. Control-freak winemaking like this will mean the most complex fruits of Chile's wine-growing paradise will remain obscured. This would be of great sadness to those who believe that Chile is as good a place to grow and make wine as any in the world.

Chilean Wine Styles (By Colour)

RED BLENDS

Chilean reds made from more than one variety revolve around Cabernet Sauvignon, with Bordeaux grapes such as Merlot, Carmenère, Cabernet Franc, Malbec (and occasionally Petit Verdot), completing the blend more often than Mediterranean ones such as Syrah or Mourvèdre. Top Bordeaux-style blends such as Almaviva, Apaltagua (Grial), Canepa (Finísimo), Casa Lapostolle (Clos Apalta), Casa Silva (Quinta Generación), Errázuriz (Don Maximiano Founder's Reserve), J.&F. Lurton Chile (Gran Araucano), Montes ("M"), MontGras (Ninquén), Morandé (House of Morandé), Quebrada de Macul (Domus Aurea), Santa Laura (Laura Hartwig Gran Reserva), and Valette Fontaine (El Principal) usually justify their high prices, while others such as Baron Philippe de Rothschild Maipo Chile (Escudo Rojo), Chadwick Estate, Córpora (Caminante), Seña, Torreón de Paredes (Don Amado), and Viña Casablanca (Neblus) remain less convincing. Red wine blends including non-Bordeaux grapes tend to show even richer, headier fruit, with Antiyal, TerraMater, Viña Leyda (all Syrah/Cabernet Sauvignon), Santa Rita's Floresta (Syrah/Merlot), Miguel Torres Chile's Cordillera (Carignan, Merlot, Syrah), Torreón de Paredes (Don Amado), and Valdivieso's oddball Caballo Loco all being noteworthy.

WHITE BLENDS

With the exception of Casa Lapostolle's dry Tanao, Chilean white wine blends tend to be made in a late-harvest (sweetish) style.

Chilean Wine Styles (By Grape Variety)

CABERNET FRANC (RED)

Cabernet Franc is used mainly to provide a floral, violet-like backdrop to red wine blends (*see* above), but Francisco de Aguirré, Tabontinaja, and Valdivieso bottle delicious varietal Cabernet Francs.

CABERNET SAUVIGNON (RED)

Cabernet Sauvignon produces Chile's most renowned red wines, and is the major contributor to red wine blends (*see* above). Cabernet Sauvignon now covers one-third of Chile's vineyard area; between 1997 and 2000, plantings of the variety doubled. Young-vine Chilean Cabernet can taste particularly hollow, especially when it comes from flat, fertile ground, where most of the new vineyards have been sited. However, well-balanced vines on good sites produce the deeply coloured, ripe, insistent-textured reds that set Chilean Cabernet Sauvignon apart. *See* Baron Philippe de Rothschild Bordeaux Maipo Chile (Mapa), Canepa (Canepa Organic), Carmen (Gold Reserve), Casa Lapostolle (Classic), Casa Rivas, Concha y Toro (Don Melchor Private Reserve), Cono Sur, Cousiño Macul (Antiguas Reservas), Errázuriz, Haras de Pirque (Elegance), La Fortuna, Miguel Torres Chile (Manso de Velasco), Montes (Montes Alpha), MontGras (Ninquén), Morandé (Vitisterra), San Pedro (Castillo de Molina, Cabo de Hornos), Santa Inés/De Martino, Santa Laura (Laura Hartwig), Santa Rita (Casa Real), Segú, TerraMater, Valle Frío, and Veramonte.

CARIGNAN (RED)

With low yields, Carignan's late-ripening berries give wild red wines of slightly astringent, edgy texture. Miguel Torres Chile, Morandé, Odfjell, Segú, and Valdivieso use Carignan to good effect.

CARMENÈRE (RED)

Carmenère vines came to Chile from Bordeaux in the 1850s and were then mixed up with Merlot, doing neither variety any favours. Chilean Carmenère was officially recognized as distinct from Merlot only in 1998. Chile is the only country openly producing Carmenère red wines (the vine has effectively disappeared from Bordeaux, where it is sometimes called Grande Vidure, but is still widespread in parts of northern Italy – where it is also mistaken for Merlot), but these have too often tasted like unripe rhubarb. This is because Carmenère needs much warmer vineyard sites than Merlot does if its thick skins are to ripen. It also needs to have its potentially high yields drastically curbed. When fully ripe, Carmenère shows a very deep colour and exudes concentrated wild redcurrant and cassis fruit mixed with coffee-bean flavours. It is one of South America's most distinctive wines. *See* Aguatierra, Apaltagua (Grial), Aresti, Calina, Caliterra, Carmen, Carpe Diem, Casa Rivas (Gran Reserva), Casa Silva (Doña Dominga and Altura), Concha y Toro (Terrunyo), Errázuriz (Single Vineyard), Los Robles (Traidcraft), Morandé, Santa Inés/De Martino (Legado de Armida), Santa Laura, Santa Rita, Segú, TerraNoble (Reserva), Valdivieso, Veramonte, Viña Casablanca, and Viña Leyda.

CHARDONNAY (WHITE)

Chilean wineries that make white wine always include a Chardonnay. Most are clean, fresh, tropical examples sold at fair prices for early quaffing. Others are made buttery from malolactic fermentation (*see* introduction to the Southern region, p.42) or creamy from oak fermentation, but few rise above the ordinary. Chile's finest Chardonnays from Aquitania (SOLdeSOL), Errázuriz (Wild Ferment and La Escultura), Haras de Pirque (Equus), and Santa Laura (Laura Hartwig) combine proficient winemaking with complex, rather than run-of-the-mill, grapes. These producers eliminated underperforming vine stocks, slashed yields, and sought new vineyard sites, not just in Chardonnay-friendly Casablanca Valley but throughout the rest of Chile as well. Casablanca Valley provides Chile's most reliable Chardonnays: examples from Concha y Toro (Amelia), Cono Sur (Visión), Laroche & Coderch, Morandé (Dueto), and Santa Rita (Medalla Real) share a cool, citrus character with

below Chile's Casablanca Valley had no vines twenty years ago. Now, this oasis of green produces Chile's finest white wines.

a rich middle of grapefruit and soft oak. Other good examples from Carmen (Reserve), Montes (Montes Alpha), and Valdivieso contain grapes from both Casablanca and from warmer regions for balance.

COT (RED)

See Malbec.

GEWURZTRAMINER (WHITE)

Gewurztraminer's strong rose petals and Turkish Delight character is toned down in Chile either by blending with other varieties or by using special fermentation yeasts to make it more consumer friendly.

MALBEC (RED)

Chilean Malbec is as deeply coloured as its famed Argentine counterpart, and its black fruit is easier on the gums than Chile's much more widely planted

below Aquitania's red wine vineyards on the outskirts of Santiago in Maipo Valley from which the "Paul Bruno" wine is drawn.

Carmenère. Malbecs from Bisquertt, Caliterra, Canepa, La Fortuna, Hacienda El Condor, Lomas de Cauquenes (labelled "Côt"), Montes, MontGras, Morandé, Santa Inés/De Martino, TerraMater, Valdivieso, and Viu Manent merit serious attention.

MERLOT (RED)

Merlot plantings more than tripled between 1994 and 1999, and by 2001 they officially accounted for twelve per cent of Chile's total vineyard area. However, in 1994, vine experts had discovered that perhaps eighty per cent of Chilean "Merlot" was really Carmenère – a much later-ripening grape – and that many vineyard plots contained a mix of the two. Mixed vineyards need to be picked separately (*see* Concha y Toro) if the wines are to taste ripe. Classic Chilean Merlot displays a ripe raspberry character, particularly (but not always) when grown on slightly cooler sites, as wines from

Carmen, Cono Sur, La Misión, Santa Laura, and Segú demonstrate. Vines that have been stressed by poor farming (too much fertilizer or irrigation), or too hot a vineyard site, turn from ripe-raspberry to baked-jam flavours (examples from Rapel's Colchagua Valley are particularly at risk). The jammy, concentrated flavours of Casa Lapostolle (Cuvée Alexandre) and Montes somehow remain elegant.

MOURVÈDRE (RED)

This thick-skinned grape needs a dry climate and moist soils to ripen. *See* San Esteban, Tarapacá, and VOE.

PAÍS (RED)

País survives in Chile from the Spanish conquest; until the mid-1990s it remained Chile's most widely planted wine grape. It is no longer being planted and Chile's wine authorities have banned its name from wine labels for export, hence Lomas de Cauquenes simply call their bottling Viñas Viejas (old vines).

PETITE SIRAH (RED)

This sturdy red grape, unrelated to "real" Syrah, is used for blending by Carmen.

PETIT VERDOT (RED)

This ultra-late ripening, but potentially super-powerful, Bordeaux variety is normally used in small quantities to season red wine blends. *See* Bisquertt, Haras de Pirque, Selentia, and Seña.

PINOT NOIR (RED)

Chile produces South America's most stylish Pinot Noirs; Uruguay is too humid and Argentina too hot for this fussy grape. In contrast, cooler areas in Chile, such as Casablanca Valley and the newly developed Leyda zone of the Aconcagua region, Chimbarongo in the Rapel Valley, and parts of the Maule Valley and the Southern region seem ideal for it. Errázuriz (Wild Ferment) and Cono Sur (20 Barrels) produce Chile's most interesting Pinot Noirs, with well-crafted examples from Laroche & Coderch, Morandé (Dueto), Viña Leyda, and Valdivieso ("V"). The overall standard should improve as Chile's Pinot Noir vineyards age. Most vines were planted from 1996 using French clones (asexually propagated vines used for selective "breeding") that give wines that are dominated by red-cherry and redcurrant flavours. Older Chilean Pinot Noir vineyards contain American clones of Pinot Noir which give more black cherry and blackcurrant flavours, and deeper-coloured wines.

RIESLING (WHITE)

Riesling is declining in Chile but good examples are made all over the country, from Bío-Bío (Cono Sur), Curicó Valley (Miguel Torres Chile), Maipo Valley (Cousiño Macul), and Casablanca Valley (Morandé).

SANGIOVESE (RED)

Errázuriz, Casa Tamaya, Francisco de Aguirré, TerraMater, and Viu Manent all work with Sangiovese vines planted in the 1990s. Aconcagua examples from Errázuriz (Single Vineyard) are Chile's most convincing so far.

SAUVIGNON BLANC (WHITE)

The weeding out of Sauvignonasse (*see* below) from Sauvignon Blanc vineyards, either through replanting or through separate harvesting, together with the use of more hygienic winemaking practices in the 1990s, has helped transform Chilean Sauvignon Blanc. Flabby wines resembling ditch-water have been replaced by more vibrant and characterful wines. Concha y Toro (Trio), Errázuriz (La Escultura), and Morandé (Dueto) produce fine, aromatic wines from Casablanca Valley, with Viña Casablanca and Viña Leyda reliable. Haras de Pirque (Character) and Santa Inés/De Martino make fuller-bodied wines from Maipo Valley. Curicó Valley provides some of Chile's best-value Sauvignon Blanc, with La Fortuna, Miguel Torres Chile, Montes, and San Pedro (Gato Blanc and 35 South) the best examples. Other dependable Sauvignon Blanc producers include Carmen, Casa Rivas, J.&F. Lurton Chile, Santa Carolina, and Santa Rita.

SAUVIGNON GRIS

Casa Silva is one of the few Chilean wineries currently working with this rarely seen grape.

SAUVIGNONASSE (WHITE)

Sauvignonasse is probably a northern Italian grape called Tocai Friulano, but was long confused with Sauvignon Blanc in Chile. Sometimes called Sauvignon Vert, Sauvignonasse is most commonly found in Curicó Valley.

SAUVIGNON VERT (WHITE)

See Sauvignonasse.

SEMILLON (WHITE)

Chile's Semillon wines (dry or sweet) can be vegetal, perhaps owing to poor nineteenth century French vine stocks. *See* Hacienda El Condor, San Pedro, Santa Inés/De Martino, Terra Andina, and Viña de Larose.

SYRAH (RED)

Syrah accounts for just one per cent of Chile's vineyard area, but plantings of it quintupled between 1997 and 1999, once growers realized that Chile's warmer Aconcagua Valley and Rapel (especially Colchagua) regions suited the variety. Syrah from Aconcagua (Errázuriz) and Rapel (Caliterra, Casa Silva, Luis Felipe Edwards, Montes, MontGras, La Ronciere, Valdivieso, Viu Manent, and VOE) show soft, rich, alcoholic fruit and firm centres (Merlot from hot regions, in contrast, can taste hollow). Syrah from cooler areas such as Casablanca (Matetic) or from further south (Carpe Diem, La Fortuna, and Tabontinaja) shows firmer red fruit.

VIOGNIER (WHITE)

Cono Sur (Visión) and Concha y Toro (Trio) produce mouthwatering Viognier from Chimbarongo and Casablanca Valley (respectively). In these areas the grapes gain complexity through late ripening and often gain concentration from spring frosts (which reduce the crop). Viognier becomes richer and more alcoholic in the warmer Limarí Valley (Casa Tamaya and Francisco de Aguirré) and in Rapel (MontGras). *See also* Anakena, Casa Silva, and Santa Inés/De Martino.

ZINFANDEL (RED)

Canepa, MontGras, and TerraMater produce easy-drinking Zinfandels, which could become more blockbuster-like as their young vines age.

Chilean Wine Styles (Other)

KOSHER WINE

Carta Vieja produces kosher wine.

LATE HARVEST

Chile's climate is not humid enough for noble rot fungus to form on grape-skins. Late-harvest wines from Miguel Torres, Montes, and Viña de Larose are sweet rather than complex. Casablanca Valley's foggy climate encourages noble rot at Morandé (Golden Harvest) and Villard Estate (El Noble). *See also* Errázuriz.

ORGANIC WINE

Chile's organic potential is finally being exploited. Santa Inés/De Martino, Cono Sur, Canepa, TerraMater, Casa Lapostolle, and Miguel Torres Chile are embracing organics. Established organic producers like La Fortuna, Lomas de Cauquenes, Carmen, and Antiyal have been joined by new ventures like Aguatierra and VOE.

SPARKLING WINE

Sparkling wine is Chile's least-appreciated wine style. Francisco de Aguirré and Miguel Torres Chile make simple, fruity examples, Valdivieso is the local market leader, and Manquehue is set to take Chilean sparkling wine to a higher level with French help. Hacienda El Condor is developing Chile's first sparkling red wines.

Chilean Wine Regions

Chile's vineyards span 1,400 km (869 miles), across twelve degrees of latitude and through five official wine regions (from north to south): Atacama, Coquimbo, Aconcagua, Central Valley, and Southern region. The first three are north of Santiago; their desert vineyards, particularly those of Atacama and Coquimbo, are mainly given to table grapes or Pisco production. Wine vineyards become more widespread in more temperate Aconcagua, covering the mainly red wine area of Aconcagua Valley, the mainly white wine area of Casablanca Valley, and the new Leyda Valley zone. South of Santiago is the Central Valley, Chile's wine heartland, and its Maipo, Rapel, Curicó, and Maule subregions. In the Southern Region, the terrain becomes more hilly and the climate wetter.

north santiago

The Atacama, the world's driest desert, marks Chile's northern border with Peru. It never rains here. It is so dry that the ground holds perfectly preserved remains of mummified Native Americans buried 3,000 years before the Egyptians embalmed their pharaohs (6,000 BC). The ground also holds mineral wealth, including copper, nitrates, and gold, all of which helped to make fortunes for the nineteenth and early twentieth-century entrepreneurs who developed Chile's wine industry. However, these entrepreneurs invested their money in the Maipo Valley, south of the capital Santiago, not this far north.

The Atacama region is one of Chile's five official vine-growing regions, but its vineyards in its Copiapó and Huasco subregions are mainly used for Pisco brandy (*see* p.22) and table grapes. The climate here is simply too hot to make fine wine. Wine production only begins in the Limarí Valley, some 1,000 km (621 miles) south of the Atacama Desert. This is another Pisco brandy stronghold, and part of Chile's official

north santiago: points of interest

The port of La Serena is **Chile's oldest town**; Mount Aconcagua is the **tallest peak** in the Andes; Aconcagua Valley is home to Seña, one of Chile's **priciest reds**; the cooler Casablanca Valley is Chile's **premier white wine region**; Casablanca also produces **top Pinot Noir**; water is so scarce **no new vineyards** can be planted.

Coquimbo region. Coquimbo is divided into three valleys: Elquí, Limarí, and Choapa. All produce Pisco brandy and table grapes, but so far only Limarí has developed wine vineyards as well. The Elquí Valley is the heartland of Chilean Pisco brandy production. It surrounds La Serena, the port founded (officially) in 1549 by conquistador Francisco de Aguirré, who planted Chile's first vineyards; he now has a Limarí Valley winery named after him.

The Aconcagua region, the third of Chile's five official vinegrowing regions, begins some 320 km (199 miles) to the south.

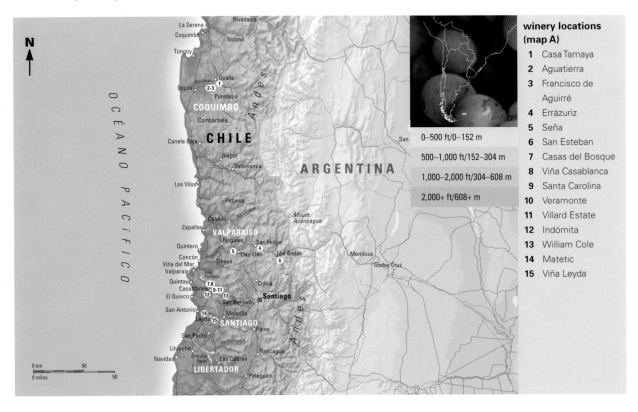

winery locations (map A)

1 Casa Tamaya
2 Aguatierra
3 Francisco de Aguirré
4 Errázuriz
5 Seña
6 San Esteban
7 Casas del Bosque
8 Viña Casablanca
9 Santa Carolina
10 Veramonte
11 Villard Estate
12 Indómita
13 William Cole
14 Matetic
15 Viña Leyda

0–500 ft/0–152 m
500–1,000 ft/152–304 m
1,000–2,000 ft/304–608 m
2,000+ ft/608+ m

limarí valley

The Limarí Valley is better known for producing the grapes for Chile's national spirit, the brandy Pisco, than for its wine. Chilean Pisco is a white spirit made mainly from Muscat grapes and a red variety called Aleatica. The juice is fermented off the skins to make a base white wine, but because it is fermented at a relatively high temperature (28–30°C/82–86°F), it is not pleasant to drink (fine white wine is normally fermented at a much cooler 14–20°C/57–68°F to maintain freshness). The base wine for Pisco is then distilled to evaporate the water in the wine, leaving behind the clear spirit (for more on Pisco, *see* introduction to Peru, p.186).

However, the marketing men recognize Pisco as a "mature market". Sales within Chile of fifty million bottles annually are healthy, but they are unlikely to increase in the future. Younger Chileans prefer to drink wine and beer rather than Pisco, and sales of Chilean Pisco abroad are miniscule. Consequently, Chile's Pisco producers must rethink their strategy. One producer who is doing just that is Pisco Capel. Capel dominates the market, but from 1993 it developed wine vineyards (and olive groves) and a winery called Francisco de Aguirré near its main Pisco production facility in the Limarí Valley.

Smaller producers such as Casa Tamaya and the organic Aguatierra have since followed Pisco Capel's lead. The Limarí Valley now has just over 2,000 ha (5,000 acres) of vineyards dedicated to wine grapes, together with 10,000 ha (24,700 acres) of vines used to make Pisco. As the Limarí Valley is some 400 km (248 miles) north of Santiago, it is closer to the Equator than any other Chilean wine region. The climate is semi-desert, so irrigation throughout the year is needed to keep the vines alive during both winter and summer.

The Pacific provides some relief from the heat. The Limarí Valley is open to the ocean and cool morning mists do collect on the valley floor in the early morning. However, temperatures rise

above Chile's capital Santiago is surrounded by mountains: the high Andes to the east, and the lower coastal range to the west.

by late morning, and the daytime heat means that acidification of wines is the norm.

In the sixteenth century, the Diaguita Native Americans populated the Limarí Valley, but they did not survive the Spanish conquest. After the Spanish ceded independence to Chile in the nineteenth century, large silver and copper mines were developed. The fortunes these mines made for Chile's new aristocratic industrial class were used to establish wine estates such as Concha y Toro and Santa Rita, around the city of Santiago in the Maipo Valley. Now, an interesting reversal is taking place. As the Maipo Valley becomes overpopulated, prospective vineyard owners are investing where land is cheaper and more freely available; as a result, the Limarí Valley should see significant further wine development in the coming years.

The valley's soils are rich in minerals and quartz fragments, and these may play a part in giving the Limarí Valley wines their powerful and very distinctive mineral-rich aromas. *See* Aguatierra and Casa Tamaya.

aconcagua valley

The Aconcagua Valley is the smallest in size of Chile's traditional fine wine regions. It lies roughly eight kilometres (five miles) north of Santiago in Chile's official Aconcagua region. The word Aconcagua means "the place where there is corn" in the Native American Mapuche language, but today's Aconcagua Valley is more reliant on table grapes, garlic, tomatoes and, increasingly, avocados, than on corn.

Although Aconcagua Valley has only 2,000 ha (5,000 acres), or around two per cent of Chile's total vineyard, the valley's potential for quality is undoubted. Flagship producer Errázuriz was founded outside the town of San Felipe in 1870, and is the only one of Chile's historic wineries outside the Central Valley (see p.26). At the time Errázuriz was founded, the Central Valley was seen as the only place in Chile suitable for wine production; Don Maximiano Errázuriz's decision to plant vineyards here was viewed with scepticism. However, Errázuriz not only survived, but it soon claimed to have the largest single vineyard under one owner in the world.

Behind Errázuriz's historic winery is the Don Maximiano vineyard. Most lies on flat ground between the winery and the hills, but in 1992 part of the hillside was planted with vines. The current winemaking team at Errázuriz has studied the Aconcagua Valley's climate and concluded that it offers wine grapes a longer growing season than the Maipo Valley does. This is because temperatures warm up earlier in the spring here, allowing the vines to bud and flower earlier without risk of spring frost.

This extended growing season suits red grapes, which account for about ninety per cent of wine grapes planted here. Carmenère, Cabernet Sauvignon, Merlot, Cabernet Franc, and Syrah enjoy longer "hang time" than in Maipo Valley, giving riper, more complex wines. With this is mind, the Errázuriz/Mondavi joint venture sited its flagship red wine vineyard of Seña in the Aconcagua Valley (although some Maipo Valley grapes are used in the Seña red).

The Seña vineyard lies at the valley's western side, where temperatures are coolest; it is planted with Bordeaux varieties. Rhône varieties such as Syrah and the Italian Sangiovese are grown twenty-four kilometres (fifteen miles) further east at San Felipe where it is warmer.

The Don Maximiano estate now comprises five parcels planted within an eighty-kilometre (fifty-mile) radius of the Errázuriz winery. They are called Max I, Max II, Max III, Max IV, and El Ceibo. Either side of the "Don Max" vineyards are three vineyards belonging to Córpora: Agustinos, Bellavista, and Colunquén. Only red grapes (Merlot, Cabernet Sauvignon, Cabernet Franc, Carmenère, and Syrah) are planted here. The most easterly vineyard in the Aconcagua Valley, very close to the Andes, belongs to San Esteban, near the town of Los Andes. Its Los Andes vineyard, protected from cool Pacific breezes, is the hottest in the Aconcagua Valley. Recent plantings include warm-climate varieties such as Syrah, Nebbiolo, Sangiovese, and Mourvèdre.

Aconcagua Valley wines are distinctive. Chardonnay and Sauvignon Blanc are grown for white wines, but it is the reds that are the most exciting. These usually show strong colour, rich, ripe fruit and appetizing structure; perfect for immediate drinking or for ageing for two-to-five years or more.

The rich, open, but rarely heavy, texture of Aconcagua wines is in part owing to the valley's fairly loose soils. Vine roots can penetrate easily, resulting in accessible wines. A good example is Córpora's top red, the Bordeaux-style blend Caminante, which is sourced from its Aconcagua vineyards. Errázuriz uses its extensive Aconcagua vineyards to excellent effect and is particularly strong on Cabernet Sauvignon, Merlot, Carmenère, and Syrah red wines, with Sangiovese becoming increasingly consistent as the vines age. It is hard to find a bad wine from the Aconcagua Valley. See Córpora, Errázuriz, San Esteban, and Seña.

casablanca valley

Casablanca Valley is Chile's most talked-about wine region, and one of its youngest. The valley is centred on Casablanca, easily Chile's ugliest wine town thanks to several large industrial plants. Casablanca's wineries are hardly beautiful, either. The valley's pioneer, Pablo Morandé (*see* Morandé), was the catalyst for the arrival of these wineries, but he can hardly be blamed for their prefabricated dullness (his modern winery is well away from Casablanca, at Pelequén in the Cachapoal Valley (*see* Rapel region, p.33). Morandé was winemaker for Concha y Toro when, in 1982, he identified Casablanca Valley's potential as a cool-climate area for white wines and Pinot Noir.

The valley begins eighty kilometres (fifty miles) northwest of Santiago on the road to Valparaíso.

below Young vines protected against frost in Casablanca Valley. The plastic allows sunlight to reach the plant, and sheathes it in heat.

Lying on the western side of the Coastal Range, it is directly exposed to the cool Pacific winds of the Humboldt Current. Morandé's cool-climate hunch proved correct; soon the thirty-kilometre-long (nineteen-mile) Casablanca Valley was transformed from vegetable and cattle farming to mainly vineyards. Land prices, which skyrocketed, have now stabilized because the land cannot sustain more vineyards. Irrigation is necessary here and there is no ready water supply (the valley lacks a major river). All local underground aquifers have been tapped and local authorities have forbidden drilling for more.

This decision has left Casablanca Valley with around 3,500 ha (8,650 acres) of vineyards, less than four per cent of the national total. Chardonnay dominates, followed by Sauvignon Blanc and Pinot Noir, with smaller proportions of Viognier,

Gewurztraminer, Merlot, and Cabernet Sauvignon. Unlike other Chilean wine regions, some of the vines here (around ten per cent) are grafted onto rootstocks, not to resist phylloxera (*see* Chile introduction, p.12), but to ward off microscopic soil worms called nematodes. These thrive in Casablanca Valley's loose, sandy soil, killing vines by poisoning the roots. Some observers believe that chemical fertilizers have destabilized the soil in Casablanca (and other regions, such as Maipo) causing nematode populations to reach plague-like proportions.

So, Casablanca Valley goes against the "Chile is a wine-growing paradise for ungrafted vines" stereotype. It goes against another stereotype, too – the one that says Chile's white wines are less exciting than its reds. Casablanca's whites are among South America's most elegant and intense, unquestionably Chile's best. The key is the Pacific-influenced climate which, in spring, is prone to hard frosts. Between mid-September and the first week in November, frost kills emerging buds and flowers, reducing yields and making the wines more concentrated. To avoid total loss, producers resort to anti-frost devices, although losses can still be severe (up to ninety per cent in some vintages).

The Pacific effect also contributes to Casablanca's long, cool autumns, which give complexity and refinement to the wines. Grapes are harvested about a month later here than in the Central Valley. Slowly ripened grapes tend to retain more flavour and more acidity, giving crisper white wines. The acidity of some whites is sometimes softened via a secondary, or malolactic, fermentation. (*See* Southern Region, p.43).

Malolactic fermentation changes tropical-fruit flavours into something more "buttery." Some producers, such as Baron Philippe de Rothschild Maipo Chile, Bright Brothers Chile, Carta Vieja, Casas del Bosque, Indómita, Montes, Santa Carolina, Santa Inés/De Martino, Santa Rita, Tarapacá, Ventisquero, Veramonte, Viña Casablanca, and William Cole, inhibit malolactic fermentation in favour of overtly tropical-fruit favours, albeit with varying degrees of richness and complexity. Wines from Casa Lapostolle, Concha y Toro, Cono Sur, Errázuriz, Laroche & Coderch, Morandé, Santa Emiliana, VIA Group, and Villard Estate show a more subdued, mineral tone. Casablanca Valley's red wines are deservedly less renowned than its whites, although Cono Sur, Concha y Toro, Errázuriz, and Morandé all make classy Pinot Noir.

Producers such as Casa Lapostolle, Casas del Bosque, Concha y Toro, Veramonte and others are now planting on slopes away from the cold, frosty valley floor. Planting here suits red grapes such as Merlot and Cabernet Sauvignon, particularly if they are planted in the warmer, eastern part of the valley, closest to the road from Santiago. The first winery one sees driving from Santiago belongs to Veramonte. Built in 1998, it, like most of Casablanca Valley's wineries, includes a visitor centre. En route to the coast and the popular seaside resort Viña del Mar, Casablanca is one of Chile's most visitor-friendly wine regions.

San Antonio and Leyda

The newest areas to emerge in the Aconcagua region are San Antonio, a coastal area due west of Santiago, and the zone within San Antonio forty-five kilometres (twenty-eight miles) southwest of Casablanca town, called Leyda. The proximity of Leyda to the coast, which is just twelve kilometres (7.5 miles) away, makes this zone significantly cooler than the Casablanca Valley. Several grape growers, including the Leyda winery, are already established here. *See* Baron Philippe de Rothschild Maipo Chile, Bright Brothers Chile, Carmen, Carta Vieja, Casa Lapostolle, Casas del Bosque, Concha y Toro, Cono Sur, Errázuriz, Indómita, Laroche & Coderch, Matetic, Montes, Morandé, Santa Carolina, Santa Emiliana, Santa Inés/De Martino, Santa Rita, Tarapacá, Ventisquero, Veramonte, VIA Group, Villard Estate, Viña Casablanca, Viña Leyda, and William Cole.

central valley

The Central Valley, the most important of Chile's five official vinegrowing regions, is home to most of Chile's best-known vineyards and wineries. It runs for 300 km (186 miles) in a north-south direction, following the route of the Pan-American Highway from the Chilean capital Santiago to the edge of the Southern region (*see* p.42). Overall, Chile is less agriculture-based than its main wine competitor and neighbour Argentina, but the Central Valley is among South America's most intensively farmed regions. The majority of Chileans who make their living off the land reside here. Nearly four million live people in the Central Valley, with another six million residing in Santiago, out of a total population of sixteen million.

About ninety per cent of all Chilean wine exports originate from the Central Valley. The Maipo River bounds it to the north and the Maule River to the south. It is divided into four subregions. From north to south these are: Maipo Valley, which includes Santiago, and is Chile's most prestigious wine region; the Rapel Valley, which covers the largely unknown Cachapoal Valley and the increasingly well-known Colchagua Valley; Curicó Valley, Chile's flattest and most productive wine valley; and the underrated but relatively isolated Maule Valley.

Most Central Valley vineyards lie in the depression between the Andes (which rise to 4,500 m/15,000 ft) in the east and the Coastal Range (which rise from 600–2,000 m/2,000–6,500 ft) in the west. Compared to California's Central Valley, Chile's Central Valley lies at a considerably higher altitude. It is narrower by fifty kilometres (thirty miles) on average but is not as hot. Generally, it produces more refined wines. Less than half of California's vineyards lie in its Central Valley, while seventy-five per cent of Chile's national vineyard, or around 75,000 ha (185,325 acres) are planted in this region.

The centre of the valley has rich, fertile soil. Wine is just one of many crops farmed here for Chile's main export markets of Europe, the USA and other Latin American countries. Agricultural crops include wheat, corn, beans, sugar-beet, and potatoes, as well as beef, poultry, nuts and wool, but fruit (apples, oranges, pears, plums, apricots, etc) and table grapes dominate.

In contrast with traditional European wine regions, the link in Chile's Central Valley between wine production and other agricultural industries is strong. Wine is the main focus for fewer than half of the Central Valley's wineries, or the people, corporations, or trusts owning them (many of which are part of diversified businesses involved in fruit, processed foods, metals, shipping, etc). For many, wine is a commodity. Not surprisingly, wine from these

left Nearly all Chile's vines are supported by posts and wires to form hedges. Free-standing vines remain only in the Maule Valley.

central valley: points of interest

Central Valley is Chile's **wine heartland**; Maipo Valley produces Chile's **ultimate Cabernets**; new vineyards are being planted in side-valleys on hill slopes for better quality; **Apalta Valley** in Colchagua is the **most talked about new region** for Carmenère and Shiraz; **cooler sites** nearer the Andes are being developed for reds and whites; Maule Valley tipped for **quality renaissance**.

33 Santa Mónica
34 Los Toruños
35 Tuniche
36 La Rosa (winery)
37 Anakena
38 Chateau Los Boldos
39 Caliterra
    (La Arboleda)
40 Totihue
41 Canepa (Trinidad)
42 Montes
    (Marchigue)
43 Bisquertt
44 Viña de Larose
45 Misiones de Rengo
46 Torreón de Paredes
47 Vina las Nieves
48 Morandé
    (Pelequén)
49 Los Vascos
50 Viu Manent
51 Siegel
52 MontGras
53 Montes
54 Casa Lapostolle
55 Apaltagua
56 Casa Silva
57 Selentia
58 Santa Helena
59 Santa Laura
60 Luis Felipe Edwards
61 Cono Sur
62 J.&F. Lurton (Chile)
63 Valdivieso
64 Miguel Torres (San
    Francisco Norte)
65 Miguel Torres
    (Chile)
66 Los Robles
67 La Fortuna
68 Hacienda El Condor
69 Aresti
70 San Pedro
71 Echeverría
72 Purisima
73 Domaine Oriental
74 TerraNoble
75 Valle Frio
76 Tabontinaja
77 Calina
78 Balduzzi
79 Cremaschi Furlotti
80 Julio Bouchon
81 Carta Vieja
82 El Aromo
83 Segú
84 Lomas de Cauquenes
    (Covica)
85 Calina Vineyards

0–500 ft/0–152 m

500–1,000 ft/152–304 m

1,000–2,000 ft/304–608 m

2,000+ ft/608+ m

winery locations (map B)
1 Aquitania
2 Quebrada de Macul
3 Cousiño Macul
  (Santiago)
4 Santa Carolina
  (Santiago)
5 Canepa (Santiago)
6 Odfjell
7 Undurraga
8 Doña Javiera
9 Manquehue (Santiago)
10 Chadwick Estate

11 Concha y Toro/Don
   Melchor (Puente Alto)
12 Almaviva
13 Casa Rivas
14 TerraMater
15 Santa Alicia
16 Manquehue (Pirque)
17 Santa Ema
18 Santa Inés/
   De Martino
19 Tarapacá (El Rosario)
20 Cousiño Macul
   (Buín)

21 Santa Rita
22 Carmen
23 Antiyal
24 Portal del Alto
25 Concha y Toro
   (Pirque)
26 La Misión
27 Valette Fontaine
28 Haras de Pirque
29 Perez Cruz
30 Ventisquero
31 La Ronciere
32 La Rosa (La Palmeria)

companies tends towards the formulaic – or, as a British Master of Wine once put it, they're "like Volvo cars: reliable, but rather dull". Yet, it is just the reliability of the Central Valley's wines that has made Chile so popular in Europe and the USA.

Central Valley wineries have done what their Australian and Californian counterparts did so successfully: they have given mainstream drinkers of everyday wines the clean, fruity, easy-to-drink, value-for-money wines they want. It is, of course, easier to deliver such wines from the Central Valley, where the dry, sunny climate, fertile soils, and abundant irrigation from the Andes combine to provide favourable and fairly regular growing conditions. These conditions allow winemakers to follow a consistent winemaking style and provide export managers and wine merchants with easier portfolios to manage.

The Central Valley is described geographically as a depression because it lies between two ranges of hills, formed by the collision of two of the earth's tectonic plates. Their continued movement towards each other makes Chile prone to earthquakes, tidal waves and volcanic eruptions. About 230 million years ago, the glaciers in the Andes melted, forming rivers. These rivers left what geologists call sedimentary deposits – what we call earth, or soil.

These soils consist of large stones and smaller pebbles on the high eastern side of the valley below the Andes, quite heavy clay and silt in the lower, main depression, and finer, looser, sandier soil toward the undulating Coastal Range. Generally, in Chile, stony soils produce refined, powerful and mainly red wines that age well; clay-rich soils produce red wines for fairly early drinking and very good white wines, while sandy soils produce quick-maturing wines of both colours.

So it is important to think of the Central Valley as three strips of land running north to south, rather than a single, low-lying depression. Differences in altitude are less significant here than in Argentina, where vineyards can vary by more than 2,000 m (6,560 ft). In Chile the difference is 600 m (1,968ft), from the Alto Maipo in Maipo Valley, at 800 m (2,624 ft) to the low-lying Teno area at under 200 m (656 ft) in Curicó Valley.

The river valleys crossing the Central Valley, which were carved out by the retreating glaciers, begin in the north with the Maipo and its tributary, the Mapocho (which runs right through Santiago, occasionally flooding it); the Cachapoal River in the northern part of Rapel, and the Tinguiririca River in Colchagua in the southern part of Rapel; the Teno and Lontué Rivers in Curicó Valley; and the Maule River (plus a large number of tributaries) in the Maule Valley at the Central Valley's southern end.

Today, these rivers bring the irrigation water that sustains the Central Valley's vineyards and other crops. The worldwide success of Chilean wine in recent years has seen the planting of many new vineyards, and the replacement and modernization of older ones. Wine producers are using water more efficiently, changing flood irrigation systems to drip irrigation. Drip systems allow growers precise control over the amount of water each vine receives, minimizing the risk of dilution. Water is less abundant for vineyards in the Coastal Range, where underground aquifers have to be tapped using drills. Soils here are less fertile, too, and yields are necessarily lower as a result.

One of the most vocal proponents of the less-fertile Coastal Range slopes is Randy Ullom, winemaker for Calina, which is owned by California's Kendall-Jackson. Ullom spent seven years exploring Chile's terrain before deciding not to plant in the Central Valley depression, and opting instead for the coastal hills of the Maule Valley, and into the Southern region. "Vines grow like weeds on the flat, fertile Central Valley floor," Ullom says, "and unless you take corrective action, such as pruning harder in winter and thinning the grape crop in summer, you get high grape yields, which limit quality." Other winemakers agree with this conclusion and increasing numbers are planting vineyards in the coastal hills where they believe more concentrated, more complex wines can be produced. Examples include Montes, with its Montes Folly (Syrah) Vineyard and MontGras, with the Ninquén Hill Vineyard, both in the Colchagua Valley. New projects are emerging in the Andean slopes on the Central Valley's elevated eastern flank, too, at the San Pedro/Château Dassault Totihue venture.

Other winemakers are challenging preconceptions about what the Central Valley is all about by planting on the western side of the coastal hills. This area, towards the Pacific Ocean, is geographically no longer the Central Valley, although it is included in the official Central Valley wine region designation. Water may be scarce here, but the cooling effects of the Pacific's Humboldt Current are keenly felt, adding potential aromatic intensity to the wines. Subregions such as the Maria Pinto Valley in the Maipo Valley and other centres, such as Marchigue, Trinidad, and Lolol in Colchagua Valley, all contain newly developed vineyards west of the Coastal Range.

The Central Valley's fertility continues to make it attractive to wine producers who are keen to avoid risks by making reliable wines from vines yielding abundant quantities of grapes. But the new vineyard developments towards the Pacific Coast, on the slopes of the coastal hills and towards the Andes, should soon mean that the historic perception of Chile's wine heartland is due for revision.

below A vineyard worker's house in Rancagua, Rapel. Its simple construction helped it survive the last major earthquake, in 1985.

maipo valley

Chile's deserved reputation as "The Bordeaux of South America" rests on the vineyards of the Maipo Valley, which were first developed on a commercial scale in the mid-nineteenth century using Chilean money and French know-how. French winemakers and viticulturalists (notably from Bordeaux) advised Chilean producers about which grape varieties to plant, and how to design, build, and equip the wineries. The French encouraged plantings of the Bordeaux vines that were to establish Chile's red wine credentials. Chilean investors made wealthy from mining (see North Santiago, p.21) adorned their vineyards with country houses and park gardens. French experts also advised on the layout and design of these gardens, some of which are still in existence today at, for example, Concha y Toro, Cousiño Macul, Santa Rita, and Undurraga.

The Spanish planted Maipo Valley's first vineyards in the mid-sixteenth century, after the conquistador Pedro de Valdivia founded the city of Santiago de Chile. Santiago is situated at 530 m (1,775 ft) above sea level, in a bowl surrounded by the Andes to the east and the Coastal Range to the west. The Andes and the Coastal Range meet in Maipo Valley, but walking around Santiago you'd never know it. It is one of the world's most polluted cities; smog blocks the sky for much of the year.

The Nobel Prize-winning Chilean poet Pablo Neruda wrote, "My country, take care of your light!" but Santiago's politicians seem unwilling to follow his wishes. They continue to license the thousands of badly maintained (and often empty) diesel buses which belch poisonous fumes, causing much of the pollution. As the bus drivers belong to Chile's biggest union,

a closed shop with significant political influence, their jobs are maintained – even if the buses are not.

Pollution is incovenient for producers with wineries in or around Santiago, such as Canepa, Manquehue, Santa Carolina, and Valdivieso, as well as for vineyards within Santiago's eastern suburb of Macul (some allege that the grapes must sometimes be washed before fermentation). The combination of pollution and an increased need for housing around the capital is taking its toll on vineyards in the immediate area.

The other vineyards and wineries within Macul's Peñalolén district belong to Aquitania and Quebrada de Macul. Aquitania's vineyard, planted from 1990, comprises eighty per cent Cabernet Sauvignon; the Quebrada de Macul vineyard, planted from 1970,

below Chile's "Mercedes Benz" may have four legs, but remains the most efficient way to move between the vineyard and the winery.

comprises more than sevety-five per cent of the variety. Cabernet is also the grape of choice in Puente Alto and Pirque. Almaviva, Chadwick Estate, Concha y Toro (for Don Melchor), and Indómita own vineyards or source grapes from Puente Alto; Concha y Toro, Haras de Pirque, Manquehue, La Misión, Portal del Alto, Santa Alicia, and Valette Fontaine own vineyards in Pirque.

Santiago's Macul suburb, Puente Alto, and Pirque form the Alto Maipo ("Upper Maipo"). This part of the Maipo Valley is closer to the Andes than any other Chilean wine region, and has the highest altitude (800 m/2,624 ft). As a result, the Alto Maipo experiences slighter cooler daytime summer temperatures and significantly greater night cooling than Rapel, Aconcagua or Curicó Valleys, while being significantly warmer than Casablanca Valley.

Cabernet Sauvignon, a late-ripening grape, has a longer growing season here. In spring, the vines bud early (mid-September) thanks to the Raco, a dry, hot Andean wind. The ripening grapes are protected from colder winds in late autumn by the Andes and by the hill spurs running off them toward the Pacific. These hills form horseshoe valleys with varied exposures, which Haras de Pirque exploits for red and white wines, and Valette Fontaine for reds. Cabernet Sauvignon needs daytime summer temperatures of over 27°C (81°F) to ripen, but at night in Alto Maipo temperatures drop to below 12°C (54°F). The grapes retain acidity and ripen steadily.

Soils here are ideal for Cabernet Sauvignon: free-draining, thanks to both the natural slopes and the large quantities of stones flushed from the Andes by the Maipo River. The gravel soils are similar to those found in the Bordeaux villages of Pauillac, St-Julien, Margaux, Cantenac, Pessac, Talence, and Léognan, sources of the world's finest Cabernet Sauvignon-dominated red wines. Some of these Bordeaux villages supplied Chile with Cabernet cuttings in the 1850s; now investment and ideas from Bordeaux can be seen at Almaviva, Antiyal, Aquitania, Valette Fontaine and others.

Alto Maipo's combination of a long growing season, steady ripening, and ideal soils makes for South America's most refined and elegant Cabernet Sauvignons. They have deep colour, powerful textures, and ripe blackcurrant flavours overlaid by eucalyptus or mint tones; the best can be aged in bottle for a decade or more. Good examples made wholly or partly from Alto Maipo Cabernet include Almaviva, Antiyal, Casa Real (Santa Rita), Domaine Paul Bruno (Aquitania), Domus Aurea (Quebrada de Macul), Don Melchor Private Reserve (Concha y Toro), Elegance (Haras de Pirque), El Principal (Valette Fontaine), Gold Reserve (Carmen), House of Morandé (Morandé), and Terrunyo (Concha y Toro).

Cabernet Sauvignon accounts for more than half of Maipo Valley's 9,500 ha (23,475 acres) of vines, followed by Merlot, Carmenère and other red Bordeaux grapes such as Cabernet Franc, Malbec and Petit Verdot, with around 2,000 ha (4,900 acres) combined. All add important flavour nuances to Cabernet Sauvignon red wines, as they do in Bordeaux. The main difference between Maipo Valley's red wines and those of Bordeaux is that the Chilean wines are more overtly fruity, with softer tannins and around 13.5–14.5% alcohol, compared to the Bordeaux norm of 12.5–13.0%.

The Alto Maipo area is becoming crowded by Santiago's ever-expanding sprawl. Land for vineyards is easier (and cheaper) to find around Alto Jahuel, Buín and Paine, forty kilometres (twenty-five miles) south of Santiago. This area is known locally as the Maipo Medio or the "middle" area between the high Alto Maipo and the lower valley floor. Antiyal, Portal del Alto, San Pedro, and Santa Rita have vineyards at Buín, as does Cousiño-Macul, while Perez Cruz is the newest development in Paine. Carmen's organic vineyard is located in Alto Jahuel. This area also produces outstanding Cabernet Sauvignon with warm, inviting but refreshing fruit and less overt mint and eucalyptus characters than are found in Alto Maipo.

Closer to the Maipo River and the valley floor is the lower Maipo, or Maipo Bajo. This centres on Isla de Maipo ("Maipo Island"), a small town on the Maipo flood-plain. It was populated in the early twentieth century by Italians, including José Canepa, the Pavone family of Santa Ema, and the De Martino family of Santa Inés/De Martino. The town is so called because it was once an island between two forks of the Maipo River, but José Canepa dammed one of these forks, permanently connecting Isla de Maipo to the rest of the valley floor. The vineyard Canepa created on the drained land now belongs to TerraMater. Isla de Maipo's rich, varied topsoil of sand and stones produces a broader, more open style of red wine than in the Alto Maipo, plus attractive whites from Chardonnay, Sauvignon Blanc, and Viognier. Tarapacá's newly developed El Rosario de Naltagua vineyard lies in a distinctive pocket of hills above Isla de Maipo and the valley floor.

Still on the valley floor, but farther west, is Talagante, where Doña Javiera, Odfjell, and Undurraga have vineyards, wineries or both. Casa Rivas is based in Maria Pinto Valley, an area west of the coastal hills of Maipo Valley that is sure to be offically recognized by Chile's wine authorities in the near future. This area has hotter summer and autumn temperatures than either Alto or Isla de Maipo, favouring Carmenère.

The southwest part of Maipo Valley is home to Ventisquero's winery on the Yali River. *See* Almaviva, Antiyal, Aquitania, Baron Philippe de Rothschild Maipo Chile, Canepa, Carmen, Casa Rivas, Casablanca, Chadwick Estate, Concha y Toro, Cousiño-Macul, Doña Javiera, Geo Wines, Haras de Pirque, Indómita, Manquehue, La Misión, Morandé, Ochagavía, Odfjell, Perez Cruz, Portal del Alto, Quebrada de Macul, San Pedro, Santa Alicia, Santa Carolina, Santa Ema, Santa Emiliana, Santa Inés/De Martino, Santa Rita, Tarapacá, Undurraga, Valdivieso, Valette Fontaine, Ventisquero, Villard Estate, and Viña Leyda.

Rapel is the only Chilean wine valley with a split personality; the region is divided into two unequal and very contrasting parts. These are the Cachapoal Valley in the north and the Colchagua Valley in the south. Growers in the Cachapoal Valley rarely use the Cachapoal designation on their wine labels, preferring to use the Rapel Valley or Central Valley designations. Colchagua Valley wine-growers, on the other hand, have in recent years become the most determined self-publicists in Chile, promoting Colchagua as Chile's premier wine region.

Rapel Valley has just over one-quarter of Chile's total vineyard area, or 27,000 ha (66,700 acres). Cachapoal Valley has 9,000 ha (22,240 acres), only one-third of that grown by its southern neighbour,

below Slightly sloping ground like this produces riper, more concentrated wines than flatter, more fertile sites.

Colchagua Valley. Both zones are mainly planted with red grape varieties. Cabernet Sauvignon and Merlot dominate, with Carmenère and Syrah gaining increasing renown. The Coastal Range forming the western border of Rapel Valley reduces the cooling influence of the Pacific, helping to maintain the Rapel Valley's dry, Mediterranean climate, which is required for these grapes to ripen fully. A number of producers from outside Rapel Valley, including Baron Philippe de Rothschild Maipo Chile, Calina, Carmen, Geo Wines, Indómita, Undurraga, Viña Casablanc, and Viña Leyda source red grapes from here.

Rapel Valley's Cachapoal Valley zone is arguably Chile's least well-known internationally, overshadowed by the historic Maipo Valley immediately to the north and the upstart Colchagua to the south. However, Cachapoal's main town of Rancagua did play a part in

Chile's war of liberation against the Spanish in 1814, during the decisive Battle of Rancagua (*see* Santa Rita). The Spanish faced two armies: a group of Chilean exiles led by Bernardo O'Higgins, and a rebel army under the command of San Martín, Argentina's liberator, who crossed into Chile from Mendoza in Argentina on the Camino Manzano Historico (*see* J.&F. Lurton in Argentina).

The town of Rancagua lies seventy-two kilometres (forty-five miles) south of Santiago, and is home to La Ronciere, Santa Mónica, and Tuniche. Unusually, all are owned by Chilean families rather than by foreign investors. Immediately to the south, the Cachapoal River, which gives the valley its name, runs from the Andes towards the Pacific via the Rapel Lake. Cachapoal is a Mapuche term meaning "mad river," owing to the river's ferocity during the spring snow-melt.

The Pan-American Highway runs south from Rancagua towards Morandé's winery at Pelequén, via Requínoa and Rengo. Requínoa is one of Cachapoal Valley's cooler areas; the valley here is narrow enough to trap cool Andean downdraughts. White grapes such as Sauvignon Blanc and Chardonnay can perform well here, giving green-tinged wines with aromas of lime and greengage. Casa Lapostolle has a vineyard here called Las Kuras, named after a Mapuche word for stones.

These stones, smoothed over thousands of years by the Cachapoal River, characterize the Requínoa soil. The deep soils retain enough of the sun's heat, and drain well enough for red grapes such as Merlot and Cabernet Sauvignon to thrive. Chateau Los Boldos has some of the best red wine vineyards here, between the Pan-American Highway and Anakena's winery in the lee of the Andean foothills. San Pedro and Château Dassault are developing a project in this area named after the hamlet of Totihue. Córpora and Viña de Larose also have vineyards and wineries here. Totihue

right Alpacas are valued for their wool. Some wine-growers use them to graze unwanted vineyard weeds.

is very dry in the summer, but cools significantly in the autumn, slowing ripening in both white and red varieties, and giving wines with plenty of flavour.

The town of Rengo is south of Totihue and closer to the centre of Cachapoal Valley. This is potentially an outstanding area for Cabernet Sauvignon. The best wines can combine the finesse of top Maipo Valley Cabernets with extra intensity; this part of the Cachapoal Valley is appreciably warmer than Maipo. The best Cabernets from Las Nieves, Misiones de Rengo, and Torreón de Paredes show these characters.

The climate becomes much cooler towards the coast at Peumo, where Concha y Toro has a vineyard planted mainly with Merlot. Peumo marks the point where the Cachapoal River turns toward the Pacific through a gap in the Coastal Range. The main road here follows the river and is one of the busiest in Chile for truckers transporting fruit to the port of Valparaíso. Called La Carretera de la Fruta ("the fruit road"), at the town of Las Cabras ("the goats") it passes directly in front of fruit-juice and wine producer La Rosa's recently modernized winery and two of its vineyards (Cornellana and La Rosa). La Rosa's third vineyard, La Palmería de Cocalan, lies some way to the northwest in an isolated pocket protected from cool, Pacific winds by the coastal hills.

As well as gearing itself up to be Chile's premier wine-producing region, Colchagua Valley is also positioning itself as Chile's premier destination for wine tourism. A wine route, a wine hotel and, one day, a wine train will all service the needs of wine tourists. Colchagua is making a bid to become South America's equivalent of California's Napa Valley. The hype is impressive – as are some of Colchagua Valley's wines, even if the quality can sometimes fall short of what is expected from wines that are generally priced rather too ambitiously. Still, because many of the wineries are either brand new or recently refurbished, facilities for visitors, such a tasting rooms, restrooms, and winery shops are commonplace.

Colchagua Valley follows the route of the Tinguiririca River. The river flows from the Andes and past Colchagua Valley's main town of San Fernando before joining the Cachapoal River at the Rapel Lake on its way to the Pacific. San Fernando lies 130 km (eighty-one miles) south of Santiago on the Pan-American Highway, and is home to Casa Silva, Selentia, and vineyards belonging to Julio Bouchon and Portal del Alto. Due south of San Fernando is the smaller town of Chimbarongo, home to Cono Sur's winery and its main vineyard. Chimbarongo is a Mapuche word meaning "foggy place;" like Teno to the south in Curicó Valley, it is relatively low in altitude. These conditions suit Pinot Noir, a Cono Sur specialty, and it is one of the few areas in the warm Central Valley where doesn't overripen.

All Colchagua Valley's other major players are found west of the Pan-American Highway, toward the coastal hills in much warmer areas. The Tinguiririca River flows past the town of Nancagua. Both Santa Emiliana with its VOE project and Luis Felipe Edwards are exploiting the sun-drenched hill slopes in this area for warm-climate, dark-skinned grape varieties, such as Syrah and Carmenère, to good effect. Merlot tends to stress on the slopes, and prefers moister ground near or on the valley floor.

Farther west is the town of Santa Cruz de Colchagua – what will be Chile's Downtown Napa if the marketers have their way. The Santa Cruz Plaza Hotel opened here in November 2000, with some of Colchagua's leading wineries as investors. The accommodation (and food) offered by some of the wineries to paying visitors on their own estates is, however, better value and more memorable (for all the right reasons) and more fun, too. Santa Laura is based just outside the town, with Santa Helena, Viu Manent, and Casa Lapostolle a few kilometres to the east.

This is the gateway to the Apalta Valley, Colchagua Valley's main piece of prime wine real estate. The centre of this side valley is actually rather poor for wine-growing thanks to a higher than desirable water table, but a plethora of old vines on the flatter land and well-exposed slopes planted during the 1990s have produced wines deserving international interest, such as Casa Lapostolle's Clos Apalta, Montes' Folly and Montes Alpha labels, and Apaltagua's Grial.

Apalta Valley forms a half-moon shape in the foothills of the coastal mountains; days are scorching hot and nights are cool. The lower reaches are given to pasture, while the foothills have now been overtaken by vines, with around 850 ha (2,100 acres) planted. The climate of the Apalta Valley enables Carmenère to ripen fully, albeit late, giving it time to build up its full flavour profile. Other late-ripening or warm-climate red grapes, such as Mourvèdre, Tannat, Shiraz, and, possibly, Montepulciano, plus Viognier (for whites) have prospered, or will do so in future. *See* Canepa, Carmen, Manquehue, Santa Rita, and Ventisquero, who are all developing vineyards here. In a bowl of hills to the north of Apalta Valley is Caliterra's new Arboleda vineyard and winery.

Grapes grown in Apalta and other Colchagua areas in the inland coastal hills are among the most expensive on Chile's open market. Grapes from the area between Peralillo and Palmilla, where Los Vascos, Siegel, Bisquertt and Viu Manent have vineyards (and in some cases wineries), as well as from Marchigue, closer to the coast where Bisquertt, Montes, Ventisquero, and Canepa have developed vineyards, are among those that fetch the highest prices. Marchigue (or Marchihue) means "a place of hard land" in Mapuche. The subsoil here is a hard pan of rock, upon which newly planted vines struggle. Canepa has planted its Trinidad vineyard on raised beds of earth to make rooting easier for vines.

Another area to watch is Lolol in the western Coastal Range where Canepa, Casa Silva, and J.&F. Lurton Chile are developing projects. Lolol has lower summer temperatures on average than Marchigue has because it is more open to the Pacific Ocean and its

cooling afternoon breezes. Lolol could produce good white wines, assuming irrigation water can be found (there is none readily available), adding another potential string to Colchagua Valley's mainly red-wine bow. *See* Anakena, Apaltagua, Baron Philippe de Rothschild Maipo Chile, Bisquertt, Calina, Caliterra, Canepa, Carmen, Casa Lapostolle, Casa Silva, Chateau Los Boldos, Concha y Toro, Cono Sur, Córpora, Geo Wines, Indómita, J.&F. Lurton Chile, Julio Bouchon, Luis Felipe Edwards, Manquehue, Misiones de Rengo, Montes, Morandé, Las Nieves, Portal del Alto, La Ronciere, La Rosa, Santa Emiliana, Santa Helena, Santa Laura, Santa Mónica, Santa Rita, Selentia, Siegel, Torreón de Paredes, Totihue, Tuniche, Undurraga, Los Vascos, Ventisquero, Viña Casablanca, Viña de Larose, Viña Leyda, Viu Manent, and VOE.

curicó valley

Curicó Valley has less than one-fifth of Chile's vineyard area, yet it produces nearly one-quarter of the country's wine. The relatively high yield of grapes per vine achieved by Curicó Valley's winegrowers is a result of three factors. First is the climate; the strong Mediterranean-like climate here enables the vines to produce significant quantities of grapes. Second is the availability of water for irrigation. Water is drawn from the Teno and Lontué Rivers, which flow down from the Andes and across Curicó Valley, (forming the Mataquito River) on their way to the Pacific. The third factor is the terrain; because Curicó Valley is a soft plateau, it is generally flat, with rich soils. Farming the vines is relatively easy with tractors and machine harvesters, which are increasingly used here.

below As night falls, cold air descends from the Andean foothills, allowing wine grapes to stay fresh and flavourful.

The flat terrain also makes flood irrigation systems highly effective; the downside is that, although irrigation stops the vines from dying of thirst, flood irrigation systems also tend to encourage vines to produce too many grapes.

Curicó Valley is divided into two subregions. The northern part, the Teno Valley, is the junior partner. Alempue's new winery is located off the Camino La Montaña ("Mountain Road"), which runs up into the Andes from the town of Teno. Like Chimbarongo to the north (*see* Rapel Valley), Teno lies next to the Pan-American Highway and experiences cool, foggy mornings, owing to its low-lying terrain. Around Teno, Sauvignon Blanc (often here Sauvignonasse, *see* p.20) is the most-favoured grape variety, followed by Merlot, which is grown by La Misión (this is "real" Merlot, not Carmenère; *see* Carmenère, p.16). On the

other, much warmer, side of Teno Valley, in the shadow of the Coastal Range, Concha y Toro has two large vineyards, Rauco and San Manuel; their grapes are used mainly to make wines sold within Chile.

The southern of half of the Curicó Valley is the Lontué Valley. This is where the majority of Curicó Valley's most important vineyards and some of Chile's most significant wine producers are located, including San Pedro and Valdivieso. Valdivieso's main winery for still wines is an unusual old-fashioned structure (containing modern equipment) in the small town of Lontué. The surrounding area really took off for wine production in the early part of the nineteenth century, when producers such as the Correa brothers replanted Spanish colonial vineyards with French grapes. These vineyards have become the largest single plot in Chile to have one owner (*see* San Pedro). The vineyards

surround San Pedro's huge modern winery next to the Pan-American highway, while billboards erected in the vineyards remind passing motorists that they are crossing the thirty-fifth parallel (after which San Pedro's 35 South brand is named).

The Molina area is also home to smaller producers such as the family-owned Echeverría vineyard and winery. Some of the vineyards belonging to Aresti and Miguel Torres are also located here. Aresti is based close to the Andes in an area that produces nuts, fruit and mineral water, as well as wine. In 1997 Santa Rita and Carmen both planted large new vineyards here. The cool air descending from the Andes, particularly in the few weeks before harvest, means that early ripening grapes such as Merlot and Sauvignon

below Drying grapes after heavy night-time dews with a tractor-mounted blower just before harvest to concentrate flavours.

Blanc are favoured over later-ripening ones such as Carmenère or Cabernet Sauvignon.

Spain's Miguel Torres bases its Chilean operation near Curicó, a market town 195 km (121 miles) south of Santiago, which gives Curicó Valley its name. Torres' arrival here in the late 1970s raised Curicó's profile significantly. Until then it was assumed that any Chilean wine valley outside of Maipo was incapable of producing fine wine. The reputation for banal wines that Curicó Valley had was probably owing to the presence of Los Robles, Chile's first wine cooperative. Now, Los Robles is adding to Curicó's allure by pioneering Chile's first fairtrade wines.

One of the four founding partners involved in Montes owns a white wine vineyard called Los Nogales, near Curicó town, which produces Montes' best white wines. Montes is gradually moving its winemaking operations from Los Nogales to its newer installation in Apalta Valley. Southwest of Curicó town is Requingua's substantial (mainly Cabernet Sauvignon) vineyard, together with an 1820s manor-house used by Requingua as an elementary school for the children of its 260 vineyard and winery workers.

Also southwest of Curicó town is the romantically named small town Sagrada Familia ("Holy Family"). Sagrada Familia occupies the banks of the Mataquito River, which has worn a gap in the coastal hills as it flows into the Pacific. This gap allows cooling afternoon breezes from the Pacific into the vineyards, which slows ripening, making for more complex wines. Vineyard owners here include Errázuriz, with its El Descanso estate, which is mainly given to Merlot and Carmenère, and a vineyard purchased by the Canepa sisters in 1996 and renamed Hacienda El Condor. Valdivieso draws some of its best Chardonnay and Pinot Noir grapes from its La Primavera vineyard. Also in Sagrada Familia is the much-improved La Fortuna, which is part of VIA Group (see p.88) for wine, but which still farms pears and other fruits along with vines.

The wine styles produced in the Curicó Valley are relatively easy to generalize about. The two main white grape varieties are Sauvignon Blanc and Chardonnay. However, most of Curicó Valley's Sauvignon Blanc is in fact Sauvignonasse (see p.20), which gives a far less interesting wine than Sauvignon Blanc does, while much of the older Chardonnay vineyards are planted with a clone (see p.17) called Mendoza, which can produce unusually concentrated wines.

Curicó's main red varieties are Cabernet Sauvignon and Merlot or Carmenère. Half of Curicó Valley's 20,000 ha (5,000 acres) of vineyard area is given over to these three varieties. Most of the Cabernet Sauvignon vines were planted from 1995 onward by, for example, San Pedro, which widely expanded vineyards such as San Miguel and others located between Molina and Lontué. Curicó Valley's official totals for Merlot and Carmenère, at 3,600 ha (8,900 acres) and 600 ha (1,480 acres), respectively, are generally agreed to be inaccurate. The later-ripening Carmenère, which is not as well adapted as Merlot to Curicó Valley's generally rich soils, almost certainly covers more than 2,000 ha (5,000 acres) here, not 600 ha (1,480 acres).

The anomaly in the official statistics arose because growers were allowed to declare their vineyards to be "real" Merlot even if they actually contained the Merlot look alike Carmenère. Carmenère gives appreciably higher yields than Merlot does, but it only tastes ripe if growers are more severe at winter pruning or if they "green prune" in summer (i.e., remove the less-ripe grape bunches just before harvest). Carmenère produces riper-tasting red wines if yields are dramatically cut, but Curicó Valley's above-average yields suggest that some producers here have yet to take this fact to heart. See Alempue, Aresti, Carmen, Concha y Toro, Echeverría, Errázuriz, La Fortuna, Hacienda El Condor, Miguel Torres Chile, La Misión, Montes, Requingua, Los Robles (cooperative), San Pedro, Santa Rita, Valdivieso, and VIA Group.

maule valley

The Maule Valley marks the limit of Spanish penetration in Chile during the conquest of South America.

The valley follows the course of the Maule River, which flows from the Andes in the east across the valley floor, and through the coastal hills, joining the Pacific at the lovely, black-sand beach resort of Constitución. Maule Valley is Chile's largest wine subregion with more than 20,000 ha (50,000 acres) of vineyards, one-fifth of the Chilean total. The traditional red grape, País, was brought by the Spanish. It is being replaced by classic varieties such as Cabernet Franc, Cabernet Sauvignon, Carmenère, Malbec, Merlot, and Syrah; white wine vineyards based on Chardonnay and Sauvignon Blanc are also being developed.

Despite its size, Maule Valley is often unfairly ignored. However, one of California's largest wine producers, Kendall-Jackson, decided that this was the best place in Chile to develop vineyards, having spent seven years testing grapes and vineyards from every region, north and south of the main Central Valley wine-production zone (*see* p.26).

Kendall-Jackson's belief in Maule Valley led to the foundation of the Calina vineyards and winery here in 1996. In the last few years, other, longer-established local wineries such as Balduzzi, Carta Vieja, Cremaschi Furlotti, Domaine Oriental, El Aromo, Purisima, and Segú, have followed Calina's lead and begun bottling wine under their own labels, rather than selling their crop in bulk. As these wineries decrease yields in the vineyard and become more consistent in winery techniques, Maule Valley may be able to forge a reputation to challenge Chile's more established regions. Calina aside, so far only Domaine Oriental, Purisima, and Segú have produced Maule Valley wines that really stand out. New projects such as Calina and San Rafael have made the kind of wines people want to drink right from the start, thanks to the long winemaking background of their founders, respectively, California's Kendall-Jackson and members of Chile's Coderch family.

above Wine in barrels ready for pumping into the vats behind. Once the barrels are cleaned, the wine will be put back for ageing.

From north to south, Maule Valley is subdivided into four sections. In the north, and on the Maule Valley's cool, Andes side, is the San Rafael Valley, a new official area. The only producer of interest is the new San Rafael vineyard and winery project (*see also* VIA Group) at Chilcas. Immediately to the south is the Claro Valley, which centres on Talca, 260 km (161 miles) south of Santiago. Talca is home to the traditional *huasos*, or cowboys, as well as to producers such as Domaine Oriental, Calina, and Purisima. Chardonnay and Merlot seem to thrive here. Concha y Toro, Miguel Torres Chile, TerraMater, TerraNoble, and Valle Frío all own important vineyards near San Clemente. This cool, humid area near the Andes produces aromatic whites and crisp reds from Cabernet

Sauvignon and Pinot Noir, but as yet no single definitive variety has emerged. San Pedro is producing ripe Carmenère, Cabernet Sauvignon, and Syrah from the drier, hotter coastal hills around Pencahue.

Maule Valley's third subregion, Loncomilla, centres on the town of San Javier, just south of the Maule River, and runs all the way to Parral, the valley's most southerly town. Balduzzi and Cremaschi Furlotti are based in San Javier, while Tabontinaja and J. Bouchon are based on the dry hills toward the coast. El Aromo and Carta Vieja are farther south, around Villa Alegre, one of the flatter, more fertile parts of Maule Valley (vine yields here need to be carefully monitored to get the grapes ripe). Segú is based on high ground near Linares in the cool Andean foothills, where Miguel Torres also has a red wine vineyard. The Maipo Valley-based Portal del Alto has two

vineyards in the far south near Parral. Maule Valley's fourth subregion, Tutuvén Valley, centres on the town of Cauquenes in the coastal hills west of Linares. The main producer here is the good-quality Lomas de Cauquenes cooperative, which sources grapes from most of the local grapegrowers. The growers' traditionally farmed vineyards are unirrigated, thanks to plentiful coastal rains, although two modern vineyards developed here by Calina have drip irrigation systems. The Cauquenes vineyards lie on a ridge running south from the town of Cauquenes toward Concepción and into Chile's Southern region (*see* p.42).

See Balduzzi, Calina, Carta Vieja, Concha y Toro, Cremaschi Furlotti, Domaine Oriental, El Aroma, J. Bouchon, Lomas de Cauquenes (cooperative), Miguel Torres Chile, Purisima, San Pedro, San Rafael, Segú, Tabontinaja, TerraMater, TerraNoble, and Valle Frío.

the southern region

Chile's Southern region is home to more than ten per cent of Chile's vineyards, or around 12,000 ha (30,000 acres) of vines. Yet, despite its size, the Southern region produces just a handful of wines that are worthy of export. The problem is that the majority of the vineyards here are planted with grape varieties such as Muscat and País. These varieties, neither the most fashionable, nor the highest-quality, are used to produce styles of wine that are difficult to sell to the domestic market, and virtually impossible to sell on the international market.

The Southern region's vineyards are shared between two main subregions, Itata Valley and Bío-Bío Valley. In addition, a new area south of Bío-Bío, called Malleco Valley, was officially recognized by the Chilean government in 2002. The Spanish planted the first vineyards in the Southern region more than 300 years ago. However, continuing rebellions by the native Mapuche people always made wine production here a precarious business.

The Mapuche, also called the Araucanian people, are unique in South America for being the only indigenous people never to have surrendered to the

below Choclo (corn) is used for "pastel de choclo" (corn and meat casserole) and "humitas" (corn paste and onion), Chilean specialities.

Spanish colonists. (The Mapuche had never succumbed to the Incas, either, even when the Inca empire was expanding rapidly just prior to the arrival of the Spanish in the early sixteenth century.) Even after Chile gained its independence from Spain in 1818, the Mapuche enjoyed a great deal of autonomy. It was not until 1883, after what became known as the Araucanian War ended, that the Mapuche recognized (but did not surrender to) the Chilean government. After peace was declared, the Chilean authorities restored the Mapuche's right to own land.

Yet, just over a century later, a new battle is being fought here, again involving the Mapuche and foreign invaders, this time in the form of foreign corporations keen to log the rich local forests to produce paper and materials for the construction industry. The Mapuche argue that paper mills and managed forests containing invasive (but quick-growing) eucalyptus trees will adversely affect both the availability and the purity of local water sources.

Foreign investors argue that the establishment of new forms of agriculture will provide more jobs for the local community. Apart from traditional dairy farming, the biggest employment activity in the region is wine. As Chilean wine producers become more export-oriented, plantings of the unfashionable Muscat and País grapes are declining. Modern vineyards growing internationally popular grape varieties, such as Chardonnay, Merlot, Pinot Noir, and Cabernet Sauvignon, have been successfully developed and are providing jobs. The most successful winery so far is Carpe Diem, which was founded as a jointventure between the Chilean government and American investors.

So what is the potential for wine-growing in the Southern region? If you ask winemakers from Aquitania, Concha y Toro, Cono Sur, Calina, and Gracia, who either own vines here, or buy Southern region grapes, the answer is an unequivocal thumbs-up. As in Maule Valley immediately to the north, the

0–500 ft/0–152 m
500–1,000 ft/152–304 m
1,000–2,000 ft/304–608 m
2,000+ ft/608+ m

winery location (map C)
1 Carpe Diem

soils here are generally less fertile than those found farther north, which means that the vines have to struggle in order to survive. A hard-working vine is usually inclined to produce lower yields of better-quality grapes. Lower yields also mean thicker grape-skins, and thus more natural resistance to pests and diseases – as well as wines with bolder, deeper colours and richer flavours

The climate is unusual, too. The main risk of being located so far south is that there is the danger of spring frosts, which can decimate yields. However, ripening is assured by hot days, although night-time temperatures drop sharply. This combination of hot and cold temperatures is especially good at providing grapes with enough natural acidity and freshness to require no addition of artificial acidity during winemaking. Grapes requiring no acidification give winemakers much more flexibility in terms of the styles of wine they can produce, too, especially in the case of white wines.

The result is that winemakers can choose to make classic, dry white wines showing crisp, mouthwatering, tropical fruit flavours, with or without the oak influence of barrel-fermentation. Or, they can produce creamier, softer whites with a richer, buttery texture by putting the wines through a secondary, malolactic fermentation; this process softens the acidity and adds a rounder mouthfeel (Aquitania's SOLdeSOL white wine from the new Malleco Valley is an excellent example). *See* Aquitania, Concha y Toro, Cono Sur, Calina, Carpe Diem, and Gracia.

the southern region: points of interest

Southern Region is the **wettest and coolest** area; with two main subregions, Itata and Bío-Bío; and a new area Malleco Valley producing one of Chile's most **highly regarded** Chardonnays; grapes like Muscat and País still dominate, but "international" varieties are increasing; the **cooler climate** slows grape ripening, and in good years leads to wines with extra **aroma and finesse**.

itata valley

The Itata Valley's few vineyards of international importance are all west of the main town of Chillán, toward the coastal hills. These coastal ridges are influenced by the Pacific Ocean in terms of rain (which can fall during the harvest) and wind. As well as drying the grapes after rain, helping to minimize the risk of disease, the wind can dehydrate the grapes, which helps to maintain flavour concentration.

The main wine producer here, Carpe Diem, trains its vines to the lyre system favoured in Uruguay (*see* p.154), which also has a maritime climate. As in Uruguay, rainfall is sufficient for irrigation to be the exception, rather than the rule. Unlike in Uruguay, though, the topsoil in the Carpe Diem vineyards consists of red, rather than black, clay. The clay contains some sand, which helps the vine roots to penetrate the clay and also helps to drain rainwater.

Granite lies beneath the topsoil in this part of Itata Valley. Once the roots reach the granite they must really struggle, which helps create wines with distinctive aromas: clove or cinnamon notes in reds from Cabernet Sauvignon, Merlot, and Pinot Noir; and cardamom, lemongrass, and coriander for Chardonnay, Gewurztraminer, and Sauvignon Blanc whites. This aromatic intensity is what attracted Calina (owned by California producer Kendall-Jackson), which sources Itata grapes for their top Bravura range. Kendall-Jackson's Randy Ullom finds the early morning fogs in the coastal hills here are reminiscent of California's Sonoma Valley. Fog cools the grapes, enabling them to warm up slowly during the day, preventing sunburn and loss of flavour. *See* Calina and Carpe Diem.

below The Andes are getting higher, by about a millimetre a decade, relatively fast in geological terms.

Bío-Bío Valley is Chile's coolest wine region (in terms of temperature), but it's not the most fashionable. That title goes to Casablanca Valley, whose cool climate made it the most fashionable wine region in South America from the late 1980s. Some Casablanca winemakers maintain that Bío-Bío is neither cool, nor cool-climate; but perhaps they feel threatened by this southern upstart. Bío-Bío's annual rainfall of 1,300 mm (fifty-two inches) is more than twice that of Casablanca, where a lack of water for irrigation means that no more vineyards can be planted by government order (see p.24).

Bío-Bío, on the other hand, has plenty of existing vineyards, and plenty of room – and water – for more. Spring and summer rainfall makes irrigation superfluous. Bío-Bío's drawback, apart from its isolation from Santiago, is that lacklustre grapes left

over from the Spanish conquest dominate its vineyards. Some potential investors are wary of planting red Bordeaux grapes such as Merlot, Cabernet Franc, Cabernet Sauvignon, Carmenère, Malbec, and Petit Verdot here; they believe these varieties are unlikely to ripen consistently this far south.

So, for the moment, Bío-Bío's white grapes (Viognier, Chardonnay, and especially Sauvignon Blanc) are forging its reputation. The red Burgundy grape, Pinot Noir, which ripens earlier than most red Bordeaux grapes, is already producing good wines. Córpora's Santa Ana vineyard, near the town of Negrete, planted in 1993, has the largest Pinot Noir plot in Chile. As well as Pinot Noir, Córpora have also planted Sauvignon Blanc and Chardonnay for white wines and are testing Cabernet Franc, Malbec, Merlot, and even Grenache (a warm-climate grape) for reds.

The hope is that these red grapes will thrive in Negrete, which has a warm local climate. The Coastal Range of hills to the west blocks cold air coming off the Pacific from the Antarctic. These hills break only where the Bío-Bío River runs into the Pacific at La Concepción, Chile's second-most populous city. Nearer the Andes, around Mulchén, is a vineyard belonging to a member of the Guilisasti family (see Concha y Toro). Cono Sur, Concha y Toro, and Santa Emiliana make use of its Riesling, Sauvignon Blanc, Gewurztraminer, and Pinot Noir.

Adolfo Hurtado, winemaker at Cono Sur, claims that the resin smell from the pine trees surrounding the Mulchén vines discourages some fungal diseases (fungal diseases normally pose a serious problem to vines grown in wetter climates). Hurtado also says that Bío-Bío's moist climate tones down the potentially overexuberant rose petal and petrol flavours that Gewurztraminer and Riesling can display, and which many wine drinkers find off-putting. Perhaps Bío-Bío's non-aromatic aromatic whites will become Chile's new white wine fashion. See Concha y Toro, Cono Sur, Córpora, and Santa Emiliana.

35 South *See* San Pedro

120 *See* Santa Rita

1810 *See* Domaine Oriental

1865 *See* San Pedro

Aguatierra (A2)

Punitaqui, Limarí Valley
Tel: (+56) 53 731494;
aguatie@attglobal.net
Canadian Jim Pryor founded
Aguatierra in the Limarí Valley in late
1999. Pryor worked in television in
North America and still runs a leisure
boating company. Now in his fifties,
Pryor first visited the Limarí Valley
through his Chilean wife, and has
fulfilled a lifetime ambition to start
an organic farm with Aguatierra.
Aguatierra is Chile's northernmost
organic wine estate. The vineyard is
surrounded by hills near the town of
Punitaqui. Cabernet Sauvignon,
Syrah, and Carmenère vines are
planted, along with olives and
mandarin oranges. Vegetable crops
such as artichokes and beans, as
well as flowers and herbs (sold as
cash crops), are grown among the
vines to create biodiversity. Waste
vegetation and grape pressings left
over after fermentation are
composted. Pryor recruited locals as
employees and they are encouraged
to make their own decisions. This
contrasts with the hierarchical
(almost feudal) decision-making
process common to most Chilean
businesses. The independent organic
produce inspector in Chile describes
Aguatierra as one of the best-
planned and executed organic

projects in the country, for its
environmental and social
contribution. Pryor will bring animals
onto the farm when practicable but
stresses that they must fulfill an
environmental function, rather than
simply be there for show. Pryor's farm
office is a far cry from the
sophisticated television studios he has
spent half his life in; it is a functional
cabin made out of what seems like
scrap building materials. The wines
are made to a good standard in a
nearby winery, and one day Pryor
hopes to build his own winery. The
Aguatierra wines include a clean,
refreshing Cabernet Sauvignon with
soft tannins, an appetizing dry rosé
Cabernet Sauvignon that benefits
from early bottling and early drinking,
and a solid Carmenère with a thick,
herby, blackberry flavour.

Alba *See* Quebrada de Macul

Albamar *See* William Cole

Alempue

Teno, Curicó Valley
asecor@entelchile.net
This modern winery in Curicó
Valley's northern zone of Teno Valley
produces very well-made, fruity,
value-for-money red and white wines
under the Alempue ("far away land")
and Maymay labels. Cabernet
Sauvignon and Sauvignon Blanc
stand out. Winemaker Serge
Candelon trained with Jacques
Lurton, first in Bordeaux and then at
San Pedro (*see* below). Most of the
grapes Candelon works with are
purchased, but he is successfully
encouraging grape suppliers to gain
official organic status and, by 2004,

15% of Alempue's purchased grapes
should have organic certification.

Aliara *See* Odfjell Vineyards

Almaviva (B12)

Puente Alto, Santiago de Chile
Tel: (+56) 02 852 9300
Chile's largest wine producer,
Concha y Toro (*see* below), and
Baron Philippe de Rothschild SA
(Bordeaux) (*see* below) created
Almaviva in a joint-venture begun in
1994 and announced in 1997.
Almaviva is a top-of-the-range,
French oak-aged red wine originating
from the best portion of Concha y
Toro's San José de Tocornal
Vineyard at Puente Alto, which is
itself in in one of the best parts of
the Maipo Valley (*see* Chadwick
Estate, below, for this vineyard's
history). Almaviva was given its own
winery, separate from either Concha
y Toro's, or Baron Philippe de
Rothschild (SA) Bordeaux's other
Chilean wine interests. Almaviva is
named after a character in "The
Marriage of Figaro," an eighteenth-
century French play by
Beaumarchais, later turned into an
opera by Mozart. The wine label also
features symbols from Chile's pre-
Columbian period. Almaviva's debut
1996 vintage produced 48,000
bottles. Blended from 75% Cabernet
Sauvignon, 19% Carmenère, and 6%
Cabernet Franc, it combines a lean
structure with ripe black fruit and
cedar notes; best drunk before 2004.
In 1997 Almaviva produced 84,000
bottles blended from 72% Cabernet
Sauvignon, 23% Carmenère, and 5%

Cabernet Franc. It has classic Maipo Valley flavours of menthol and eucalyptus, as well as the herbaceous character that marks much of the best red Bordeaux. In 1998, Almaviva produced 120,000 bottles, blended from 72% Cabernet Sauvignon, 26% Carmenère, and 2% Cabernet Franc. This was a difficult, wet vintage; the wine shows commendable refinement, if somewhat flat texture. In 1999, 156,000 bottles were produced, blended from 78% Cabernet Sauvignon, 19% Carmenère, and 3% Cabernet Franc. Drought conditions during the growing season and sixteen months in oak barrels have left the fruit flavours rather parched. The obvious concentration and richness of Almaviva 1999, however, will certainly appeal to fans of woody, ripe wine styles. The first Almaviva vintage to be both fermented and aged in the new Puente Alto winery was 2000. It produced 192,000 bottles, blended from 86% Cabernet Sauvignon and 14% Carmenère (with no Cabernet Franc), and is the best Almaviva to date. Redcurrant fruit and French oak flavours combine in an even-textured wine with appealing richness. The 2001 Almaviva was blended from 70% Cabernet Sauvignon, 27% Carmenère, and 3% Cabernet Franc. A hot summer produced a thick blackcurrant note to the fruit; this vintage needs several more years to settle. Almaviva is certainly an excellent wine. The location of its vineyard is first class, on a par with Concha y Toro's Don Melchor and

superior to the neighbouring Chadwick Estate, and with appreciably older vines than Chadwick Estate, too. Almaviva's winery has a simple but effective design, incorporating minimal use of pumps, and air-conditioned, barrel-ageing cellars. The wine needs more wildness to its fruit for it to become great rather than very good.

Altum *See* TerraMater

Amelia *See* Concha y Toro

Anakena (B37)

Requínoa, Rapel Valley
Tel: (+56) 02 426 0608;
info@anakenawines.cl
Jorge Gutiérrez founded Anakena in the Rapel Valley town of Requínoa before creating, and then selling, his Porta wine brand to Córpora (*see* below). Anakena was originally a fruit farm, but Gutiérrez, together with a friend from school, entrepreneur Felipe Ibañez, converted it to vineyards and a winery in the mid-1990s, just as Chile began successfully developing wine exports. The Anakena winery contains small fermentation tanks suited to quality winemaking; the winery is designed to minimize pumping (which can damage the wine). Whites from Chardonnay and Viognier are notably rich, while red wines show consistently clean fruit flavours and have an approachable texture. The wines are sold under the Tekena and Anakena labels (Anakena is the name of a beach on Chile's mysterious Easter Island).

Andes Peaks *See* Santa Emiliana

Antiguas Reservas *See* Cousiño-Macul

Antiyal (B23)

Buín, Maipo Valley
Tel: (+56) 02 821 4224;
alvaroespinoza@entelchile.net
Antiyal is the name of Alvaro Espinoza's garden-like, organic Cabernet Sauvignon vineyard planted in 1996 in front of his family home near Buín, in the Maipo Valley. From 1993, Espinoza put first Carmen (*see* below), and then its organic Nativa project, on Chile's wine map, before leaving to begin his own projects, including Antiyal and Geo Wines (*see* below). Antiyal's red wine reflects Espinoza's experiences of winemaking in Bordeaux and organic grape-growing in California, as well as his Chilean origin. It combines a firm Bordeaux-style backbone and exuberant Californian character, allied to elegant, Chilean fruit. Espinoza makes Antiyal from his own Cabernet grapes and from organic grapes grown in his mother's organic vineyard at Isla de Maipo, called San Lorenzo. In 1999 Antiyal produced around 4,000 bottles, blended from 70% Cabernet Sauvignon and Merlot, with 30% Syrah. This wine can be drunk now, but will start to show all its nuances from around 2005. Antiyal has been described as a "hippie wine," but this description suggests that it may be slightly unhygienic. Nothing could be further from the truth, even though alpacas and geese roam the Antiyal

vineyards and their manure is composted to nourish the soil. Antiyal is a modern wine with clear, concentrated fruit, and an indefinable, wild quality that many Chilean wines strive for but few attain. It admirably exploits Chile's vast organic potential. Although concentrated, Antiyal is not overbearing, making it easy to drink and enjoy. Both vineyards used for Antiyal are unirrigated (dry farmed) and free of chemical sprays. At picking, the grapes display what wine scientists would call "perfect physiological and analytical maturity". In other words, the flavours in the grapes and the sugar (for the alcohol) ripen together. This means the grapes do not require the winemaker to intervene, by adding acid or sugar, during fermentation, leaving a natural wine. Small-scale vineyards farmed along sustainable lines, such as Antiyal and San Lorenzo, are the alternative future of wine-growing, not just in Chile but worldwide, too. The soil at these establishments will remain healthy, rather than eroding. Soil erosion is the biggest problem in modern, industrially farmed vineyards in which heavy tractor use and chemical residues are irreversibly turning layers of precious topsoil to dust. Antiyal sacrifices quantity (big yields) for quality (big, but balanced flavours). It is a "back to basics" wine; it says to consumers and critics, "It's the vineyards, stupid". It provides the reality check needed in a wine world increasingly dominated by global brands whose cheap prices disguise their huge cost to the environment. Few could argue with Espinoza, who says, "I want to make great wine first, and an environmentally sound wine second."

Antu Mapu *See* Lomas de Cauquenes

Apaltagua (B55)

Apalta Valley, Rapel
Tel: (+56) 02 241 9222
Apaltagua belongs to a branch of the Donoso family, but is distinct from Domaine Oriental, which produces the Casa Donoso wines. Apaltagua produced bulk wine until 1999, when Hugo Donoso gave his Fundo San José vineyard and winery, in Rapel's prized Apalta Valley, to his children. The vineyard grew Cabernet Sauvignon and Carmenère vines planted from 1945–1950. In 2000, the Donosos fermented these grapes for the first time in the new winery. Around 100,000 bottles of very good red wine are made using three labels. The first, a Carmenère called Apaltagua, comes from Fundo San José's youngest vines and shows vibrant, elegant red fruit for early drinking. Second is Envero, a blend of almost equal amounts of Carmenère and Cabernet Sauvignon from older vines, aged in French oak. Envero is the Spanish word for what French wine-growers call *véraison,* the moment when the grapes change from hard green berries into soft purple grapes, four to six weeks before picking. Envero offers excellent value for money, and combines the best characteristics of Chilean red wine, with its deep, ripe black-fruit flavour, refreshing mouthfeel and pleasant aftertaste. The top wine Grial ("grail") is an attempt to make the best Carmenère in Chile, although up to 15% Cabernet Sauvignon may be blended in. Carmenère specialist Alvaro Espinoza (*see* Geo Wines, below) oversees blending. Although Grial has plenty of concentration, it is far from being a top-heavy blockbuster style, with an alcohol level of around 14%. This is higher than one would find for top red Bordeaux but is far from excessive in Chile. Grial displays Carmenère's essential characteristics: deep ruby colour, distinctive red fruit flavours (wild redcurrant, cassis) and herbaceous overtones. The wine ages in new French oak barrels and is best consumed within three to six years of harvest.

Aquitania (B1)

Maipo Valley
Tel: (+56) 02 284 5470;
info@aquitania.cl
Two high-profile Bordeaux winemakers, Paul Pontallier and Bruno Prats, founded Aquitania in 1990 with highly regarded Chilean winemaker Felipe de Solminihac as a minority partner. A red wine vineyard and winery were developed in the Maipo Valley, within Santiago's Peñalolén suburb, near Cousiño-Macul and Quebrada de Macul (*see* below). Pontallier is winemaker at Bordeaux's first growth Château Margaux, while Prats was (until 1997) owner-winemaker of Bordeaux's second growth Château Cos d'Estournel.

wines of south america

Pontallier's wines are seen as elegant, while Prats favoured (especially in his latter years at Cos) a more obvious, blockbuster style. Their Chilean wine, under the Domaine Paul Bruno label, initially bore little resemblance to Bordeaux, even though it was made with Bordeaux varieties (Cabernet Sauvignon, Merlot, and Carmenère). Early vintages, when the vines were young, were ultra-soft, with a pronounced but one-dimensional blackcurrant juice character. In recent years, Domaine Paul Bruno has become a much more interesting, more Bordeaux-like, wine. Its texture remains soft and juicy, but now has sufficient depth and complexity to withstand ageing in oak barrels without the risk of the fruit drying

out. Around 150,000 bottles are produced. A new development is SOLdeSOL, a Chardonnay sourced from Felipe de Solminihac's small vineyard in the Traiguén area in the far south of Chile's Southern region. This is Chile's southernmost commercial vineyard. During harvest the grapes are trucked overnight to Santiago where they are fermented in 100% new French oak barrels. The cool Southern region climate creates Chardonnay with character, intensity, and freshness. Barrel fermentation in new French oak softens the natural crispness of the enticing green apple fruit into something creamier. SOLdeSOL is Chile's most distinctive dry white wine.

Araucano *See* J.&F. Lurton Chile

above Horses outside Talca in Maule Valley belonging to the local cowboys or *"huasos"*.

Arboleda *See* Caliterra

Aresti (B69)

Tucapel 3140, Santiago de Chile
Tel: (+56) 02 680 6771;
bellavta@entelchile.net
The Aresti family bought their first of four vineyards in Curicó's Molina area in 1952. They built a solid reputation for bulk wine before deciding, in 1999, to bottle wine under the Aresti and Montemar labels. Aresti now makes around 1.5 million bottles of attractive, reliable wine under the guidance of foreign consultants. The Bellavista Vineyard surrounds Aresti's family hacienda on a dry, open site on clay soils.

Bellavista is noted for Carmenère red wines displaying notably ripe characters, and for Sauvignon Blanc (actually Sauvignonasse) whites with appealing, light, tropical flavours. It also produces underrated Gewurztraminer. La Favorita Vineyard has poorer, rockier soils than Bellavista, ideal for Cabernet Sauvignon. Here, this late-ripening grape variety produces dense, mineral-scented wines with ripe tannins, useful for blending. Aresti's Micaela Vineyard was the first one purchased by the family in 1953; it lies nearly opposite Viña San Pedro's winemaking headquarters. Aresti's Peñaflor Vineyard is divided roughly in two between vines planted before 1978 (when Aresti bought it) and those planted after 1985. Its Merlot wines are light but highly aromatic, because this site is on cooler, higher ground close to the Andes.

Armador *See* Odfjell Vineyards

Aventura *See* Morandé

Balduzzi (B78)
Av Balmaceda 1189, San Javier
Tel: (+56) 073 322138
Balduzzi provides a typical example of a traditional Maule Valley winery that has switched from selling bulk wine to large Santiago wineries, to selling wine in bottle under its own label. The change from bulk to bottle occurred in 1986 when a winery was built in San Javier. The Balduzzi family are trying to run their vineyards, which are planted mainly with Sauvignon Blanc, Chardonnay, and Cabernet

Sauvignon, on environmentally friendly lines. Their wines are steady, rather than spectacular.

Baron Philippe de Rothschild SA (Bordeaux)
This French holding company is responsible for the first growth Château Mouton-Rothschild in Bordeaux, and the world's largest-selling Bordeaux brand, Mouton-Cadet. Baron Philippe de Rothschild SA (Bordeaux) also began the fashion for joint-venture agreements between foreign wine companies in 1979, when, with California's Robert Mondavi Winery, it created Opus One in Napa Valley. Opus One's partners are now friendly rivals in Chile where both have joint ventures: Baron Philippe de Rothschild SA (Bordeaux) with Concha y Toro for Almaviva and Robert Mondavi with the Chadwick family of Errázuriz for Caliterra and Seña. In a further twist, Almaviva is produced next door to the Chadwick family's own prestige project, Chadwick Estate. NB: Baron Philippe de Rothschild SA (Bordeaux) and Baron Philippe de Rothschild Maipo Chile are not to be confused with Domaines Barons de Rothschild (Lafite, *see* Los Vascos).

Baron Philippe de Rothschild Maipo Chile
Quilicura, Santiago de Chile
bprchile@rdc.cl
Baron Philippe de Rothschild SA (Bordeaux) (*see* immediately above) also makes a range of other wines in Chile via its Baron Philippe de Rothschild Maipo Chile subsidiary. The wines, called Mapa, Mapa

Reserva, and Escudo Rojo, are made from purchased grapes. Mapa's Casablanca Valley Chardonnay shows distinctive sherbet firmness, while Maipo Valley Cabernet Sauvignon and Rapel Valley Merlots show smooth summer fruit flavours. The top red Escudo Rojo ("red shield") is a well-made, cedar-scented, oak-aged blend of Cabernet Sauvignon, Cabernet Franc, and Merlot. Production of both Mapa and Escudo Rojo jumped substantially between 2000 and 2001, and the quality of both seems to have diminished as a result somewhat.

Bisquertt (B43)
Fundo Lihueimo s/n, Palmilla
Tel: (+56) 02 233 6681
Bisquertt is one of Rapel Valley's oldest and largest wine producers. The Bisquertt family has Basque origins and first grew wine grapes in Rapel's Colchagua Valley in the nineteenth century, but only since 1991, under Don Osvaldo Bisquertt, did the family bottle wine under its own name. Bisquertt annually produces approximately five million bottles of dependable, clean, easily appreciated wines. The main wine labels are Casa (or Chateau) La Joya ("the jewel"), and Don Osvaldo. Oak-aged examples are labelled Reserva, while top selections carry a Gran Reserva designation. Whites made from Chardonnay and Sauvignon Blanc improved dramatically from the mid-1990s, becoming much cleaner, with a chalky texture suited to immediate consumption. Oak-aged (Reserva) Malbecs show an

appealing mix of soft, ripe fruit and firm oak; Carmenère gets its characteristic firmness from the grape, softened or made to taste riper by barrel-ageing. Bisquertt's Cabernet Sauvignon and Merlot wines have that slightly overripe character typical of these varieties in Colchagua Valley, and which contemporary wine drinkers find so appealing. As Bisquertt's first hillside vineyard, called Rinconada, matures, Syrah and Petit Verdot reds will be added to the range.

Bright Brothers Chile

Tel: (+351) 219 583192
www.brightbrothers.pt
The Australian Bright Brothers produce a range of clean, fresh-tasting wines made for early drinking. They include an attractive cherry-scented Pinot Noir from Casablanca Valley, made in a winery recently acquired by Tarapacá. *See also* Bright Brothers Argentina (p.124) and Bright Brothers Uruguay (p.165).

Brio *See* Indómita

Caballo Loco *See* Valdivieso

Cabo de Hornos *See* San Pedro

Calina (B77 & B84)

Fundo El Maiten, Talca
Tel: (+56) 71 263126
California's Kendall-Jackson assessed Chile's potential by working with grape-growers throughout the country's wine regions. Then, in 1993, it planted its own vineyards around Talca and in the coastal hills

near Cauquenes in Maule Valley. Some grapes are still bought in (*see* Carpe Diem) for the Calina wines, but only from hill sites, which give better quality than grapes from the valley floor, according to winemaker Randy Ullom (*see* Central Valley Introduction, p.28). Around five million bottles are produced annually under the Calina and the more expensive Calina Elite labels. Calina Cabernet Sauvignon is sourced from two regions. The Southern region's Itata Valley grapes bring black-fruit flavours overlaid with spice, while Colchagua Valley grapes bring cherry and mint nuances. Nine months in American oak barrels harmonizes the two elements, providing a smoky overlay. A Calina red blended from Cabernet Sauvignon and Carmenère has rich tannin and soft oak flavours. A varietal Carmenère is soft and warm. Calina Chardonnay is an overtly tropical dry white toned with obvious, but not clumsy, oak use. The Calina Elite Merlot shows ripe berry fruit and firm French and American oak nuances. Calina Elite Cabernet Sauvignon is blended from several areas and includes a portion of Merlot. A similar red, called Bravura (meaning "daring") from the 1999 vintage comprised 71% Cabernet Sauvignon sourced from Carpe Diem in the Itata Valley, and a private grower in Colchagua Valley, with 29% Merlot from forty-year-old Maule Valley vines. The wine was aged for eighteen months in new French oak and is Kendall-Jackson's most complex and naturally textured South American wine. Three

thousand bottles were produced. (*See also* Tapiz in Argentina).

Caliterra (B39)

Palmilla, Santa Cruz
info@caliterra.com
Caliterra is an invented name, meaning "quality land," or "quality soil," from the two Spanish words for quality (*calidad*) and earth (*tierra*). California's Robert Mondavi Winery and Chile's Errázuriz have produced Caliterra since 1996, although Errázuriz and another Californian joint-venture partner, Franciscan Vineyards, originally founded Caliterra in 1989. Franciscan ultimately started its own Chilean venture, Veramonte. Today, Caliterra produces more than seven million bottles annually under the Caliterra, Caliterra Reserve, and Arboleda labels. Grapes purchased under contract account for 70% of Caliterra's needs (*see* Haras de Pirque). The rest come from Caliterra's own vineyard, sculpted into hills in Colchagua in the Rapel Valley. This estate, called La Arboleda, is where Caliterra's red wines are made. The whites are still made in Errázuriz's wineries in Curicó and Aconcagua Valleys. Caliterra's Chardonnays are made in the buttery style popular in North America, while whites made from Sauvignon Blanc are earthier. Until recently, Caliterra's Merlots and Cabernet Sauvignons lacked the vitality of those produced when Franciscan Vineyards was Errázuriz's Californian partner a decade ago. However, Caliterra is starting to hit form with red wines

made from Carmenère, Malbec, and Syrah, which show attractive black olive, violet, and menthol flavours, respectively. Caliterra's current owners also produce Seña (*see* below).

Campero *See* Hacienda El Condor

Canepa (B5 & B41))

Cerillos, Santiago de Chile
Tel: (+56) 02 557 9121;
josecanepa@canepa.cl
Canepa remains one of Chile's biggest wine names, despite a potentially terminal family split following the of José Canepa II, son of the company's founder, in 1992. By 1930, Canepa Snr had planted substantial vineyards and olive groves around Isla de Maipo in Maipo Valley. When Canepa II died his three sisters and widow, Luciana, inherited the business, but attempts to work together failed. Eventually, the Canepa sisters took most of the vineyards (from which they founded TerraMater, *see* below) and Canepa's olive oil business. Canepa's widow, meanwhile, retained the Canepa brand name and Canepa's modern Santiago winery, but was left with only a small portion of vineyards. She soon developed new vineyards in Rapel Valley's Colchagua zone. A vineyard was planted in Apalta Valley, and a winery and vineyard were installed at Trinidad, near Marchigue, from 1997. This estate's slopes were left natural rather than bulldozed flat (as is usually the case with industrialized vineyard developments in Chile's Central Valley). Other crops grown here

include oranges, lemons, peaches, and other fruits. Beef cattle and eggs are also produced. Further vineyards are due to be developed in Rapel Valley's western coastal hills at Lolol. Canepa produces the equivalent of eighteen million bottles, but the Canepa brand name is only used for its best wines, from grapes grown in its own vineyards. Other wine labels include Peteroa, named after the vineyard surrounding Canepa's Santiago winery. Part of Canepa's Trinidad estate is managed organically, and four wines are made called Canepa Organic: a clean Chardonnay with a citrus character; a Cabernet Sauvignon with pleasant, light, black-fruit flavours; a deeper Merlot with chocolate and fruitcake flavours; and an appealing Zinfandel with a strong, ripe, plum and cinnamon character. Canepa's conventionally farmed wines are made to a good standard, and will improve further once its new vineyards mature. The Malbec Private Reserve is consistently rich, as is an oak-aged Semillon. The top wine, Finísimo, is a red blended mainly from Cabernet Sauvignon. Like Canepa wines in general, it is reasonably priced for the quality.

Carmen (B22)

Camino Padre Hurtado 0695, Alto Jahuel
Tel: (+56) 02 362 2122;
mlecaros@carmen.cl
Carmen claims to be the oldest Chilean wine brand, having existed since 1850. In 1986 it was acquired by Santa Rita (*see* below) and was given its own, separate, Maipo Valley

winery in 1992. The winery was designed by Alvaro Espinoza, who quickly established Carmen as one of Chile's most exciting producers. Espinoza was one of the first modern Chilean winemakers to spend most of his time in the vineyards, where he felt that the real quality of the wines was ultimately determined. In an era of ego-driven winemakers, this vineyard-oriented approach was both refreshing and effective. It eventually led to Carmen launching its organic Nativa range. These are made from hand-picked grapes grown near Carmen's winery in Alto Jahuel in Maipo Valley. Nativa Chardonnay is a clean, rich, ripe mix of mineral-scented tropical fruit and new French oak. Around 20,000 bottles are produced. Like the equally good but stylistically different Errázuriz Wild Ferment Chardonnay (*see* below), this wine is not seeded with a commercial yeast culture but is allowed to ferment using native yeast. The Nativa red wine is a classic and delicious Maipo Valley Cabernet Sauvignon. It has a deep colour and a ripe blackcurrant, blackberry, and mint flavour that is juicy but not overripe or jammy. The wine stands out for its textured concentration and for the wild note to its fruit (some might called it brambly or hedgerow-like). Carmen's top Cabernet Sauvignon is the Carmen Gold Reserve. This hand-picked wine comes from vines planted in 1957. Its rich, smooth fruit has the elegance and intensity of top red Bordeaux, but in texture it is more obviously voluptuous and open. Carmen's basic range, sometimes called Carmen Insigne, includes: a tidy, lightly oak-aged Cabernet Sauvignon; a rich Merlot with a balanced (rather than excessively alcoholic) aftertaste; a refreshing Sauvignon Blanc blended from Carmen vineyards in Rapel, Curicó, and Maipo Valleys; and an easy-drinking Chardonnay blended from vineyards in Rapel, Casablanca, and Maipo Valleys. An intermediate range called Carmen Reserve is oak-aged, but the oak influence is deliberately underplayed. This is because the fruit flavours present in the grapes, sourced from various regions, are sufficiently characterful not to need much of an oak veneer. No one at Carmen would claim that the winery is a specialist producer of Pinot Noir, but Carmen's Reserve Pinot Noir has notably stylish fruit with a judicious amount of oak influence. The key wine in the Carmen Reserve range is blended from Cabernet Sauvignon and Carmenère, the latter labelled until 2001 by Carmen under its Bordeaux synonym (Grande Vidure). Carmen immediately championed Carmenère after 1994 when vine experts discovered that most Chilean Merlot was in fact this much later-ripening grape variety. As Alvaro Espinoza's approach was vineyard-oriented, it was natural for Carmen to take the lead in working with Carmenère and actively promoting it by featuring its name on labels. Espinoza took the very un-Chilean step of drastically cutting back the yields to help ensure that the grapes would ripen fully, as

unripe Carmenère tastes vegetal and green. Soon, Carmen was producing outstanding Carmenère wines from the "new" discovery. Carmenère also features in the Carmen Winemaker's Reserve, a distinctive, peppery red blended from Cabernet Sauvignon, Grande Vidure (Carmenère), Petite Sirah, and Merlot. The Petite Sirah had been planted in a Carmen vineyard by accident, but, like a good chef, Espinoza made a virtue out of it, as he had with Carmenère. Although these were ingredients he had never expected or planned to work with, both add a deep-coloured, tannic element to the blend. Espinoza left Carmen in 1999 to pursue his own projects (*see* Antiyal and Geo Wines). Carmen's wine production increased by 400% between 1994 and 2003 to six million bottles and the new winemaking team under the experienced María del Pilar González has the challenge of maintaining the consistently high standards established here. Carmen has high expectations for its new hillside vineyards established in the Apalta Valley area within Rapel's Colchagua Valley.

Carpe Diem (C1)

Fundo Las Cañas, San Javier
vinsur@entelchile.net
Carpe Diem is based near the town of Chillán in the Southern region's Itata Valley. The project was set up in 1995 using American investment in conjunction with finance from the Chilean government. The aim was to redevelop wine-growing in this part of Chile, it having stagnated since

the Spanish colonial period. Grapes from Maule Valley are also used in the wines. Chardonnay and Sauvignon Blanc wines have a marked buttery character that contrasts with the inherent citrus character of the grapes. The red wines have an aroma of oak, beneath which are ripe, but firm, fruit flavours, especially in the case of Carmenère and Syrah. Carpe Diem sells some of its grapes to other wineries such as Calina (*see* above).

Carta Vieja (B81)

Villa Alegre de Loncomilla
Tel: (+56) 073 381612;
vicar@ctc-mundo.net
A Spanish family called del Pedregal founded Carta Vieja in the Maule Valley in 1825, not long after Chile gained independence from Spain. Seven generations later, Carta Vieja is still run by the same family. Their estate is based at Villa Alegre in the Loncomilla Valley near the family's late-nineteenth century adobe manor-house featured on their wine labels. Historically, the del Pedregals geared their vineyards to the production of simple wines sold within Chile, usually in Tetrapack, but this style of wine now accounts for only 10% of Carta Vieja's annual sales. More than eight million bottles are produced annually under the Carta Vieja and El Otro labels, including kosher wine. Carta Vieja's most popular wines internationally are light reds smelling of undergrowth and smoky wood, made from Merlot and Cabernet Sauvignon. Its most interesting

wines are produced from Chardonnay and Sauvignon Blanc grapes bought in from Casablanca Valley.

Casa Donoso *See* Domaine Oriental

Casa La Joya *See* Bisquertt

Casa Lapostolle (B54)

Santa Cruz, Colchagua
Tel: (+56) 02 242 9774;
www.casalapostolle.com
Casa Lapostolle was created in 1994 by two influential French and Chilean families: France's Marnier-Lapostolle, who own vineyards and distilleries in France and produce the Grand Marnier liqueur; and Chile's Rabat family who own Manquehue (*see* below). The Rabat family had prime vineyards in the Apalta Valley area of Rapel's Colchagua Valley and owned a winery close by, which was renovated once the joint-venture was signed. Within five years, Casa Lapostolle's wines were obtaining the highest average prices of any Chilean winery. This is no mean achievement, considering Casa Lapostolle produces around two million bottles annually. Casa Lapostolle's allure was augmented when Michel Rolland, the world's most influential red winemaker, was hired as "consultant winemaking partner." Rolland's white wines deservedly arouse less critical interest than his reds, and Casa Lapostolle's are a case in point. They come from estate vineyards in Casablanca Valley and the Requínoa area of Rapel, supplemented by

purchased grapes. The Tanao Blanc is a firm, slightly vegetal dry blend of Chardonnay, Semillon, and Sauvignon Blanc, named after a word used by Easter Islanders meaning "spirit of the earth." Casa Lapostolle Classic Chardonnay, Casa Lapostolle Classic Sauvignon Blanc, and Cuvée Alexandre Chardonnay are hand-picked and barrel-fermented. All show clean, tropical-fruit flavours consistent with cool fermentation, but also a slight hardness, which may be seen as a "French style." Casa Lapostolle's red wines are more diverting, especially for fans of a rich, extracted style (*see* profile of Alta Vista in Argentina, p.122). They come from Requínoa and Apalta in Rapel Valley, again supplemented by grapes bought in from local growers. The Tanao Rouge blends Merlot, Cabernet Sauvignon, and Carmenère, with vegetal Carmenère notes apparent in the aroma and firm, blackcurrant fruit from the Cabernet dominant on the palate. The Casa Lapostolle Classic range of red wines includes a Cabernet Sauvignon and a Merlot, both of which balance direct fruit and oak flavours. More consistent (and more expensive) examples of these two grape varieties sell under the Cuvée Alexandre label. Michel Rolland preferred the elegance of the 2000 Cuvée Alexandre Merlot to the concentration of the 1999, and this may signal a welcome change in style to wines with more obvious freshness. Casa Lapostolle's flagship wine, called Clos Apalta, blends Merlot, Carmenère, Malbec, and

Cabernet Sauvignon from a core of fifty- to eighty-year-old, dry-farmed vines in the Apalta Valley. Some of the vines are so gnarled and mis-shapen as to make entry by tractor impossible, so a horse is used to plough instead, and fully organic farming methods are being adopted. Clos Apalta displays powerful fruit and oak flavours (the wine often has more concentration than elegance) that require several years in bottle to become fully resolved.

Casa Real *See* Santa Rita

Casa Rivas (B13)

Maria Pinto Valley, Maipo
Tel: (+56) 02 225 4506;
oficinacentral@casarivas.cl
Casa Rivas is the only wine producer in the Maria Pinto Valley at the north-western, coastal limit of the Maipo Valley. The vineyards were planted from 1998 on low-lying hills which rise eighty-five metres (280ft) on gentle slopes, allowing excellent drainage and exposure to the sun. The vineyard will eventually produce 1.3 million bottles. The basic Casa Rivas label includes two white wines made from Chardonnay and Sauvignonasse (labelled as Sauvignon Blanc). Both are clean, elegant examples with crisp, rather than excessively fat, textures thanks to early harvesting. A British Master of Wine likened the Sauvignon Blanc's mineral tones to a French Loire Valley white wine such as Sancerre. Both Casa Rivas white wines also appear in barrel-fermented Reserva forms, and are

notable for an appealing, exotic twist of lime in the aftertaste. The Casa Rivas reds are this estate's strongest style. Casa Rivas and Casa Rivas Reserva, made from Cabernet Sauvignon and Merlot, exhibit appetizing, firm, black fruit flavours. The Carmenère has an extra dimension to its bitter cherry fruit. Carmenère specialist Alvaro Espinoza (see Geo Wines) oversees the top wine, called Casa Rivas Gran Reserva Carmenère. This wine is aged for just ten months in French oak; any longer would prematurely dry its concentrated ripe fruit.

Casa Silva (B56)

Hijuela Norte, Angostura
Tel: (+56) 072 716519
Casa Silva claims to be one of the few remaining Chilean wineries in family hands, and can trace its wine origins back five generations. The company dates back to the arrival in Chile of wine-grower Emilio Bouchon, who came to Chile from Bordeaux in the nineteenth century. Casa Silva still owns part of the Angostura estate in the San Fernando area of Rapel Valley (*see also* Selentia, below) first planted by Bouchon. Since 1997, Casa Silva has also developed two new vineyards in Rapel's Colchagua Valley. The first is in Los Lingues, on gentle slopes north of San Fernando. The second is near Lolol, a potentially interesting area between San Fernando and the Pacific coast. Casa Silva currently produces around four million bottles, but only began bottling wine under its own name in 1997. Among the

most interesting is a blend of Chardonnay, Viognier, and Sauvignon Gris, which has an unusual aroma thanks to the combination of Viognier, which provides exotic peach fruit, and Sauvignon Gris, which is noted for its musky character. Sauvignon Gris is one of the few wine grapes (along with Muscat) that can be eaten as a table grape, as well as used as a wine grape. For red wines, Casa Silva is particularly noted for engagingly full-bodied Carmenère, labelled Doña Dominga when unoaked, and Casa Silva Reserva or Casa Silva Altura when barrel-aged. Casa Silva's best red wine is Quinta Generación ("Fifth Generation"), a blend of Cabernet Sauvignon, Carmenère, and Petit Verdot exhibiting agreeably firm oak tannins and ripe black-fruit flavours reflecting Rapel Valley's warm to hot climate.

Casa Tamaya (A1)

Ovalle, Limarí Valley
Tel: (+56) 2650 8490;
vina@tamaya.cl
The Casa Tamaya winery, built in 2001, is named after a Native American word meaning "High Lookout Point." The name refers to a hill site near Ovalle in the Limarí Valley used by the Diaguita tribe in the fourteenth century. Casa Tamaya's Chilean owners aim to produce just over one million bottles from their own vineyards. Initial results seem promising. White wines made from Viognier, Chardonnay, and Sauvignon Blanc show clean, rich fruit flavours and interesting

aromas. Red wines from Sangiovese and Carmenère are light, pleasant wines. All should develop greater complexity as the vines mature.

Casa Viva *See* Viña Casas del Bosque

Casal de Gorchs *See* Manquehue

Casas del Bosque (A7)

Santa Rosa, Casablanca
www.casasdelbosque.cl
Chilean shop owner and businessman Juan Cuneo developed the Casas del Bosque estate in Casablanca Valley from 1991. Cuneo is also a racehorse owner and got to know Casablanca Valley as he travelled through it from his Santiago office on his way to race meetings at Viña del Mar. The estate includes horses and beef cattle, as well as vegetables, plus alfalfa and wheat. From the outside, the modern winery resembles a country supermarket. On the inside it is spacious and well maintained, and produces around 360,000 bottles annually under the Casas del Bosque and Casa Viva labels. The wines are light on flavour and are designed for immediate drinking, as the ephemeral nature of the tropical fruit in the Chardonnay and Sauvignon Blanc whites shows. The best red is a Rapel Valley Cabernet Sauvignon made from purchased grapes. It has a more natural texture than the Casas del Bosque Casablanca Valley Merlot, which has pleasant, if hollow, prune-like fruit. The best wine overall is a sweet white Sauvignon Blanc called "Late Harvest" which

combines creamy fruit and vanilla flavours.

Casillero del Diablo *See* Concha y Toro

Castillo de Molina *See* San Pedro

Chadwick Estate

Torre Sur, Santiago de Chile
Tel: (+56) 02 203 6688

The Chadwick family, who own Errázuriz (*see* below) and who are also involved in Seña with California's Robert Mondavi Winery (*see* below), acquired the San José de Tocornal vineyard in 1945. It is in Puente Alto, in the Maipo Valley. In the mid-1960s, the Chadwicks sold the San José de Tocornal Vineyard to Concha y Toro, who now use it to produce their top wine, Don Melchor, as well as Almaviva with partner Baron Philippe de Rothschild SA (Bordeaux). The Chadwicks retained the San José de Tocornal manor-house and the surrounding park, to which a polo field was added. They converted this polo field into a Cabernet Sauvignon, Cabernet Franc, and Carmenère vineyard from October 1994. There are three main sections surrounded by a wall. As Chadwick Estate Vineyard is lower-lying and further from the Andes than the Don Melchor and Almaviva vineyards, the soils are less uniform and drain less easily. To try to maximize ripeness, the vineyard is picked vine-by-vine rather than row-by-row or block-by-block, as is usual.

left Winemaking crews celebrate after harvest with a wine-crushing competition.

Despite these attempts, Chadwick Estate is inferior to both of its "neighbours," Don Melchor and Almaviva, and also to Errázuriz's Don Maximiano Founder's Reserve and the Errázuriz-Mondavi joint-venture wine, Seña. The debut vintage in 1999 produced 18,000 bottles from a blend of 92% Cabernet Sauvignon and 8% Carmenère. Commentators have detected tastes of blackberry, black cherry and tobacco, with toasted almonds and caramel notes from the oak, but the dominant feature here is one of unripe fruit tannins. The 2000 Chadwick Estate produced 13,200 bottles and was made from 100% Cabernet Sauvignon. Its black fruit was much clearer and riper than in the 1999 example, but it remains a rather unconvincing wine – especially for one asking such a high price.

Chateau La Joya *See* Bisquertt

Chateau Los Boldos (B38)

Requínoa, Cachapoal
Tel: (+56) 072 551230;
boldos@clb.cl

The French Massenez family, who own a distillery in Alsace producing *eaux de vie* (brandy) and fruit liqueurs, acquired Chateau Los Boldos in 1990. Although the French owners produce pear distillate at Chateau Los Boldos, their focus here is wine, and fruit orchards on the estate are being converted to vineyards. These are located around Requínoa, in the Rapel Valley's Cachapoal zone, on gently sloping, rich, pebbly soils first planted with

vines by Basque immigrants in the 1850s. The vineyards were known as Santa Amalia until the Massenez takeover, when the name was changed to sound more French. The oldest vineyards contain a significant percentage of vines planted prior to 1976. Younger vines are being re-trellised to produce lower yields, and to facilitate machine-picking, without which the vine trunks might snap. Around 2.5 million bottles are produced annually under the Chateau Los Boldos Tradition, Vieilles Vignes ("old vines") and Grand Cru labels. White wines made from Chardonnay and Sauvignon Blanc show earthy, rather than fruity, flavours. Red wines from Cabernet Sauvignon and Merlot are superior, with Merlot showing greatest richness. The top wine, Chateau Los Boldos Grand Cru, is a red blend of hand-picked Merlot and Cabernet Sauvignon aged in French oak barrels. Behind some strong oak aromas are deep and very interesting black-fruit flavours; these give a wine best appreciated within five years of the harvest.

Chicureo Estate *See* J. Bouchon

Chileno *See* Ventisquero

Clos Apalta *See* Casa Lapostolle

Clos Centenaire *See* Domaine Oriental

Concha y Toro (B11 & B25)

Las Condes, Santiago de Chile
Tel: (+56) 02 821 7000;
webmaster@conchaytoro.cl

Concha y Toro rivals Argentina's Peñaflor as South America's largest wine company, producing around 145 million bottles annually. Half of all Chilean wine exported to the USA, Chile's biggest customer, and over one-quarter of all wine sold in Chile, comes from Concha y Toro. Unusually for Chile, Concha y Toro is a public limited company, so, as well as delivering wine each vintage, it must also deliver "shareholder value"; but since the company went fully public, Concha y Toro's profits and wine quality have risen steadily. The company owes its late-nineteenth century origins to a Frenchman called Subercaseaux who invested his profits from northern Chile's silver mines in land and vineyards at Pirque in the Maipo Valley. His daughter Emiliana and her wealthy husband, a *marquis* (*marqués*) called Don Melchor de Concha y Toro, soon made Concha y Toro the leader of Chile's late-nineteenth century wine boom. In the 1970s, clever manoeuvring by Concha y Toro's major investors from the influential Guilisasti and Larraín families protected Concha y Toro's interests, first under Allende and then under Pinochet's dictatorship. As Chile widened its horizons in the 1990s, Concha y Toro raised cash by selling shares and bought all the vineyard land it could find between Casablanca in the north and Bío-Bío in the south (*see* Maipo, Rapel, Curicó, and Maule Valley profiles). It hired renowned winemakers including Ignacio Recabarren (*see* Viña Casablanca and Quebrada de Macul, below) and styled its wines for the USA and Europe. Chile's stable economy meant that Concha y Toro could "overdeliver" on quality, while remaining competitive on price. Money from share issues was also invested in Concha y Toro's highly successful, separately run projects: Cono Sur, Santa Emiliana, and Almaviva (*see* those individual entries). Concha y Toro's basic range Casillero del Diablo ("Devil's Cellar") is sourced from vineyards all over Chile. To prevent theft of wine from the main Pirque wine cellar in the 1880s, Don Melchor de Concha y Toro told his workers a devil (*diablo*) lived among the barrels, hence the name. Concha y Toro's Trio range comprises several single-varietal wines blended from a number of vineyards within a specific valley and using moderate oak influence. Highlights include rich Chardonnay, Viognier, and Sauvignon Blanc from Casablanca Valley, and balanced Merlot from Rapel Valley. Concha y Toro's Marqués de Casa Concha range comes from single vineyards owned by Concha y Toro: a soft, balanced, barrel-fermented Chardonnay from Santa Isabel Vineyard in Maipo Valley; a ripe Cabernet Sauvignon with a warm alcoholic aftertaste from Puente Alto in Maipo Valley; a Merlot from a vineyard in Peumo in Rapel Valley's Cachapoal Valley, in which vines of Merlot and its "impersonator" Carmenère are mixed. The Carmenère gives the wine a fresh edge to its succulent, overripe fruit. The Terrunyo ("terroir") range takes the Marqués de Casa Concha concept a stage further by sourcing grapes from specific blocks of vines in single vineyards. Highlights include a commendably ripe Carmenère from the best block of the vineyard in Peumo (cited immediately above), and Casablanca Valley Sauvignon Blanc, from a vineyard called El Triángulo, a deep, serious wine for those who doubt that Chile can make great whites. A Casablanca Valley Chardonnay from the same vineyard, sold under the Amelia label, is one of the few Chilean white wines whose rich complex flavours become fully apparent only after decanting. The Terrunyo Cabernet Sauvignon from Pirque, in the Maipo Valley, is a well-made and intense junior partner to Concha y Toro's top wine, Don Melchor Private Reserve Cabernet Sauvignon from Maipo's Puente Alto area. This deep-coloured, lush but well-structured red exudes juicy blackcurrant and vanilla flavours and pleasant, soft texture. Don Melchor comes from the San José de Tocornal vineyard (*see* Chadwick Estate) planted in 1978 next to Almaviva, which Concha y Toro co-owns (*see* above). Other labels used by Concha y Toro include Explorer, Frontera, Sendero, Sunrise, and Subercaseaux. Concha y Toro also owns Trivento in Argentina (*see* p.146).

Cono Sur (B61)

Chimbarongo, Rapel Valley
Tel: (+56) 02 203 6100;
query@conosur.com
Cono Sur is justifiably regarded as one of Chile's most innovative, forward-thinking and dynamic

wineries. Concha y Toro, Chile's biggest and most traditional wine producer, created Cono Sur in 1993, locating it in an old, badly designed winery called Tocornal in Chimbarongo, in the Rapel Valley, with adjacent vineyards called Santa Elisa. Cono Sur now produces more than five million bottles annually, and is one of Chile's flagship export brands (its main second-label is Tocornal). Crucially, Cono Sur broke the mould by being given a young winemaking team, who were told to style innovative wines for export, with bright, ripe fruit flavours. The first winemaker, Ed Flaherty, was hired from California and gained instant critical acclaim for Cono Sur's Pinot Noir. No one at Concha y Toro had known just how well-adapted this red Burgundian grape was to Cono Sur's cool, foggy Chimbarongo vineyard. Flaherty's "non-interventionist" winemaking style, in which the fermentation was largely left to take its own course, resembled that used in Burgundy. In 1997, Flaherty joined Errázuriz (*see below*) and was replaced by a young Chilean winemaker called Adolfo Hurtado. He took the Burgundian concept a stage further, making regular visits to Burgundy and saving himself "thirty years of trial and error." He learned that Pinot Noir is sensitive enough to exhibit subtle character changes according to where it is grown. So, Cono Sur's Pinot Noirs are now sourced from Casablanca Valley and Mulchén in the southern Bío-Bío Valley, as well as from Chimbarongo in Rapel. No

other Chilean winery comes close to Cono Sur as a producer of vibrant, clean, complex and, crucially, enjoyably risk-free Pinot Noir (Burgundian Pinot Noir can be contemptibly inconsistent and poor-value). Cono Sur was forward thinking by being the first Chilean producer to use artificial (plastic) corks to avoid the risk of mustiness from real cork. It was also one of the first Chilean wineries to run livestock as part of its organic vineyard programme. Sheep graze weeds and geese eat insect pests, reducing the need for tractors and chemicals. Livestock also provide manure for compost that can be used as fertilizer. Cono Sur reasons that the savings made on chemical herbicides and fertilisers can pay the salary of the shepherd and the goose manager. Thus, Cono Sur can remain profitable and environmentally aware at the same time. Winery waste water is recycled and employees are educated in improving their environmental awareness. Most impressive of all is that wine quality here for both red and white wines keeps improving. The old Tocornal winery has been modernized, and the Pinot Noir grapes have their own dedicated open fermentation tanks, which enable the grapes to be foot-trodden as in Burgundy. Cono Sur is the only Chilean winery producing Pinot Noir by this method. Foot-treading gives a gentle fermentation, soft fruit textures, a good level of colour, and enables the bottled wines to develop over several years.

Cono Sur produces more Pinot Noir than any other Chilean winery, but its first Pinot Noir experiments under Ed Flaherty's tutelage in 1995 produced just twenty barrels of wine (6,000 bottles). In remembrance of this, Cono Sur produces a 20 Barrels range in Reserve and Limited Edition tiers. The name Cono Sur refers to the "southern cone," a geographic metaphor for the shape of Latin America. Cono Sur's basic range offers excellent-value wines including a diverting, mineral-scented Gewurztraminer sourced from the Bío-Bío Valley; an inviting Syrah with wild fruit tempered by about 10% Cabernet Sauvignon, and a dry Viognier with an attractively lean texture. Cono Sur's Reserve range includes a lively Chardonnay from Casablanca Valley, and two dynamic oak-influenced reds from Merlot and Cabernet Sauvignon. These offer, unusually, black and red fruit respectively (the opposite is more usual). It is also rare to find that a New World Pinot Noir specialist such as Cono Sur is capable of (or interested in) making equally good wines from Bordeaux varieties such as Merlot or Cabernet. The Cono Sur Visión range is another step up in quality. A barrel-fermented Chardonnay retains its freshness, while the Pinot Noir has genuine richness. Visión Riesling, grown in Chimbarongo, has crisp, pine-scented fruit. The Cono Sur 20 Barrels range comprises Cabernet Sauvignon, Merlot, and Pinot Noir, in which vibrant fruit and oak flavours from barrel-ageing combine effortlessly. The Cabernet Sauvignon is ripe, but not overripe or "jammy". The Merlot has fine-grained texture. The Pinot Noir 20 Barrels, and Pinot Noir 20 Barrels Limited Edition, show clear, refined, expressive fruit beneath evident oak.

Co-operativa Agrícola Vitivinícola de Curicó *See* Vinos Los Robles

Cooperative Vitivinícola Lomas de Cauquenes (COVICA) (B84)

See Lomas de Cauquenes

Copihue *See* Miguel Torres Chile

Cordillera *See* Miguel Torres Chile

Cornellana *See* La Rosa

Córpora

Camino a Totihue km 4, Requínoa
Tel: (+56) 02 206 7868;
www.gracia.cl

Córpora is a powerful agro-industrial group owning universities and hotels as well as producing tea, salmon, fruit, and tin. Córpora owns extensive vineyards in Chile's Aconcagua and Central Valleys, as well as in Bío-Bío in the Southern region. Córpora sells its wines under the Porta and Gracia (or Gracia, de Chile) labels. Red wines come mainly from Aconcagua and Maipo Valleys, while white wines and Pinot Noir come from the cooler Bío-Bío Valley. The grapes are processed in Córpora's Totihue winery in Rapel Valley. The wines are clean, overtly fruity and with moderate oak

influence, criteria designed to appeal to contemporary wine drinkers consuming wine with food. This is especially true of the whites, made from Chardonnay and Sauvignon Blanc, which contain the merest hint of sweetness to accentuate any tropical fruit character present in the grapes at picking. The Gracia, de Chile label translates as "thank you, from Chile" and each wine is also given a Chilean epithet: Reposado ("quiet, slow down"), Celebrado ("celebrated"), Curioso ("curious"), Luminoso ("bright"), Cercanía ("closest"), Relativo ("relative"), Murmullo ("whisper"), Pasajero ("passenger"), Temporal ("storm"), Sereno ("calm"), Eventual ("eventually"), Porquenó ("why not"), Ocasión ("occasion"), Callejero ("someone who likes walking"). Red wines from Cabernet Sauvignon, Carmenère, Merlot, Syrah, and Pinot Noir are light and crisp, with just enough depth to survive drinking with a main course. The top wine under the Gracia label is the dry red Caminante ("walker"), a blend of Aconcagua Valley Cabernet Sauvignon, Merlot, and Carmenère aged in new oak barrels. It has a ripe, firm taste but without the depth or complexity that its ambitiously high price suggests.

Cousiño-Macul (B3 & B20)

Peñalolén, Santiago de Chile
Tel: (+56) 02 284 1011;
www.cousinomacul.cl

The Spanish first planted Cousiño-Macul's sloping vineyard in a sun-trap in Santiago's Peñalolén suburb

in 1554. The vineyard was replanted with vines imported from Bordeaux from 1856, and by the end of the nineteenth century it had become Chile's most respected wine under the direction of a Cousiño widow, Doña Isadora Cousiño. Cousiño-Macul became admired as Chile's "first growth", for the quality of the wines matched the potential of the vineyard. However, by the 1990s, the Cousiño-Macul wines had become dirty, oxidized, and inconsistent, although few commentators seemed prepared to say so in public. In the mid-1990s, the Cousiño family decided to convert gradually most of the Santiago vineyard, one of the greatest in the New World, to real estate. Only 10% of the original vineyard and the surrounding park will remain by 2020. A new vineyard in Buín has been developed using original cuttings from the Santiago vineyard, and a new winery has been built there, too. But Cousiño-Macul's owners cannot realistically expect to retain their "title" of Chile's first growth, because, although the new Buín vineyard is on a good site, the land in this part of the Maipo Medio is flatter than the original vineyard in Peñalolén; since the time of the Ancient Greeks, we have known that the best wines generally come from sloping ground. Also, the Buín vineyard has been designed with (at least partial) machine-picking in mind. No first growth anywhere in the world picks by machine, for this method does not allow substandard grapes to be eliminated from the fermentation vats. The Cousiños defend their decision to move to Buín. They say they are moving in order to make better wine on a better terroir, and that, in terms of rainfall and soil types, Buín is better than Peñalolén. Less controversially, Cousiño-Macul's wines have improved beyond recognition since the move to Buín was completed just before the 2002 harvest. A team of young winemakers have corrected the old winemaking faults, and are making cleaner, better-balanced wines. Cousiño-Macul's basic range includes promising fruity white wines from Chardonnay and Sauvignon Blanc, with subtle oak influence, and a clean, dry Riesling labelled Doña Isadora. Reds from Merlot and Cabernet Sauvignon show attractive, rich fruit. Cousiño-Macul's Antiguas Reservas range includes an elegant, barrel-fermented Chardonnay and a refined, oak-aged Cabernet Sauvignon with bold fruit and characterful tannins. The top wine is the Cousiño-Macul Finis Terrae blend of Cabernet Sauvignon and Merlot, made from the oldest Santiago vines. This wine at least has the potential to remain Chile's greatest red wine, and vat samples from 2002 augur well. The 2002 wines are the first for a decade in which Cousiño-Macul's winemaking has preserved the integrity of its grapes, whether from Buín or Santiago. However, as prefabricated supermarkets are built on top of the original historic, and indisputably great, sixteenth-century vineyard, one cannot help but think what might have been.

COVICA *See* Lomas de Cauquenes

Cremaschi Furlotti (B79)
San Javier, Maule Valley
Tel: (+56|) 02 633 0776;
winecris@chilesat.net
The Cremaschi family owns two wineries and substantial vineyards around San Javier in the Maule Valley. In 1998, a refurbishment programme began at their main winery. The winemaking is improving, although the wines lack some texture and balance. Whites from Sauvignon Blanc and Chardonnay are attractively chalky, if somewhat dilute, while red from Merlot, Carmenère, Cabernet Sauvignon, and Syrah can taste somewhat "boiled". Once the winemaking problems are ironed out, the reds in particular should provide some interesting flavours, for the Cremaschi family has some very fine vineyards.

Cuvée Alexandre *See* Casa Lapostolle

Darwin's Path *See* Manquehue

De Martino *See* Santa Inés/ De Martino

De Solminihac *See* Santa Mónica

Domaine Oriental (B73)
Talca, Maule Valley
Tel: (+56) 02 233 1056;
www.domaineoriental.cl
Domaine Oriental takes its name from its geographic position at the east (orient) of the Maule Valley's biggest town, Talca. A member of the Donoso family acquired it in 1810, built a colonial mansion, and, from the mid-nineteenth century, planted vineyards with French grape varieties. A group of French-Tahitian investors acquired the business in 1989. They renovated the existing "Oriental" vineyard, added another one nearby called Las Casas de Vaquería, and built a new winery in the architectural style of Señor Donoso's original colonial mansion. In order of ascending price, the wines are sold as Casa Donoso, Casa Donoso Reserve, Casa Donoso 1810, and Casa Donoso "D" Casa Donoso 1810 and Casa Donoso "D" are red blends of Cabernet Sauvignon and Carmenère aged in French oak for more than twelve months; both display the tannic pepper character often found in these two grape varieties. The Casa Donoso range was formerly known as Domaine Oriental, while the Domaine Oriental Reserve was known as as Clos Centenaire. Domaine Oriental uses the Maule Valley denomination for all its wines. Overall, the winemaking is well handled, almost managing to make lightweight fruit taste genuinely substantial. Red wines from Cabernet Sauvignon, Carmenère, and Merlot show more texture than whites from Chardonnay and Sauvignon Blanc, but all are crisp and approachable soon after bottling. Please note that Domaine Oriental has no connection with the branch of the Donoso family owning Apaltagua (*see* above).

Domaine Paul Bruno *See* Aquitania

Domus Aurea *See* Quebrada de Macul

Don Amado *See* Torreón de Paredes

Don Maximiano *See* Errázuriz

Don Melchor Private Reserve *See* Concha y Toro

Don Miguel *See* Miguel Torres Chile

Don Osvaldo *See* Bisquertt

Don Sebastien *See* Valle Frío

Doña Bernarda *See* Luis Felipe Edwards

Doña Isadora *See* Cousiño-Macul

Doña Javiera (B8)
Fundo San Miguel, El Monte
Tel: (+56) 02 818 1470;
t_global@entelchile.net
This historic, family owned estate in the Talagante area of Maipo Valley is starting to hit form. The vines are relatively young, having been replanted in the 1990s, making the wines potentially slightly uneven. At their best they show well-rounded fruit and well-integrated oak. The white wines from Chardonnay and Sauvignon Blanc have a slight edge on the Merlot and Cabernet Sauvignon reds. Doña Javiera produces wine under the Río Claro label.

left Roberto Echeverria Jnr., winemaker at the Echeverria winery in Curicó Valley.

Dueto *See* Morandé

Echeverría (B71)

Viña La Estancia, Molina
Tel: (+56) 02 207 4327;
info@echewine.com
This welcoming, family-owned
winery is based near the town
of Molina in the Curicó Valley. The
Echeverrías became involved in
wine in the eigtheenth century,
but only began bottling their own
wine from 1993. Their vineyard
surrounds the functional winery
in a single block, and grows the
main Bordeaux grape varieties as
well as Chardonnay. Around one
million bottles are produced each
year. Echeverría wines are steady
rather than spectacular, but are
generally clean, reliable, and
easy to drink.

Edición Limitada *See* Morandé

El Aromo (B82)

17 Oriente 931, Talca
Tel: (+56) 02 335 9077;
exports@elaromo.cl
Founded near Villa Alegre in the
Maule Valley in 1922 by a French
company, El Aromo is now
Chilean owned. Most of its wines
are sold within Chile, and initial
attempts at bottled wine for
export were somewhat
disappointing and lacking
real clarity.

El Bosque *See* Viña Casablanca

El Ceibo *See* Errázuriz

El Crucero *See* Siegel

El Descanso *See* Errázuriz

El Oriente *See* Portal del Alto

El Otro *See* Carta Vieja

El Principal *See* Valette Fontaine

El Triángulo *See* Concha y Toro

Enigma *See* Santa Inés/De Martino

Envero *See* Apaltagua

Errázuriz (A4)

Panquehue, San Felipe
Tel: (+56) 02 203 6688;
www.errazuriz.com
Don Maximiano Errázuriz planted his
first vineyard at Panquehue in the
then-barren Aconcagua Valley in
1870, using vines imported directly
from France. The firm is now owned
by his descendents, the Chadwick
family, who produce about five
million bottles annually under the
Errázuriz label. Errázuriz's Wild
Ferment Chardonnay and Pinot Noir
wines provide examples of how
calculated risk-taking by the
winemaker delivers something that
is both outstanding and different.
The grapes for both Wild Ferment
wines come from Errázuriz's La
Escultura vineyard in Casablanca
Valley and are usually fermented
without being seeded with
commercial wine yeasts. Wines
seeded with commercial yeasts
ferment quite quickly, usually within
ten days. Errázuriz Wild Ferment
Chardonnay ferments over a period
of five weeks because the yeasts take
longer to multiply into a colony
capable of digesting grape sugar and

converting it into alcohol (or wine).
This means that the grapes must be
picked slightly earlier, at a lower
level of ripeness or potential alcohol,
at 12.5%, rather than over 13.5%;
otherwise the wild yeasts cannot
ferment the wine fully. But
a slow fermentation creates a
Chardonnay with richer texture and
more interesting flavours of jasmine
and honeysuckle, rather than the
one-dimensional, tropical fruit-
flavour so common to the majority
of modern Chardonnays. After
fermentation, the wine is aged in
new and used French oak barrels for
nine months or so, which
accentuates its gentle, refined
texture. The current winemaker at
Errázuriz, the Californian Ed Flaherty,
was Cono Sur's first winemaker.
Flaherty's Wild Ferment Pinot Noir at
Errázuriz offers a real contrast in
style to the excellent Pinot Noir
wines now produced by his
successor Adolfo Hurtado at Cono
Sur. The Errázuriz Pinot Noir displays
a bright floral or raspberry character
found in good red burgundy,
whereas Cono Sur's Pinot Noirs are
generally deeper coloured and
exhibit black-cherry or plum
influences. As well as pioneering
winemaking styles, Errázuriz was the
first Chilean winery to plant vines on
hill slopes when its historic Don
Maximiano vineyard behind the
winery was enlarged. Errázuriz
developed other sloping vineyards in
Aconcagua Valley such as Las
Vertientes and El Ceibo. Errázuriz
also owns flatter vineyards in Curicó

Valley, such as El Descanso, and the La Escultura vineyard in Casablanca. The names of these vineyards sometimes feature on Errázuriz labels as part of a Single Vineyard range. This includes increasingly good oak-aged Sangiovese and Carmenère wines with very subtle character. White wines in the Single Vineyard series from Chardonnay and Sauvignon Blanc grown at the La Escultura estate show clean, well-balanced, integrated mineral and oak flavours. Sweet late-harvested whites are only made infrequently, but they are probably Chile's most underrated of this difficult (for Chile) style. However, most of the glory goes to Errázuriz's Cabernet Sauvignon, Syrah, and Merlot red wines labelled Errázuriz Estate, Don Maximiano Estate Reserva, or Max Reserva. These wines show well-judged levels of ripeness, considering that in the heat of the Aconcagua Valley it is easy for grapes to become overripe and prune-like. The company's top wine is the Don Maximiano Founder's Reserve, sourced from vines grown on the hill slopes behind the white-washed Panquehue winery. Ed Flaherty's first vintage of "Don Max" (as it is known) in 1997 produced a rich wine with spicy Californian flavours. The cooler 1998 vintage produced a fresher, less exuberant, more Bordeaux-like wine. The 1999 was blended from 90% Cabernet Sauvignon, 5% Cabernet Franc, and 5% Merlot, and has elegant, firm, textured fruit, leaving a blackberry and briar aftertaste. The

2000 was blended from 95% Cabernet Sauvignon with 5% Cabernet Franc, of which 84,000 bottles were produced, double the quantity of 1999, even after a huge amount of grape thinning in the vineyards before harvesting. Ed Flaherty says the 2000 vintage taught him that a small vintage (1999) is not always superior to a bigger one (2000), although he adds that, without thinning off some of the grapes, 2000 would have been a poor year. The result is a concentrated, elegant wine with fine, rather than blockbuster, texture. It tastes riper than Chadwick Estate (from Maipo Valley) and more elegant and interesting than Seña (from Aconcagua Valley), yet is the least expensive wine of the three.

Escudo Rojo *See* Baron Philippe de Rothschild Maipo Chile

Explorer *See* Concha y Toro

Finis Terrae *See* Cousiño-Macul

Finísimo *See* Canepa

Floresta *See* Santa Rita

Francisco de Aguirré (A3)
Camino a Puntiqui, Ovalle
Tel: (+56) 02 462 2000;
www.vinafranciscodeaguirre.cl
Chile's leading producer of Pisco brandy, Pisco Capel, developed Francisco de Aguirré in 1993 as its wine arm (*see* North Santiago, p.21). In the middle of the vineyard is Francisco de Aguirré's visitor

centre and gravity-fed winery. This produces more than four million bottles of still and sparkling wines annually. The main labels are Misty Peak, Palo Alto, and Tierra Arena. The overall standard for both red and white wines is encouraging. The most appealing reds are made from Cabernet Franc, which mixes floral, fruit and slight herbaceous flavours, and Sangiovese, which is unusually vibrant considering the vines are less than a decade old. Carmenère also performs well, giving wines of deep purple colour but approachable tannins, while Merlot exhibits an overripe fruitcake character. Syrah is consistent, with subdued aromas of soft-red fruit (raspberry, strawberry). Cabernet Sauvignon and Pinot Noir seem a little stretched in terms of texture, possibly a result of heat-induced stress in the vineyard. Francisco de Aguirré's dry white wines include a critically acclaimed Chardonnay combining rich tropical fruit with an austere, mineral texture, and a Sauvignon Blanc that, like its Cabernet Sauvignon counterpart, can be lifeless. Viognier, however, shows increasing depth and harmony. Francisco de Aguirré's top range of wines is called Tempus. These are blended from two varieties: Cabernet Sauvignon and Merlot for Tempus Red; Chardonnay and Viognier for Tempus White. Both wines are aged in French oak barrels, but the wood flavours imparted by the oak are well integrated and do not dominate the fairly refined mineral and fruit flavours. One specialty wine produced here is a sweet, simple,

wines of south america

tangerine-flavoured white wine called "Late Harvest". This is made from Muscat, the main grape from which Pisco brandy is distilled.

Fresita *See* Manquehue

Frontera *See* Concha y Toro

G Butron *See* Tuniche

Galope *See* Indómita

Gato Blanco/Negro *See* San Pedro

Geo Wines
Las Condes, Santiago de Chile
Tel: (+56) 02 207 9166;
sereymo@entelchile.net
Sergio Reyes and winemaker Alvaro Espinoza (*see* Antiyal, above) formed Geo Wines in March 2000 to advise Chilean wineries on any or all of the following aspects of wine production: grape growing, wine fermentation, blending, labelling, and wine sales. Clients have included Haras de Pirque, Casa Rivas, Viña Leyda, Apaltagua, and Santa Emiliana's VOE project. Espinoza's belief in more sustainable farming methods influences his work with these clients. He argues that healthy soils help vines produce more interesting, riper-tasting wines. Espinoza's father, a respected Chilean winemaker, trained him, but later Jacques Boissenot, a publicity-shy Bordeaux winemaker, honed his style. So, for red wines Espinoza favours a ripe, but subtle style in which oak nuances from barrel-ageing support the wine's fruit flavours but do not dominate, while

concentration comes from ripe grapes, rather than from extractive winemaking and heavy oak-ageing. Espinoza feels this latter style of wine wins wine competitions but is too extracted to be drunk with pleasure and is totally unsuited to Chile. Geo Wines produces its own wines under a number of labels, including Quiltro ("stray dog"), Pargua ("full moon" in the native Mapuche language), Coyam ("oak" in Mapuche), Kuyen ("moon" in Mapuche), Novas (a group of stellar constellations), and Nazca (after the mysterious prehistoric Nazca lines in southern Peru). The main grape varieties Geo works with are Merlot, Cabernet Sauvignon, Syrah, Petit Verdot, Carmenère, and Pinot Noir. Geo own no vines, but do consult and advise to growers. Grapes are sourced from specific vineyards and growers within Rapel and Maipo Valleys. The wines are well-made, ripe, clear, mouthwatering examples of Chile's potential.

Gillmore *See* Tabontinaja

Gold Reserve *See* Carmen

Gracia, de Chile *See* Córpora
Gran Araucano *See* J.&F. Lurton Chile

Gran Tarapacá *See* Tarapacá

Grial *See* Apaltagua

Hacienda Cunaco *See* Viu Manent

Hacienda El Condor (B68)
Santiago de Chile
Tel: (+56) 02 233 2505

The owners of TerraMater (*see* below) founded Hacienda El Condor by acquiring a vineyard and a nineteenth century winery at Sagrada Familia in the Curicó Valley in 1996. The winery was modernized and the wines are sold under the Campero and Condor labels, or as Millamán, which means "golden condor" in the native Mapuche language. As parts of the El Condor vineyard were last replanted in the 1960s, "Old Vine" selections from Semillon, Cabernet Sauvignon, and Malbec are produced. These wines share the clean, fruity characteristics of the TerraMater wines, but have an extra degree of depth and complexity. Old Vines Semillon Reserva has an attractive, rich, earthy texture overlaid by substantial flavours of new French oak barrels, but is not vegetal or resinous. Old Vines Cabernet Sauvignon/Malbec shows how Cabernet Sauvignon's firm fruit can become softer and broader when allied to Malbec's more obviously rich texture. A Syrah/Malbec aged in new and older oak also offers rich, balanced fruit and oak flavours. Delicious sparkling Malbec reds are being developed.

Haras de Pirque (B28)
Correo Pirque, Pirque
Tel: (+56) 02 854 7910;
ww.harasdepirque.com
In 1991, Chilean businessman Eduardo Matte bought a thoroughbred horse farm in a valley at Pirque in the Maipo Valley's Andean foothills. Matte added a horse-training area and running track

for his racehorses. The slopes around the estate remained unused, so from 1992 Matte consulted one of Chile's most respected wine authorities, Alejandro Hernández of Portal del Alto, before deciding to plant a vineyard. Initially, Haras de Pirque sold its grapes to wineries such as Caliterra, but soon built its own winery. It is cut into the side of a hill in a horseshoe shape and is gravity-fed. It features an underground barrel cellar offering cool, humid surroundings, ideal for keeping wines fresh while they mature or ferment in wood, which all Haras de Pirque's wines do. The first wines were produced in 2000, with Alvaro Espinoza of Geo Wines (*see* above) consulting. The Equus range includes two white wines (Chardonnay and Sauvignon Blanc) partly fermented in French oak barrels, and an oak-aged Cabernet Sauvignon. All three show clean, full, rich textures and strong individuality. The Haras Character range includes the same three wine styles as at the Equus level, but the wines are more intense. Oak-fermented Sauvignon Blanc is one of the most difficult wines to make, but the Haras Character Sauvignon Blanc, which is partially fermented in French and American oak barrels, has enough freshness not to be overpowered by the wood. The Haras Character Chardonnay is partially fermented in French oak and has the tropical fruit flavours so common to this variety in the New World; but it also has the mineral tones found in the best white Burgundy. Haras de Pirque labels its two best wines

Haras Elegance. The first, a Chardonnay, has intense fruit with refined texture and demonstrates that Maipo Valley can produce more than just great red wines. The second, the Haras Elegance Cabernet Sauvignon, has a full, satisfying, firm texture; the black-fruit flavours reveal themselves slowly. Haras Elegance Cabernet Sauvignon is partially fermented in oak vats, then aged in smaller oak barrels. The oak vats allow the wine to ferment steadily preserving elegance, while the oak barrels provide the wine with its vanilla overtones. Haras de Pirque's excellent range is due to be extended once plantings of Carmenère, Merlot, Cabernet Franc, Syrah, Petit Verdot, and Viognier reach maturity.

House of Morandé *See* Morandé

Hugo Casanova *See* Purisima

In Situ *See* San Esteban

Indómita (A12)

Ruta 68 km 64, Casablanca
indomita@entelchile.net
A Chilean company owning extensive fruit orchards and vineyards throughout the country founded Indómita in 1996. This is one of the few Chilean wineries to draw on grapes from all parts of the Central Valley (Maipo, Rapel, Curicó, and Maule) as well as from the Casablanca Valley. A gravity-fed winery designed to produce three million bottles was built in Casablanca Valley. The wines, sold under the Brio and Galope labels, or as Indómita Gran Reserva, are lively

and well made. The best examples are: Casablanca Valley Chardonnay, Maipo Valley Cabernet Sauvignon (sourced from vines in Puente Alto), and Rapel Valley Carmenère.

Insigne *See* Carmen

J.&F. Lurton Chile (B62)

Domaine de Poumeyrade, France
Tel: (+33) 05 57 55 12 12;
jflurton@jflurton.com
The Bordeaux-based Lurton brothers, Jacques and François, are developing a well-designed boutique winery at Lolol, in the Rapel's Colchagua Valley. Open fermentation tanks allow grapes for red wines to be foot-trodden or punched down for softer textures (*see* Cono Sur). A vineyard will be planted from 2003. In the meantime, wines are made from purchased grapes under the Araucano and Gran Araucano labels. White wines from Chardonnay and Sauvignon Blanc are characteristically clean, crisp and full-flavoured. Reds from Cabernet Sauvignon and Carmenère show hints of wild fruit. The top Gran Araucano red, a Cabernet Sauvignon, Merlot, and Carmenère blend, shows concentrated fruit and understated oak. *See* J.&F. Lurton Argentina (p.134) and J.&F. Lurton Uruguay (p.169), as well as San Pedro, below, where Jacques Lurton oversaw winemaking between 1994 and 2001.

J. Bouchon (B80)

Camino a Constitución, km 30
San Javier
jbouchon@jbouchon.cl

Like Selentia and Casa Silva, Julio Bouchon owes its origins to nineteenth century immigrant French wine-grower Emilio Bouchon. Of these three domaines, J. Bouchon produces the least interesting wines. J. Bouchon owns two vineyards – Chicureo near San Fernando in Rapel Valley, and Las Mercedes in Maule Valley. The names of these vineyards sometimes feature on the labels of J. Bouchon's wines. White wines made from Chardonnay and Sauvignon lack fruit. Red wines from Cabernet Sauvignon, Merlot, and Malbec are finer than the whites but can still be inconsistent.

La Escultura *See* Errázuriz

La Fortuna (B67)

Camino a la Costa, Sagrada Familia
fortuna@tnet.cl
La Fortuna is a family owned vineyard, recently modernized winery, and extensive fruit farm based at Sagrada Familia in Curico's Lontué Valley. A partnership with the VIA Group (*see* below) has added extra impetus to La Fortuna's wine quality, thanks to a much-needed winery upgrade. La Fortuna has three separate Curicó Valley vineyards: El Semillero, La Cabaña, and San Jorge. El Semillero vineyard was one of the first in Chile in the modern era to be officially run on organic lines, and La Fortuna hopes that all its vines will be under certified organic management by 2005. The youngest vines in the El

right Chile's Patagonia region, unlike Argentina's, has no vineyards.

Semillero vineyard are Syrah, and already these show good potential. Red wines made from El Semillero Malbec vines planted in the 1960s show deep colour, and intense, sensual black fruit. White wines from Sauvignon Blanc have improved greatly since the mid-1990s, and rank with the best from Curicó Valley (which, apart from Casablanca Valley, is the most consistent area for Sauvignon Blanc in Chile). Wines from conventionally farmed grapes include clean, tropical and naturally rich Chardonnay, plus Carmenère, Cabernet Sauvignon, and Pinot Noir reds with upfront fruit and light, easy-drinking textures.

La Misión (B26)

San Luis de Pirque
www.wfchile.cl
La Misión is co-owned by a Chilean shipping magnate, a French conglomerate owning Champagne Henriot, and other luxury lifestyle brands, together with Chablis producer William Fèvre. The estate takes its name from an old French mission in Pirque, in the Maipo Valley, within which the winery is housed. The vineyards are mainly in Maipo Valley, while some Merlot grapes are sourced from Teno in Curicó Valley. Initially, La Misión's vineyards contained a significant proportion of white grapes, but the world trend toward red wines means that some Chardonnay and Sauvignon Blanc vines have been grafted over to Cabernet Sauvignon and Pinot Noir, respectively. La Misión produces white wines of high

quality from the remaining vines, including Chardonnay, Sauvignon Blanc, and a Sauvignon/Chardonnay blend. The Chardonnay in particular has a distinctive, firm, mineral character reminiscent of good Chablis. La Misión's red wines made from Carmenère, Merlot, Pinot Noir, or Cabernet Sauvignon are equally elegant. They display moderate ruby colours, with suitably refreshing fruit. The oak tones in the La Misión Gran Cuvée range need two to four years in bottle to settle. Around one million bottles are produced annually, labelled La Misión or La Misión del Clarillo. For another winery named after the Spanish Jesuits missions, *see* Misiones de Rengo (below).

La Palmería *See* La Rosa

La Quinta *See* Santa Inés/De Martino

La Ronciere (B31)

Av San Martín, Rancagua
Tel: (+56) 072 230136;
info@laronciere.com
Family owned La Ronciere vineyard and winery is based in Rancagua in Rapel's Cachapoal Valley. The wines are made in an easy-drinking, value-for-money style. Oak-influenced Reserva reds include peppery Cabernet Sauvignon and Syrah.

La Rosa (B32 & B36)

Fundo La Rosa, Ruta H,
66-G km 37, Peumo
Tel: (+56) 02 670 0600
SOFRUCO, one of Chile's largest producers of fresh and dried fruits,

owns La Rosa. The Ossa family, which controls SOFRUCO, have been growing wine grapes in Chile since the mid-nineteenth century. The Ossas sold their grapes to Santa Rita until the mid-1990s when they began making their own wine under the La Palma or La Palmería labels. These names come from La Rosa's finest vineyard, the isolated La Palmería de Cocalan, in the coastal hills of Rapel's Cachapoal Valley. The vineyard surrounds a "palmería" or palm forest containing the southernmost palms in the world, some over 1,000 years old. This estate was acquired from Santa Alicia (*see* below) in the 1960s. La Rosa's other Rapel Valley vineyards are called Cornellana and La Rosa; these names also feature on La Rosa's wine labels. About twelve million bottles are produced annually, and quality is very consistent. Chardonnay and Sauvignon Blanc under the La Palma/La Palmería label are clean, light-textured wines with no oak influence. La Rosa's best reds are firm, oak-aged Merlot and Cabernet Sauvignon wines labelled as Reserva or Gran Reserva.

Laroche & Coderch

c/o Valdivieso
www.valdivieso.cl
French producer Michel Laroche, who produces Chablis and Languedoc wines, and Chilean Jorge Coderch, one of the owners of Valdivieso, formed this joint venture in 2001. Early releases of Pinot Noir and Cabernet Sauvignon show

marked wood influence, beneath which are some complex fruit flavours. Casablanca Valley Chardonnay shows vibrancy and richness, again with pronounced oak.

Las Casas del Toquí
See Viña de Larose

Las Lomas *See* Lomas de Cauquenes

Las Mercedes Estate *See* J. Bouchon

Las Nieves (B47)
Fundo Santa Teresa, Rengo
www.torreon.cl
Brothers Javier and Alvaro Paredes set up Las Nieves in 1997 as a venture separate from their family's wine business, Torreón de Paredes (*see* below). The wines are made from grapes coming from either Javier and Alvaro's own vineyards in Rengo in the Rapel Valley, or from purchased grapes. The wines have uncomplicated fruit flavours and offer value for money; wines made from Cabernet Sauvignon are the best.

Laura Hartwig *See* Santa Laura

Le Dix *See* Los Vascos

Legado de Armida *See* Santa Inés/De Martino

Leyenda *See* Viña de Larose

Lomas de Cauquenes (COVICA)
Tel: (+56) 73 512 026;
www.covica.cl
This is one of only a handful of wine cooperatives in Chile (*see also* Los Robles). The vineyards occupy the rolling coastal hills in the Maule Valley, where Chile's Central Valley ends. Lomas de Cauquenes makes a fascinating red wine from the much-maligned País variety. The vines were last replanted in the late nineteenth century. Called Las Lomas Viñas Viejas ("old hillside vineyards"), it comes from an organic, unirrigated vineyard ploughed by horse in the traditional way. The wine has great density, owing to extremely low yields of grapes per vine, and displays unusual deep, leathery fruit. Comparing this wine to a classic Chilean Central Valley Cabernet Sauvignon or Merlot is as sensible as comparing chalk with cheese. Other wines made from certified organic grapes under the Las Lomas label include reds from Cabernet Sauvignon and Malbec (labelled as Cot Rouge), and whites from Chardonnay and Sauvignon Blanc. All are made in a clean, modern style while retaining a wild element to their fruit. This cooperative also makes a range of conventionally farmed wines called Antu Mapu. Highlights here include Chardonnay and Sauvignon Blanc, and reds from Cabernet Sauvignon, Carmenère, Merlot, and Pinot Noir.

Los Pocillos *See* Valle Frío

Los Robles (B66) (Cooperative Agrícola Vitivinícola de Curicó)
Blamaceda 565, Curicó
vinoslosrobles@losrobles.cl
A group of small wine-growers founded this wine cooperative in Curicó in 1942, after a serious earthquake devastated their vineyards (*see* Lomas de Cauquenes, above, for another cooperative). More than fifty vineyard owners still bring their grapes to this to this (recently modernized) winery each vintage. The vineyard owners, plus the staff working in the winery, are free to join a trade union. This is significant because most vineyard and winery workers in Chile have only temporary employment contracts, so the wine companies they work for do not automatically provide them with health insurance or union membership. Many are unable to claim for loss of earnings or medical care when industrial accidents occur, involving either badly maintained machinery or inadequately labelled pesticides. The Los Robles cooperative is the only Chilean winery producing wines accredited under guidelines drawn up by the fair trade organisation Traidcraft. These stipulate that working conditions for the producers must be safe and non-exploitative, and that a fair price must be paid for the product (in this case grapes) so that producers can trade themselves out of poverty. The Los Robles Traidcraft Fair Trade range includes a rich, dry Sauvignon Blanc, a warm, inviting Carmenère, and a pleasant red blend of Cabernet Sauvignon and Merlot. All are clean, well-made wines for early drinking. Under the Traidcraft scheme, grape growers can invest in replanting unproductive vineyards. Some of these growers were caught in a poverty trap in 1973

after financial support promised under Salvador Allende's democratically elected socialist government was withdrawn, following Pinochet's military coup. The cooperative produces the equivalent of ten million bottles annually. Also of interest is its Barrel Selection Sauvignon Vert, a crisp oak-influenced dry white made from Sauvignonasse.

Los Vascos (B49)

Peralillo, Colchagua Valley
Tel: (+56) 02 314 372

The Los Vascos vineyard is named after a Basque family who first worked it from the mid-eighteenth century. The estate lies mainly on flat ground near the Colchagua Valley town of Peralillo, in the lee of the coastal hills. In 1988, the Basque family's descendents sold a part-share in Los Vascos to Domaines Barons de Rothschild (Lafite), owners of the famous Bordeaux First Growth, Château Lafite-Rothschild. The Lafite-Rothschild investment in the winery and vineyards, plus some astute marketing, has made Los Vascos one of Chile's more profitable wineries. In 1995, Santa Rita acquired the remaining share in Los Vascos. Santa Rita, the Maipo Valley wine producer, is considered by many to be currently Chile's "First Growth," or best producer, noted particularly for its rich, succulent red wines. However, the style of the Los Vascos wines has remained essentially as it was before Santa Rita became involved. Chardonnay and Sauvignon Blanc resemble the dreary white Bordeaux wines of the 1970s, in the dark age before the arrival in the 1980s of Australia's fruit-driven whites, which brightened our perceptions. The Los Vascos red wines are scarcely better, prompting one of the world's most respected wine writers, Hugh Johnson, to describe Los Vascos as a "Lafite-Rothschild-Santa Rita operation, but no Chilean first growth" (*Hugh Johnson's Pocket Wine Book 2000*, Mitchell Beazley, p.243). The Los Vascos red wines are made predominantly from Cabernet Sauvignon, which can be, as it is here, austere. Vanilla flavours from oak ageing dominate, leaving what fruit there is in the wines rather dry and bitter. In order of ascending price, the Los Vascos reds are called Los Vascos, Los Vascos Réserve or Grande Réserve, and a wine called Le Dix, a special bottling released in 1998 to mark ten years of Lafite-Rothschild's involvement in Chile. Demand for the Los Vascos wines worldwide is so strong that it is expanding its vineyard area; this style of wine obviously has an eager market. Château Lafite-Rothschild is also involved in the CA-RO project in Argentina (*see* p.125).

Luis Felipe Edwards (B60)

Santiago de Chile
Tel: (+56) 02 208 6819

This increasingly reliable Rapel Valley winery is named after its Chilean businessman owner. There are two vineyards of near-equal size in Rapel's Colchagua Valley. One is called San José de Puquillay, and lies in its own valley surrounding the Luis Felipe Edwards winery near Nancagua. The oldest vines here lie on the valley floor where the soil is quite rich (arable crops such as maize and wheat are grown in neighbouring fields), so new vineyards have been terraced into the surrounding horseshoe of hills, on poorer soils well-suited to late-ripening red wine grapes such as Carmenère and Syrah. The second vineyard, called Santa Bernadita de Pupilla, lies much closer to the Pacific Ocean on flat ground, which is easy to work. It produces a rich, dry Chardonnay for early drinking. Luis Felipe Edwards produced bulk wine until 1994, when the winery was established with French advice. In 1999, an Australian winemaking consultant was hired, and as a direct result the Luis Felipe Edwards wines made from Merlot, Carmenère, and Cabernet Sauvignon have become fruitier. The biggest leap forward has been made with the Syrah (Shiraz). The best examples, labelled as Pupilla (after Santa Bernadita de Pupilla vineyard), or Terraced (after the new terraced vines) acquire a rich vanilla influence from ageing in American (rather than French) oak barrels, in the manner of Australian Shiraz. The top red wine here, Doña Bernarda, is a firm blend of Cabernet Sauvignon, Carmenère, Shiraz, and Malbec, with a resinous tone from ageing in French and American oak barrels.

Manquehue (B9 & B16)

Santiago de Chile
Tel: (+56) 02 750 4000;
www.manquehue.com

The Rabat family founded Manquehue in 1886, and it is now one of the most important suppliers of wine to the Chilean market. Manquehue's profile increased after the Rabat family founded Casa Lapostolle with France's Marnier-Lapostolle family (*see* above). Manquehue has wineries in Santiago and at Pirque in the Maipo Valley. These produce wines under the Casal de Gorchs and Rabat labels. The best Casal de Gorchs wines are made from Cabernet Sauvignon and Merlot sourced from Manquehue's vineyards in the Apalta Valley in Rapel. The still wines lack a degree of finesse and depth; however, they should improve as winemaking consultants from France exert their influence. By far the best wines from Manquehue are its sparkling wines, which come in two forms. The first, called Fresita and Mont Piñas, are sweetened with strawberry and pineapple juice, respectively. The second style comprises a more classic range of dry white sparkling wines blended from Chardonnay, Sauvignon Blanc, and Pinot Noir grapes, using secondary fermentation in bottle (as it is done in Champagne) to produce the bubbles. The grapes are sourced from several of the coolest Chilean wine subregions, in the same way that most Champagne is blended from a number of different villages, rather than from one specific vineyard. This allows a consistent flavour and texture or "house style" to be maintained. These sparkling wines are sold under the Casal de Gorchs, Darwin's Path, and Southern Star labels. After several years of experimentation with input from French winemakers, the 2001 vintage produced 40,000 bottles of clean wine with balanced, mineral-rich fruit flavours, and elegant fizz.

Manso de Velasco *See* Miguel Torres Chile

Mapa *See* Baron Philippe de Rothschild Maipo Chile

Maquehua *See* Miguel Torres Chile

Marqués de Casa Concha *See* Concha y Toro

Matetic (A14)
Fundo El Rosario, Lagunillas
Casablanca
Tel: (+56) 02 232 3134
The Matetic family arrived in Punta Arenas, in the far south of Chile, in the late nineteenth century from Croatia. Over time, the family developed a farm in hilly, forested land near the port of San Antonio in the Aconcagua region. The farm produced corn, hay, beans, blueberries, wheat, and beef cattle. In 1999, a vineyard was planted with Sauvignon Blanc, Pinot Noir, Syrah, and Merlot. Matetic is certified organic and is run on integrated, self-sustaining lines. Compost to fertilize the soil is made from cow manure and hay produced on the farm, together with the grape-stems left over from winemaking. Cover crops such as vetch, barley, and flowering plants are sown between the vine rows to control erosion. From the start, the vines have been pruned hard to maintain low yields. This builds up the vines' natural resistance to pests and diseases by keeping them strong, and also means that wines with concentrated flavours can be produced. New World Syrah can end up smelling of egg or rotting cabbage when fermented in closed fermentation tanks, so Matetic and its Californian winemaking team decided to ferment their Syrah in open-top fermentation tanks. Some winemakers believe that open-top fermentation tanks risk oxidizing the Syrah (turning it to vinegar) but this only really occurs if the grapes come from high-yielding, poor-quality vines, which is not the case here. Syrah needs to be able to breathe during fermentation to show its floral character to full effect, and to allow its red-fruit flavours to dominate the palate. Otherwise, it develops characters such as cedar, meat, or leather.

Maymay *See* Alempue

Medalla Real *See* Santa Rita

Memorias *See* Valette Fontaine

Miguel Torres Chile (B64 & B65)
Curicó, Curicó Valley
www.torreswines.com
Miguel Torres, one of Spain's most famous wine producers, acquired his first Chilean vineyard just south of Curicó town in 1979. He was the first modern European wine-grower to invest in this country, which was

then still isolated under Pinochet's dictatorship. Torres equipped his winery with stainless steel tanks, rather than the traditional *raulí* (a local beech) vats that were then common in Chile, but which were difficult to keep clean. This change sparked a revolution. Within fifteen years, Chilean wineries had burned their raulí vats and Chile's hitherto dirty, musty wines became cleaner and fruitier. The original Torres vineyard, called Maquehua, lies on heavy ground next to the winery and is planted with Merlot and Cabernet Sauvignon. The San Francisco Norte vineyard, planted on volcanic ground just west of Lontué in Curicó Valley, was acquired in 1984. It grows mainly Cabernet Sauvignon, Pinot Noir, and Chardonnay, plus Syrah and Sauvignon Blanc. San Francisco Norte's oldest Cabernet Sauvignon plot was last replanted in the 1890s, and is called Manso de Velasco, after the Spanish governor who founded Curicó in 1743. Fundo Cordillera, planted on volcanic soil east of Molina, was acquired in 1991. This cool area is close to the Andes and suits white grapes such as Sauvignon Blanc, Chardonnay, Gewurztraminer, and Riesling. Since 1991, Torres has acquired two mainly red-wine vineyards in the Maule Valley areas of Linares and San Clemente. The San Clemente vineyard is home to Torres' first fully organic project. Through this project, Torres is changing the way it fertilizes all of its vines. It is avoiding the use of nitrogen-rich chemical fertilizers that exacerbate the overly fertile nature of Chile's valley soils. Instead, compost containing lower levels of nitrogen is being used. The main Torres labels, Copihue, Santa Digna, and Maquehua, produce Sauvignon Blanc and Chardonnay whites, and Merlot and Cabernet Sauvignon reds with clear fruit and light oak. A fruity white called Don Miguel is a blend of Gewurztraminer and Riesling. Torres also uses Riesling in a tempting sweet, late-harvest white fermented and aged in French oak. A weighty red aged in French oak called Cordillera contains around 15% Syrah, 20% Merlot, and 65% Carignan. The Carignan vines are more than fifty years old, and are unirrigated. They provide Cordillera with the wild red fruit and leather flavours associated with reds from the southern Rhône Valley or from northern Spain. The top red wine, Manso de Velasco, shows an elegant mix of blackcurrant fruit from old-vine Cabernet Sauvignon and attractive French oak flavours. Torres also makes some of Chile's most appealing sparkling wines, blended from Chardonnay and Pinot Noir with a second fermentation in the bottle, the same way as Cava is made (Cava comes from Spain's Penedés region, where Miguel Torres is based). Miguel Torres says he invested in Chile partly because Chilean workers had unrivalled knowledge of vineyard management in the New World. Torres's annual wine festival for its workers in Curicó town lasts three days and is one of Chile's major wine tourism events. Torres recently opened Chile's first public winery restaurant at its Curicó winery, handily located just off the Pan-American Highway.

Millahue *See* Portal del Alto

Millamán *See* Hacienda El Condor

Misiones de Rengo (B45)
Torre Santa María, Santiago de Chile
www.tarapaca.cl
Compañía Chilena de Fósforos produces the Misiones de Rengo range of wines from a winery in the Cachapoal Valley in the town of Rengo. During the eighteenth century, Rengo was a resting place for missionaries travelling to southern Chile. The grapes are purchased, and the winemaking is totally separate from that of Tarapacá (*see* below), which Compañía Chilena de Fósforos also owns. Early Misiones de Rengo releases from the 2000 and 2001 vintages showed clean, attractive fruit and well-handled oak ageing.

Misty Peak *See* Francisco de Aguirré

Mondavi/Errázuriz
This joint-venture partnership between Chile's Errázuriz winery and California's Robert Mondavi Winery produces the Caliterra range (*see* above) and Seña (*see* below).

Montemar *See* Aresti

Montes (B42 & B53)
Huechuraba, Santiago de Chile
www.monteswines.com
Four Chileans intent on producing top-quality wine for export founded

Montes in 1988; it was then referred to as "Chile's first boutique winery". Since then, it has grown from being an 80,000-bottle brand to one of about four million annually. Standards have been maintained, as one of the four original partners, winemaker Aurelio Montes, has adapted his winemaking style during this time. New vineyards have been developed in Apalta and Marchigue, in Rapel's Colchagua Valley. Montes' original vineyards in Curicó Valley provide Chardonnay and Sauvignon Blanc for white wines. These show more obvious levels of fruit than they did in the mid-1990s, even when oak fermented (they are labelled Montes Reserve, Fumé or Barrel Fermented). The American oak used for fermentation imbues deep straw tones to the wines' colour and a rich, flattering texture. From the Curicó vineyards also comes a late-harvest sweet white blended from Gewurztraminer and Riesling, with a fresh, slightly "baked" tangerine sweetness. Montes has styled its red wines to show quite overt oak influence from barrel-ageing over the last decade, but the oak becomes more subdued once the wines are given at least two years' bottle age. Red wine highlights at the Montes Reserve, Montes Oak Aged Reserve, or Limited Selection level are sourced from the Colchagua Valley. They include a Malbec with initially dusty, but ultimately bold fruit, a succulent Merlot with 15% Cabernet

Sauvignon to tone down its exuberance, and a commendably even-textured Cabernet Sauvignon. A Cabernet Sauvignon/Carmenère blend sourced from the Apalta Valley shows Bordeaux flavours of cedar and cigar box, together with Chilean ripeness. A Reserve Pinot Noir made from purchased Casablanca grapes is rich and slightly wild. The Montes Alpha range comprises concentrated and often complex Cabernet Sauvignon, Chardonnay, Merlot, and Syrah, which are fermented or aged in French oak. Montes Alpha Cabernet Sauvignon shows how ripe and thick-tasting this variety can become on the hot slopes surrounding the Apalta Valley. Montes Alpha Chardonnay from Curicó Valley is almost exotic, with rich, creamy oak. Montes Alpha Merlot, from the Apalta Valley, has rich alcohol and needs drinking soon after it is bottled. Montes Alpha Syrah from the Apalta Valley is outshone by Montes Folly, a superior (and more expensive) Syrah bottling, which has tremendous depth, yet somehow retains its balance. Grapes come from the winery's best and steepest plot in Apalta. The top wine from Montes is called "M" It is a Bordeaux-style blend from Cabernet Sauvignon, Merlot, Cabernet Franc, and Petit Verdot vines planted in the Apalta Valley in the early 1990s. About 9,000 bottles of "M" were produced in 1996, and 36,000 in 1999. In texture, "M" is less obviously polished than Santa Rita's Casa Real, Concha y Toro's Don Melchor, or Quebrada de Macul's

Domus Aurea; but these are Maipo Valley reds from close to the Andes, whereas "M" is from Rapel's warmer coastal hills. Oak and hot berries combine in "M", along with glycerol and eucalyptus, all in concentrated doses, rounded out by elegant, wild-fruit flavours.

MontGras (B52)

Providencia, Santiago de Chile
Tel: (+56) 02 520 4355;
www.montgras.cl

Although MontGras was only established in 1992, it is already considered one of Chile's leading wineries, thanks to a combination of vineyard innovation, solid winemaking, and bullish marketing. Brothers Eduardo and Hernán Gras founded MontGras with Cristián Hartwig, whose family also owns another leading winery, Santa Laura (*see* below). Both MontGras and Santa Laura are at the forefront of promoting Rapel Valley's Colchagua zone. MontGras has pioneered the planting of vineyards along the tops of hills, rather than just on the hillsides, with its Ninquén Hill project. The Ninquén plateau gets more sun but also receives more of the sea breezes coming off the Pacific to the west than the valley floor does. The cooling influence should prevent the grapes from overheating as they ripen. The MontGras winery works on a gravity system, and recycles its waste water for use on the vines as drip irrigation. The vineyard is divided into small blocks, each oriented slightly differently to the angle of the

sun, so that the vines ripen at different times. This way of planting is a help to the winemakers, who can find it difficult to cope if all the grape varieties ripen at the same time. Whites from Chardonnay and Viognier are clean, rich, and balanced, with subtle oak. Oak-aged reds dominate at MontGras, and are labelled as MontGras Reserve and MontGras Limited Edition. The Syrah is particularly notable for its combination of ripe fruit and generous, rather than overpowering, American oak, and shows how well-adapted this grape is to the Colchagua Valley's warm, coastal hills. The Limited Edition wines are sometimes called Single Vineyard when they come from a single block of MontGras' vineyards: Malbec from block 141, Syrah (144), Zinfandel (116), a Cabernet/Merlot blend (172 and 173), and Viognier (165). The Malbec has a much firmer character than its Argentine counterpart, while the Zinfandel shows succulent cherry fruit. MontGras makes a solid red blended from four varieties (Cabernet Sauvignon, Carmenère, Malbec, and Merlot) called Quatro, but the flagship MontGras wine is called Ninquén. This is a blend of the best grapes available at each harvest, and can be made from a grape blend, or from a single variety, as was the case with the 100% Cabernet Sauvignon produced in 2000. It is aged in new French and American oak barrels and is not fined or filtered. Ninquén has fine texture and generous fruit. The wine will gain extra dimension when the vineyards mature.

Mont Piñas *See* Manquehue

Morandé (B48)

Huechuraba, Santiago de Chile
Tel: (+56) 02 443 1024;
www.morande.cl

Pablo Morandé was the first to recognize the potential of the Casablanca Valley when he developed experimental vineyards for Concha y Toro here in the 1980s. Morandé now has his own vineyard in Casablanca Valley called El Ensueño ("the dream"), as well as others in Maipo Valley and Rapel Valley, where his modern winery is located. Morandé produces nearly five million bottles annually. His wines are carefully styled to suit contemporary drinking fashion, yet with labels such as Aventura ("adventure") and Pionero ("pioneer") he reminds consumers of his past contribution to Chile in general and to the Casablanca Valley in particular. The unfiltered Aventura range of red wines demonstrates that Morandé's desire to experiment is alive and well, for Aventura is made from non-traditional grape varieties such as Carignan, Cinsault, Malbec, César, and Blauer Portugieser. Morandé's Dueto ("duet") range comes from Casablanca Valley. Chardonnay, Riesling, and Sauvignon Blanc whites have biting freshness, but texture, too. Merlot is bright, while Pinot Noir combines juicy fruit and a wild note of coffee. Some of the Pinot Noir grapes are frozen before fermentation for up to three weeks to capture the fruit flavours present in the skins without taking on any of their astringency. The Terrarum range ferments in, or is aged in, American oak, and shows that Morandé can make Chardonnay from Maipo Valley, too; it is well crafted, fatter, and more obviously intense than his Casablanca version. Morandé's Edición Limitada wines are one-off releases from the best barrels ("barricas") of those grape varieties that performed well in any given year (similar to Valdivieso's "V" range, *see* below). These wines can be outstanding, as is the Maipo Valley Malbec "88 Barricas" 1999. This wine was made from Malbec vines that were planted in 1935 and are still worked by horse. It compares well to Noemía from the Argentine Patagonia (*see* p.140), with concentrated tar and wild damson fruit, and great elegance. Another one-off wine, the Golden Harvest Casablanca Sauvignon Blanc, "48 Barricas" 2000, is a delicious, concentrated, but balanced sweet white with incredible vitality – Chile's most complete late-harvest white. Morandé's Vitisterra range comes from single-vineyard, single-lot wines aged in French oak. French oak makes Maipo Valley Merlots and Cabernet Sauvignons approachable and elegant. The top wine, House of Morandé, is a single-vineyard Maipo Valley Cabernet Sauvignon aged in French oak, blended with small amounts of Merlot and Cabernet Franc. This is a refreshing wine with thick fruit and good character. Morandé's other labels include Vistamar, Subsol, and Niebla.

Nativa *See* Carmen

Neblus *See* Viña Casablanca

Niebla *See* Morandé

Ninquén *See* MontGras

Nuevo Mundo *See* Santa Inés/De Martino

Ochagavía

Santiago de Chile
www.santacarolina.com

Ochagavía's first vineyard was planted twelve kilometres (7.5 miles) southwest of Santiago by Don Silvestre Ochagavía, the "father of the Chilean wine industry," in 1851. Ochagavía became the first Chilean grower to replace poor-quality grapes left over from the Spanish conquest with classic French vines, kick-starting Chile's modern wine revolution (*see also* the work of Tiburcio Benegas for Trapiche in Argentina, p.145). Ochagavía is now part of the group which owns Santa Carolina (*see* below); its original vineyard in Santiago has now been converted to real estate for housing.

Odfjell Vineyards (B6)

Santiago de Chile
Tel: (+56) 02 811 1530;
info@odfjellvineyards.cl

Odfjell is owned by a family of Norwegians who were among the first to ship wines in bulk from South America in the 1950s. They no longer ship wine but they do ship liquid chemicals. The family founded Odfjell Vineyards in 1991, but only produced their first bottled wine in 1999. Odfjell's vineyard, near Talagante in the Maipo Valley, supplies most of the grapes, with the rest coming from purchased grapes sourced from further south. In order of ascending price, wines are labelled Rojo, Armador, Orzada, and Aliara. The Orzada range includes three soft red wines from Maule Valley, made from Cabernet Franc, Carmenère, and Carignan, with obvious but not excessive oak overtones. The top red wine, Aliara, is a potentially decent blend of Cabernet Sauvignon and Carmenère.

Orzada *See* Odfjell Vineyards

PachaMama *See* TerraMater

Palmeras Estate *See* Santa Emiliana

Palo Alto *See* Francisco de Aguirré

Peñalolén *See* Quebrada de Macul

Perez Cruz (B29)
Fundo Liguai, Camino Los Morros s/n
Huelquén, Paine
furibe@perezcruz.com
Eleven brothers and sisters from the Perez Cruz family founded this estate near Paine, in the Maipo Valley, in 2000. The winery has been described as "an extraordinary hull-like structure, built completely out of pine, and close up, one felt one was viewing IKEA's flat-packed interpretation of the Guggenheim museum in Spain." The owners say that they wanted to make an environmental commitment by building the winery from renewable,

organic materials; so it came as a surprise to learn that Perez Cruz's vineyards are farmed conventionally, particularly as Chile is one of the few wine regions in the world in which one can easily grow wine grapes organically. Commendably, however, the vines are cropped at very low yields, demonstrating the owners' commitment to producing concentrated red wines. These are made from Cabernet Sauvignon, Syrah, Merlot, Carmenère, and Malbec. Once Perez Cruz's winemaking style evolves from dense, heavy wines into something more refined and elegant, this property could become one of Maipo's star wineries.

Peteroa *See* Canepa

Porta
Tel: (+56) 02 206 7868;
www.gracia.cl
Jorge Gutiérrez created the Porta wine brand before selling it in 1997 to concentrate on Anakena (*see* above). Porta then became part of Córpora (*see* above).

Portal del Alto (B24)
Alto Jahuel, Buín
Tel: (+56) 02 821 3363
Alejandro Hernández founded Portal del Alto in 1970, when he bought a Cabernet Sauvignon vineyard in Buín, in the Maipo Valley. Hernández is a respected and well-liked professor of winemaking at one of Chile's leading universities. He also consults to Chilean wine producers in need of guidance (*see* Haras de Pirque,

above). He chose the Buín vineyard from which to make his own wine because it had been planted using vine cuttings first brought to Chile from Bordeaux and other French vineyards in the mid-nineteenth century. Hernández has three other vineyards. One is in Maipo Valley, at Pirque; another, in the Rapel Valley's San Fernando area, contains Cabernet Sauvignon vines dating from 1902, and Merlot from the 1940s; and in 1992, Hernández inherited a fourth estate called El Oriente. This lies at the southern limit of the Central Valley, in the Loncomilla zone of the Maule Valley. Portal del Alto produces around 800,000 bottles annually. Its white wines are solid and rich, but lack the balance of Chile's best. Reds from Merlot and Cabernet Sauvignon are labelled Reserva and Gran Reserva to signify ageing in oak barrels. These have the distinctive flavours of wild hedgerow fruit one always hopes to find in wines from healthy, old vines. They have the soft mouthfeel popular among Chilean drinkers; if they were styled more toward foreign palates, with more bite, freshness, and clarity to the fruit, they would surely be among Chile's most sought-after wines. Portal del Alto also labels its wines as El Oriente and Millahue.

Primus *See* Veramonte

Privada Last Edition *See* Tarapacá

Pupilla *See* Luis Felipe Edwards

Purisima (B72)

Camino las Rastras, Talca
Tel: (+56) 712 66540;
www.casanova.cl
The Casanova family have made wine in Chile since they arrived here from northern Italy in the late nineteenth century. Their vineyard near Talca in the Maule Valley is planted to mainly Sauvignon Blanc and Cabernet Sauvignon. Purisima's owner, Hugo Casanova, releases wines as Purisima Estate or under his own name. White wines from Sauvignon Blanc and Chardonnay show crisp, clean, light asparagus flavours and, increasingly, Maule Valley richness. Reds from Merlot and Cabernet Sauvignon improved dramatically since 2000, showing clean, increasingly ripe textures.

Quebrada de Macul (B2)

Peñalolén, Santiago de Chile
The Quebrada de Macul vineyard, in the Santiago suburb of Peñalolén, is adjacent to Aquitania's (*see* above) and to Cousiño-Macul's (*see* above) vineyards. (Quebrada de Macul was once part of Cousiño-Macul's vineyard.) Quebrada de Macul's owner, a lawyer, sold his grapes to other wineries until 1996, when he invited leading Chilean winemaker Ignacio Recabarren (*see* Concha y Toro, above, and Viña Casablanca, below) to become a minority partner. Now, around 100,000 bottles of distinctive red wines are produced, mostly from Cabernet Sauvignon planted in 1971. Alba ("dawn"), aged in older oak barrels, has crisp, wild berry fruit. Stella Aurea ("star") is

aged in new and second-year oak barrels and displays a juicy, ripe texture, with aromas of menthol, in classic Maipo Cabernet Sauvignon style. The top wine, Domus Aurea "house of the sun", is blended with tiny amounts of Merlot and Cabernet Franc. It has all the elements of good Chilean red wine: crisp fruit, solid, ripe texture and an elegant aftertaste.

Quinteros *See* William Cole

Rabat *See* Manquehue

Requingua

Santiago de Chile
Tel: (+56) 75 310 047;
requinguavineyards@entelchile.net
The Chilean family that owns Requingua ("corner of the winds") is gearing its substantial Cabernet Sauvignon vineyards in the Curicó Valley towards a range of easy-drinking red wines, made with the help of winemaking consultants from several foreign countries. Sauvignon Blanc, Chardonnay, Merlot and Carmenère have become increasingly fine-tuned, too.

Río Claro *See* Doña Javiera

Rojo *See* Odfjell Vineyards

Rosario Estate *See* Tarapacá

San Carlos de Cunaco *See* Viu Manent

San Esteban (A6)

2074 La Florida, Los Andes
sanesteban@vse.cl
San Esteban owns a significant hillside vineyard called Paidahuen in

the warmest and most easterly part of the Aconcagua Valley. It contains Cabernet Sauvignon, Merlot, Carmenère, Syrah, Nebbiolo, Sangiovese, Mourvèdre, Chardonnay, and Sauvignon Blanc. The San Esteban winery was upgraded in the mid-1990s, and San Esteban hopes to challenge the historic domination of Errázuriz in the Aconcagua Valley. The top red wines, labelled In Situ, include Cabernet Sauvignon, Syrah, and Carmenère. These show soft, ripe fruit flavours overlaid with a more obvious amount of new French oak than found in the Errázuriz red wines.

San José de Tocornal *See* Almaviva, Chadwick Estate, and Concha y Toro

San Pedro (B70)

Fundo San Pedro, Curicó
Tel: (+56) 02 373 4300;
info@sanpedro.cl
Compañías Cervecerias Unidas (CCU), Chile's largest brewer, largest mineral water producer, and second-largest soft-drinks manufacturer, acquired San Pedro, one of Chile's largest wine producers, in 1994. San Pedro's two Curicó Valley wineries produce one hundred million bottles of wine annually. San Pedro's San Miguel Vineyard, which surrounds its ultra-modern winery in Molina, covers 400 ha (988 acres) and is the largest single vineyard in Chile. San Pedro also has another 2,000 ha (4,942 acres) of vines in the Central Valley (*see* Maipo, Rapel, Curicó and Maule Valley profiles). San Pedro's Gato ("cat") wine brand is the

largest selling Chilean brand worldwide, with annual sales of twenty-four million bottles. The Gato Blanco ("white cat") range includes Semillon and Chardonnay, but the Sauvignon Blanc is the best-known white wine and is Chile's best-value example of this grape variety. It is made from Sauvignonasse and Sauvignon Blanc and exudes ripe gooseberry flavours. A similar but more concentrated Sauvignon Blanc called 35 South (or 35 Sur) contains a higher proportion of Sauvignon Blanc to Sauvignonasse. Around 50% of San Pedro's vineyards are planted with Cabernet Sauvignon, and this variety produces the company's best red wines in the Gato Negro ("black cat") range and under the 35 South label. This brand is named after the 35th parallel, which runs through San Pedro's San Miguel vineyard. San Pedro's oak-aged Castillo de Molina Cabernet Sauvignon red is consistently San Pedro's most attractive and versatile wine, showing classic Chilean Cabernet Sauvignon blackberry fruit and a crisp texture. Other red wines from San Pedro, such as Merlot, Carmenère, and Syrah, have improved since 2000, but still show unripe peppery (rather than overtly ripe) fruity characters. San Pedro's 1865 range is aged in new oak barrels and honours the year in which San Pedro uprooted poor-quality vines left over from the Spanish conquest and replaced them with grapes such as Cabernet Sauvignon and Merlot from

Bordeaux. San Pedro's top wine Cabo de Hornos ("Cape Horn") comes from its oldest Cabernet Sauvignon vines and develops appealing cedar and lead-pencil flavours after three to six years in bottle. This style reflects the Bordeaux-New Zealand influence that revolutionized San Pedro's previously rather old-fashioned wines between 1994 and 2001 (see J.&F. Lurton Chile, above, and Valdivieso, below, for more detail). With new Chilean winemaker Irene Paiva at the helm from 2001, Cabo de Hornos should develop a riper, more Chilean personality. San Pedro also co-owns Totihue in Chile, and owns Chile's Santa Helena and Argentina's Finca La Celia (see p.133).

San Rafael

Fundo Las Chilcas, Talca
www.viawines.cl
San Rafael was founded by Jorge Coderch and members of his family, who part-own Valdivieso and who also created the VIA Group (see below). San Rafael is the VIA Group's flagship vineyard and winery, located at Chilcas, near Talca in the Maule Valley's new San Rafael area. The Chilcas vineyard is part of a larger farm that also raises cattle. The hills were planted with vines, and the low-lying areas, which are fertile and more humid, were left for maize and pasture for the cattle. The cattle also consume the grape seeds and skins left over from winemaking, and provide manure for composting into fertilizer. This is applied in autumn, immediately after harvest. Two

natural reeds, one called *totora* and the other called *pita*, are used for tying the vines to the supporting wires, instead of plastic-based ties. Part of the vineyard is under organic management. The site for Chilcas was chosen because it is set on rolling hills, rather than on the fertile plain; the quality potential here is extremely high. A new, state-of-the-art winery has been built at Chilcas.

Santa Alicia (B15)

PO Box 301 - V, Santiago de Chile
www.santa-alicia.com
Santa Alicia produces around 1.8 million bottles of adequate, easy-drinking wine from two Maipo Valley vineyards called El Ciprés and Los Maitenes, located near Santa Alicia's main winery in Pirque. Santa Alicia was known as Las Casas de Pirque when it was owned by a Chilean businessman and politician called Valdés. After his death in the 1960s the reputation of the estate underwent a hiatus. The La Palmería de Cocalan vineyard in the Rapel Valley, which Valdés had owned, was sold to La Rosa (see above). Today Santa Alicia is part-owned by descendents of Valdés, who are gradually improving wine quality.

Santa Amalia See Chateau Los Boldos

Santa Carolina (A9 & B4))

Santiago de Chile
www.santacarolina.com
Santa Carolina was founded in 1875 and is one of Chile's most renowned wine names. The company produces

the equivalent of thirty million bottles annually. A conglomerate producing jam, powdered milk, yogurt and fresh fruit owns Santa Carolina, Ochagavía (*see* above), and Viña Casablanca (*see* below), and was also, briefly, the owner of Santa Ana in Argentina (*see* p.142). Santa Carolina has vineyards and wineries across the Central Valley, and in the Casablanca Valley. Its oldest winery, near Chile's national stadium in Santiago, is a historic monument; its vaulted underground brick cellars are now used for the ageing of wine in barrel. Santa Carolina's oak-aged wines, labelled Reserve, Family Reserve, or Barrel Selection ("Barrica Selection") are of more interest than its unoaked Classic range. The oak gives the wines time to breathe before it is bottled, adding extra nuance to light fruit flavours and harmonizing any unevenness of texture. White wines from Chardonnay are made in an obvious, buttery style and with marked, but integrated, alcoholic warmth behind. The Sauvignon Blanc whites are broader and weightier than those made under the Casablanca Winery label. Red wines include adequate Carmenère, richer Merlot, lean Cabernet Sauvignon, and lush Syrah with profound oak influence. The top wine, VSC (for Viña Santa Carolina), is a Maipo Valley red blended from Cabernet Sauvignon, Syrah, and Merlot, with slightly overripe fruit and a simple oak veneer.

Santa Digna *See* Miguel Torres Chile

Santa Ema (B17)

Izaga 1096, Isla de Maipo

Santa Ema is the least significant of the three wineries founded by Italian immigrants in the 1930s in Isla de Maipo (the others being Canepa and Santa Inés). Santa Ema has a steady market for its traditionally-made wines in Chile and in the USA, and is still owned by its founding Pavone family.

Santa Emiliana

Las Condes, Santiago de Chile
Tel: (+56) 02 235 7715

Concha y Toro created Santa Emiliana in 1986 as a source of value-for-money wines to be made independently of Concha y Toro. Santa Emiliana was named after the wife of Don Melchor, the Marqués de Casa Concha, who founded Concha y Toro in the late nineteenth century. Santa Emiliana produces about twenty million bottles annually, and enjoys strong sales of its Andes Peaks, Palmeras Estate, and Walnut Crest brands in the USA. These offer value for money and are sourced from a dozen vineyards and wineries in the Casablanca and Central Valleys, as well as the Southern region. The top-selling whites are crisp, mouthwatering Casablanca Valley Chardonnay and Central Valley Sauvignon Blanc. Popular reds are simple, juicy Cabernet Sauvignon and Merlot labelled Maipo, Rapel, or Central Valley. Santa Emiliana also has a stake in Villard Estate (*see* below) and a new organic project called VOE (*see* below).

Santa Helena (B58)

Providencia, Santiago de Chile
Tel: (+56) 02 362 1526

Santa Helena is to San Pedro what Cono Sur is to Concha y Toro: a vineyard and winery which has been hived off from the main body of a much larger wine company in order to produce smaller amounts of more distinctive wines under a separate brand name. The logic is that, because foreign wine drinkers are "trading up," or drinking less wine but of better overall quality, brands such as Santa Helena could represent the future of the wine market. San Pedro created Santa Helena in 2001 from six of its vineyards (*fundos*) in the Rapel Valley, and a winery near Santa Cruz de Colchagua, which was upgraded. The first wines produced by Santa Helena from the 2001 vintage were ordinary at best. In 2002 the wines remained dilute, but the Chardonnay and Sauvignon Blanc did show more clarity, and the Cabernet Sauvignon, Merlot, Pinot Noir, Carmenère, and Malbec reds had healthier-looking colours if underripe textures. The wines are sold under the Santa Helena, Santa Helena Siglo de Oro ("golden century") and Santa Helena Selección del Directorio labels.

Santa Inés/De Martino (B18)

Manuel Rodriguez 229, Isla de Maipo
Tel: (+56) 02 819 2959;
www.demartino.cl

An Italian called De Martino founded Santa Inés in the Maipo Valley town of Isla de Maipo in the 1930s. Grape juice, grape concentrate and wine are produced in two separate plants that were the first in Chile to recycle their waste water. Around fifteen million bottles of wine are produced each year. Grapes are purchased from Casablanca and Maipo Valleys, or are sourced from the De Martino's Isla de Maipo Vineyard, La Quinta. The family began an organic trial here in 1999 on a small part of the vineyard, but then decided it made no sense to have part of the vineyard organic and the rest conventional, so it became 100% organic. Organic Cabernet Sauvignon, Malbec, and Carmenère grapes are blended in a bright red wine with firm red fruit called Nuevo Mundo ("New World"). Other wines produced here are labelled De Martino, Santa Inés, and Enigma, with the top range from the oldest vines called Legado de Armida or Reserva de Familia. The

below San Pedro's ultra-modern winery also has cellars dating from the ninteenth century.

winemaking is consistent and has evolved steadily from the mid-1990s. White wines from Chardonnay and Viognier are clean, rich and slightly buttery, while Sauvignon Blancs express a crisp, green fruit character. Red wines from Cabernet Sauvignon and Merlot are deservedly popular for their clear fruit, while Malbec and Syrah show the most obvious depth. The Carmenère Legado de Armida shows persistent bramble and black cherry flavours, and well-integrated oak. A late-harvest sweet Semillon white shows pronounced, grassy character and delicate sweetness.

Santa Isabel *See* Viña Casablanca

Santa Laura (B59)

Santa Cruz de Colchagua
Tel: (+56) 72 823179;
vslaura@entelchile.net
Santa Laura is named after Laura Hartwig, a member of the Bisquertt family (*see* above), who planted a

vineyard on land she inherited near Santa Cruz de Colchagua in the Rapel Valley. Together with her husband Alejandro Hartwig, they have made Santa Laura a source of some of Chile's most elegant, full-flavoured wines. Only around 120,000 bottles are produced, making Santa Laura one of the smallest wineries in the Colchagua Valley. Unusually for Chile, both red and white wines are equally good. Surplus grapes are taken by MontGras (*see* above), in which Santa Laura has a shareholding. Laura Hartwig Chardonnay shows clean, concentrated fruit, and a lively, rich texture. It is partly fermented in French oak barrels before being aged on the lees (dead yeasts left over after fermentation) to soften it. This technique only adds to the wine if the grapes are healthy and ripe at picking. Otherwise, the dead yeast cells give the wine dirty, sour milk flavours. This wine proves that even though Colchagua Valley is known for its red wines, its white wines can be outstanding. Three oak-aged red wines are made under the Laura Hartwig label. Cabernet Sauvignon is from the oldest vines, first planted at the end of the 1970s. Its texture, deep red colour, and black-fruit flavours are just the qualities one would hope to see in a top Colchagua Valley Cabernet. Carmenère is more obviously rich, and the use of oak is well handled. The Merlot, perhaps the least comfortable of the Bordeaux grapes in Colchagua Valley's hot climate, retains freshness, despite its evidently rich level of alcohol. Again, the use of oak ageing supports the fruit, rather than disguises it. Santa Laura's top wine is the Laura Hartwig Gran Reserva, a blend of Cabernet Sauvignon, Merlot, and Carmenère. This combines the best elements of the three red wines mentioned, as well as producing an extra dimension to the grape flavours – which is just what one would hope for in a winery's top wine.

Santa Mónica (B33)

Rancaugua, Rapel Valley
Tel: (+56) 72 224951;
www.santamonica.cl
Santa Mónica is a Chilean-owned family winery producing around one million bottles of wine from estate-grown grapes from in and around the Rapel Valley town of Rancagua. Owner Emilio de Solminihac studied winemaking in Bordeaux in the 1950s; an old-fashioned winemaking style characterizes the bottled wines (more wine is sold in bulk). The wines could become more expressive once Emilio's daughter finishes her winemaking studies in Bordeaux and returns to Chile. Wines are sold under the de Solminihac, Santa Mónica, and Tierra del Sol labels.

Santa Rita (B21)

Las Condes, Santiago de Chile
Tel: (+56) 02 362 2000;
www.santarita.com
A mining entrepreneur founded Santa Rita in the nineteenth century. Now Santa Rita is one of Chile's five largest wineries, with annual sales of around sixteen million bottles. It is also believed to be one of Chile's best-managed, both in terms of the wines it produces under head winemaker Cecilia Torres, and the prices it obtains for them in North America and the UK. Santa Rita has vineyards in Casablanca, Maipo, Rapel, and Curicó Valleys, but is based at Buín in the Maipo Valley, where it owns a historic underground wine cellar. In 1814, "the liberator," General Bernardo O'Higgins, sought refuge here with 120 of his men during the Battle of Rancagua (*see* Rapel Valley, p.34). They survived and then fought successfully for Chile's independence, which the Spanish granted in 1818. The Chilean heroes are honoured in Santa Rita's most widely sold wine brand, called "120." The highlight in this range is the increasingly consistent Sauvignon Blanc. More interesting wines with deeper fruit and moderate oak influence are sold under the Santa Rita Reserva label, particularly with regard to red wines made from Merlot, Syrah, and Cabernet Sauvignon; Carmenère and Pinot Noir are also sound. Santa Rita's Medalla Real range provides an interesting oak-fermented Chardonnay and an oak-aged Merlot, both from Casablanca Valley. Medalla Real red wines sourced from Maipo Valley grapes include a flamboyant Cabernet Sauvignon, which combines mint, black fruit and French oak, as well as a more subdued Syrah that smells of little but is richly flavoured. Santa Rita's most exciting current project is a French-oak aged red called Triple C, blended from Maipo Valley Cabernet Sauvignon, Cabernet Franc, and Carmenère. The first vintage, in 1997, showed thick fruit texture and appealing oak flavours. Red wines sold under the Floresta label include a rather strongly oak-flavoured Cabernet Sauvignon from the Apalta area of Colchagua Valley, and better-balanced reds blended from two varieties, such as Syrah/Merlot and Petite Sirah/Merlot. Santa Rita's top wine, Casa Real, comes from the firm's best Cabernet Sauvignon vineyards. Casa Real is probably Chile's most consistent "icon" red in the sense that the jump in quality between 1989, Casa Real's first vintage, and 1999, Casa Real's best vintage to date, is much smaller than the leap made through the years by Concha y Toro's Don Melchor or Errázuriz's Don Maximiano Founder's Reserve, for example. Chilean Cabernet Sauvignon from Maipo Valley is always associated with black fruit; Casa Real is no exception. It certainly has more "aristocratic" textures and flavours compared to Don Melchor, being much firmer on the finish. Compared to Don Maximiano, which is sourced from warmer, coastal hills in Aconcagua, Casa Real has the extra clarity and freshness one would expect from vines grown in the cooler Andean foothills. Casa Real is named after the house built in 1880 by the

company's founder, which is now a luxury hotel and restaurant. Santa Rita also owns a part-share in Los Vascos (*see* above), and wholly owns both Carmen (*see* above) and Terra Andina (*see* below). Santa Rita's project in Argentina is called Doña Paula (*see* p.129). It is named after the lady who, sympathetic to the cause of independence from Spain, allowed the 120 fugitive soldiers to hide in her wine cellar in 1814.

Segú (B83)

Fundo Mirador, San Javier
Tel: (+56) 73 210078;
www.vinosegu.com
Segú has Spanish origins but is now run by two branches of the Segú family, based in Linares, in the southern part of the Maule Valley. Two vineyards, located on rolling coastal hills, are planted with mature, increasingly well-maintained vines; about 70% are red varieties. About one million bottles are produced annually. The Segú winemaking style has evolved of late. White wines made from Chardonnay, Sauvignon Blanc, and Gewurztraminer, show consistent texture, clean fruit, and satisfying, ripe aftertastes. Cabernet Sauvignon and Merlot Reserve styles aged in French oak effortlessly combine wood and dark fruit. Carmenère reds are lighter, but suffer no lack of ripeness. A Carignan, lifted by the addition of 10% Cabernet Sauvignon, has endearing leather flavours and mouthwatering tannins.

Selentia (B57)

Villa Angostura, San Fernando
selentia@byb.es
Selentia is a joint venture between the Spanish drinks giant Bodegas y Bebidas and the Mayol Bouchon Chilean family, who owned extensive vineyards in the San Fernando area of Rapel Valley. These vineyards cover an estate called Angostura and were first planted in the nineteenth century by Emilio Bouchon after he left Bordeaux in France. Emilio Bouchon's Angostura estate has ultimately spawned three wineries: Casa Silva (*see* above), J. Bouchon (*see* above) and Selentia. Selentia's new winery was built from 1999; the first wines were released in 2000 under the Viña Selentia, Viña Selentia Reserva, and Viña Selentia Reserva Especial labels. The majority of the vineyard is planted with Cabernet Sauvignon, Carmenère, Merlot, and Petit Verdot for Bordeaux-style red wines. A smaller amount of Chardonnay and Sauvignon Blanc is used for whites. The top wine is the Viña Selentia Reserva Especial, a Bordeaux-style red blend. The owners say it is made to be matured in bottle before drinking; in fact, it is sufficiently light in texture to be drunk almost immediately.

Seña

Panquehue, San Felipe
www.errazuriz.com
Chile's Errázuriz winery and California's Robert Mondavi Winery founded Seña in 1996; the two also produce Caliterra (*see* above). Seña is one of Chile's most expensive red wines. It is sourced from Aconcagua Valley grapes that are fermented and matured in oak barrels at Errázuriz's Aconcagua Valley winery; the Mondavi team oversee the blending. In 1999, a vineyard on rolling ground forty-one kilometres (twenty-five miles) from the Pacific in the western Aconcagua Valley was planted for Seña. The site was chosen because a grower who sold grapes for Seña was based here, and his grapes were consistently among the best. Only one-quarter of the Seña Vineyard had been planted by 2002. By 2005, it will be fully planted with Cabernet Sauvignon (60%), Merlot (20%), Cabernet Franc (10%), Carmenère (5%), Petit Verdot (3%), and Malbec (2%). This grape selection is broadly similar to that found in a Médoc vineyard in France's Bordeaux region, although Carmenère is rarely found there today. The soils in the Seña vineyard are sandier than those of the Médoc, where generally there is more gravel. Wines from sandy soil are generally lighter and more open textured than those from gravel, as a tasting comparison between Seña and a top Médoc red shows. Vine rows at Seña have been contoured across the slope to aid mechanization. Seña's owners believe that vines ripen more uniformly when planted this way, although there is greater risk of erosion. Seña's vineyard has been landscaped to incorporate habitat breaks for biodiversity, and perches have been installed for birds of prey, which act as a natural form of pest control. However, Seña will not be managed on organic lines. A winery

specifically for Seña will be built here in 2004. The debut 1997 Seña was a crisp, slightly uneven blend of 84% Cabernet Sauvignon and 16% Carmenère. Seña 1998 was blended from 90% Cabernet Sauvignon, 5% Carmenère, and 5% Merlot, but suffered dilution due to a wet El Niño vintage. The 1999 was blended from 75% Cabernet Sauvignon, 17% Merlot, and 8% Carmenère. It included Maipo Valley grapes for the first time, which gave the wine broader texture but failed to provide it with the depth or diversity of flavour expected of one of Chile's priciest wines. Seña 2000 was blended from 77% Cabernet Sauvignon, 17% Merlot, and 6% Carmenère. One can find more interesting and concentrated flavours than Seña for around half the price in Errázuriz's 2000 Don Maximiano Founder's Reserve. Around 100,000 bottles of Seña were produced in 2001. Perhaps by 2020, when the Seña vineyard has matured and the wine is made in Seña's own, self-contained winery, this "icon" wine will start to deliver. On current form, it is difficult to discern what Seña, meaning "sign," "signature," "distinguishing feature," or "signal," is trying to tell wine drinkers about Chile's potential for high-quality red wines or its ability to deliver value for money.

Sendero *See* Concha y Toro

Siegel (B51)
Santa Cruz de Colchagua
Tel: (+56) 72 822532

Siegel is named after Alberto Siegel, one of Chile's leading wine brokers. Siegel has produced the El Crucero range of wines from his modern winery near Palmilla in Colchagua Valley since 1999. The wines are fruity and clean, but so far have shown little of the Colchagua Valley's potential to produce wines of substance.

SOLdeSOL *See* Aquitania

Southern Star *See* Manquehue

Stella Aurea *See* Quebrada de Macul

St Morillon *See* Valdivieso

Subsol *See* Morandé

Sunrise *See* Concha y Toro

Tabontinaja (B76)
Santiago de Chile
Tel: (+56) 02 245 6500;
tabontin@cepri.cl
Chilean Francisco Gillmore produced Tabontinaja's first wines in the modern era in 1993. His estate near San Javier in the Maule valley is named after the large earthenware jars (*tinajas*) that seventeenth century Spaniards once used here for fermenting their wines (*tinajas* are still used in southern Spain today). The vineyard, next to the winery, is located on a fine site that epitomizes the rolling, well-drained slopes of the Maule Valley. Gillmore sells the majority of his grapes to Calina, but also makes around 100,000 bottles of his own wine under the Gillmore name. His Cabernet Franc, Cabernet Sauvignon,

Carmenère, Merlot, and Syrah red wines are often compared to the wines of Calina. One key difference between the two is that the Gillmore reds are firmer and more leathery compared to Calina's more obviously fruit-driven style.

Tanao *See* Casa Lapostolle

Tarapacá (B19)
Torre Santa María, Santiago de Chile
www.tarapaca.cl
A Chilean consortium called Compañía Chilena de Fósforos (Chilean Match Company), which produces asparagus and timber as well as other products, bought Tarapacá (formerly Tarapacá Ex-Zavala) in 1992. It was one of Chile's oldest wine producers, but its reputation had waned, particularly after the economic upheavals following Pinochet's military coup in 1973. Tarapacá's new owners sold its existing vineyards and winery in Santiago, first developed in the late nineteenth century, for real estate. Tarapacá then moved farther south, into the Isla de Maipo area, to a new estate called El Rosario de Naltagua. The estate is enclosed by the Maipo River on one side and by mountains on the others. The El Rosario name appears on Tarapacá's wine labels, as do the vineyard plots: El Ciruelo is named after plum orchards once grown here, and now grows Merlot and Mourvèdre vines; El Rosal is planted with Pinot Noir; El Tranque grows Cabernet Sauvignon and Merlot; La Cuesta ("the hill") is planted with Cabernet Sauvignon and Syrah; La Isla ("the island")

grows Sauvignon Blanc; Piritas, at the foot of an old pyrite mine, grows Chardonnay; and San Jorge grows Cabernet Sauvignon. Around twelve million bottles are produced each year, under the Rosario Estate, Viña Tarapacá, Viña Tarapacá Reserva, Viña Tarapacá Gran Reserva, Viña Tarapacá Privada Last Edition and Gran Tarapacá labels. White wines display an unusually sweet aftertaste, while reds have an unfortunate mousy character that blurs the fruit. Tarapacá's owners have recently acquired vineyards and a winery in the Casablanca Valley (now used by Bright Brothers Chile (*see* above)) and are investigating organic farming practices. In a separate development, Tarapacá's owners produce the Misiones de Rengo range (*see* above).

Tekena *See* Anakena

Tempus *See* Francisco de Aguirré

Terra Andina

Santiago de Chile
Tel: (+56) 02 333 0735;
www.terraandina.com
The French Pernod Ricard group (*see* Etchart, Argentina, p.131) created Terra Andina in 1996. The wines were originally made from purchased grapes in rented wineries. Santa Rita (*see* above) acquired the Terra Andina name in 2001 and is building it a dedicated winery. Around two million bottles of value-for-money wine are produced each year. As Terra Andina can now draw grapes from the Santa Rita and Carmen vineyards, we can expect better quality in the future.

Semillon and Cabernet Sauvignon are currently Terra Andina's most diverting wines. Terra Andina's new owners are looking to focus on Syrah and on red blends of Cabernet Franc with Merlot, and Syrah with Cabernet Sauvignon.

Terraced *See* Luis Felipe Edwards

TerraMater (B14)

Providencia, Santiago de Chile
Tel: (+56) 02 233 1311
Sisters Gilda, Edda, and Antonieta Canepa (*see* Canepa, above) founded TerraMater in 1996. The vineyards are located on three estates in the Maipo, Curicó, and Maule Valleys. Wines are made in the Maipo Valley, at a new winery capable of producing six million bottles. Since the 2000 vintage, TerraMater's wines have been much more consistent and are starting to show the potential of the company's higher-than-average proportion of old vines. Monitoring TerraMater's extensive vineyards block by block has allowed identification of plots which give the best grapes. The basic TerraMater range includes a creamy Chardonnay and Sauvignon Blanc, as well as Malbec, Merlot, Syrah, Cabernet Sauvignon, Sangiovese, and Zinfandel red wines, which show vanilla and resin scents from oak influence. Shiraz/Cabernet and Zinfandel/Shiraz blends provide extra complexity. TerraMater Reserva and Gran Reserva wines show more refined oak and riper fruit flavours. The top wines, called TerraMater Altum, include generous Cabernet

Sauvignon and Merlot sourced mainly from vineyards planted in the 1950s at Los Niches in the Curicó Valley (for Cabernet) and from San Clemente in the Maule Valley (for Merlot). The TerraMater Mighty Zinfandel comes from Maipo Valley vines that were grafted over to the variety onto existing old vines. It receives rather less oak barrel-ageing than the Altum reds, which allows its vivacious red-cherry fruit and soft texture to shine. A recent development at TerraMater is the PachaMama organic range of Sauvignon Blanc, Chardonnay, and Cabernet Sauvignon wines made from purchased grapes. These are clean, vibrant wines for immediate drinking. TerraMater's owners also own Hacienda El Condor (*see* above).

TerraNoble (B74)

San Clemente, Maule Valley
Tel: (+56) 02 203 3360
French winemaker Henri Marionnet, who is based in the Loire Valley, founded TerraNoble with a group of Chilean investors in 1992. A vineyard was planted near San Clemente in the Maule Valley and TerraNoble's first wines were produced in 1994. The grapes are picked by hand and TerraNoble claims to use a minimal amount of vineyard chemicals, although its own vineyards are not officially certified as organic. More than one million bottles are produced under the Valle Andino and TerraNoble labels. Unusually, TerraNoble's entire production is exported. The TerraNoble Merlot is made without oak influence and

from grapes that are uncrushed as they enter the fermentation vats. This process produces a wine with good colour and soft texture, with an aroma not dissimilar to Beaujolais Nouveau: a mix of banana and bubblegum. In the Loire, Marionnet is known for his fruit-filled Gamay wines. Oak-aged red wines under the TerraNoble Reserva and Gran Reserva labels are fermented in the more classic manner, using crushed berries. Of these, both Cabernet Sauvignon and Carmenère show ripeness and balance, while Merlot's briary flavours have a noticeable alcoholic warmth. The San Clemente area experiences relatively cool night-time temperatures, which leave TerraNoble's white wines made from Chardonnay and Sauvignon Blanc with a noticeably crisp texture.

Terrarum *See* Morandé

Terrunyo *See* Concha y Toro

The Don *See* Valdivieso

Tierra Arena *See* Francisco de Aguirré

Tierra del Sol *See* Santa Mónica

Tocornal *See* Cono Sur

Torreón de Paredes (B46)
Fundo Santa Teresa, Rengo
Tel: (+56) 02 211 5323;
torreon@torreon.cl
The Chilean Paredes family founded the Torreón de Paredes vineyard and winery outside the town of Rengo in the Rapel Valley in 1979. The land

was once an arable farm growing almonds and wheat as well as vines. The estate takes its name from a tower, or *torreón*, built on the property before Chile's independence from Spain. A wine cellar dating from the end of the eighteenth century also survives. The oldest vine plots contain Cabernet Sauvignon, Chardonnay, Merlot, and Sauvignon Blanc, while Carmenère, Pinot Noir, Syrah, and Viognier are now being planted. To have greater control over yields, the owners are installing drip irrigation in place of the flood system. Around three-quarters of a million bottles are produced annually, and only estate-grown grapes are used for the wines. These are sold mainly under the Torreón de Paredes, Torreón de Paredes Reserve, and Torreón de Paredes Private Collection labels. White wines are broad and occasionally resinous, especially where the juice has been fermented in oak barrels, as in the case of the Private Collection Chardonnay. Among the reds, Merlot and Cabernet Sauvignon show deep colour and are warm, rich, and peppery. The Paredes family has been fortunate that a number of talented winemakers have worked here from the mid-1990s onwards, but there has been a lack of consistency. The top wine, a Bordeaux-style red blend made from Merlot and Cabernet Sauvignon aged in French oak, is named after the estate's founder, Don Amado Paredes. It displays some of the

cedar character one finds in Bordeaux's red wines, but with a softer, more approachable mouthfeel. Don Amado had seven sons; two of them, Javier and Alvaro, run the family business and have also established Las Nieves (*see* above).

Totihue (B41)
Fundo San Pedro, Curicó
www.sanpedro.cl
San Pedro and Bordeaux's Château Dassault created Totihue in a joint venture. From 2004, Totihue will produce around 800,000 bottles of prestige, oak-aged, Cabernet Sauvignon-dominated red wines. A vineyard is being planted in Totihue in the Cachapoal Valley. The vines are on the Andean slopes, where good drainage and exposure to the sun assures ripeness, while distinct night cooling provides intensity of flavour.

Trio *See* Concha y Toro

Triple C *See* Santa Rita

Tuniche (B36)
Camino a Tuniche, Rancagua
Tel: (+56) 72 250818;
info@tuniche.com
Tuniche was founded in 1969 by the Butron family, and is based in the Rapel Valley town of Rancagua. Value-for-money wines are sold under the G Butron and Tuniche labels. Recent investment in new vineyards and modernization of the winery has improved wine quality. The most interesting wine is a late-picked, sweet white blended from Riesling and Gewurztraminer, called Tuniche Late Harvest.

Undurraga (B7)

Camino Melipilla, Santa Ana

info@undurraga.cl

The Basque Undurraga family acquired their first vineyard at Talagante in the Maipo Valley after a rival bidder from Cousiño-Macul failed to turn up at an 1882 land auction. The Undurraga family now owns three other vineyards, in Maipo and Rapel Valleys, but its wines have not moved with the times. Compared to wines made today by other famous Chilean wine names dating from the end of the nineteenth century, such as Santa Rita, Concha y Toro, and Errázuriz, Undurraga's seem dull and out of focus. This is despite Undurraga upgrading its winery in 1997, and employing renowned French winemaking consultants for its top wine, Undurraga Founders Collection Cabernet Sauvignon. The original Undurraga winery is a beautiful white-washed building thirty-four kilometres (twenty-one miles) southwest of Santiago. It is worth visiting, partly for its collection of wine-related artifacts, but mainly for the surrounding garden, laid out in French classical style. It contains palms, monkey-puzzle and eucalyptus trees, as well as Sequoia oaks, and it is arguably superior to similar nineteenth century park gardens at the Santa Rita and Concha y Toro wineries. It is a pity that, in wine terms, Undurraga does not compete with its historic peers.

V *See* Valdivieso

Valdivieso (B63)

Santiago de Chile

www.valdivieso.cl

Valdivieso is the dominant producer of sparkling wine in Chile, but it is recognized internationally as an increasingly fine source of still wines. Having travelled to Champagne, Don Alberto Valdivieso produced the company's first sparkling wines in 1897, in cellars in Santiago that are still in use today. In 1950, Valdivieso was acquired by Mitjans, a family group producing distilled drinks, liqueurs and (dull) wine under the St Morillon label. Valdivieso makes twelve million bottles of still and sparkling wine, from both estate and purchased grapes. Consistency has been its problem recently, especially for Sauvignon Blanc and Chardonnay white wines. In 2002, the whites underwent a renaissance, and are much fresher and cleaner, after New Zealander Brett Jackson, formerly of San Pedro, became winemaker. Valdivieso's reds historically have provided its most interesting bottles, including The Don, a wild, concentrated oak-aged blend of 50% Carignan plus Malbec, Cabernet Sauvignon, and Syrah from the Colchagua Valley. Valdivieso's Reserve, Single Vineyard, and Barrel Selection wines provide solid reds such as Pinot Noir, and usually enjoyable examples of Malbec, Carmenère, Cabernet Sauvignon, Cabernet Franc, Carignan, and Merlot. Valdivieso's top red is called Caballo Loco ("crazy horse"), the nickname given to Jorge Coderch, who is one of Valdivieso's co-owners (*see also* Laroche & Coderch, above). Caballo Loco blends different grape varieties from different years, so the bottle does not state a specific vintage. The Caballo Loco No 5 was blended mainly from Cabernet Sauvignon lots from the 1999 and 2000 vintages. It has an appetizing texture, with a number of distinct flavour influences, and complex tannins which ultimately provide a satisfying whole. Some traditionalists frown on this kind of creative blending, but Valdivieso shows how well it can work. In contrast to the Caballo Loco principle, Valdivieso releases single-vintage, single-vineyard, single-varietal wines from its oldest vines under the "V" label. These 3,000-bottle lots, such as the rich, tannic Pinot Noir sourced mainly from vineyards in Sagrada Familia in Curicó Valley, are usually worth searching out for their individuality, as well as their quirkiness.

Valette Fontaine (B27)

Santiago de Chile

Tel: (+56) 02 242 9800

Valette Fontaine is a red-wine-only joint venture that produced its first wine from vineyards in Pirque, in the Maipo Valley, in 1999. The Valette family, who were owners of Château Pavie in the Saint-Emilion region of Bordeaux, provide winemaking expertise, while the Fontaine family own the vineyards. These lie at 800 m (2,640 ft) on the foothills of the Andes, in an area with unusually stony soil. The vines are planted at a density of 5,000 vines per hectare (or 2,220 vines per acre). Traditional Chilean vineyards are planted at around half that density. High-density vineyards such as Valette Fontaine's force the vines to compete with each other for root space, producing vines which root more deeply. This technique should produce healthier vines and more complex wines. Two wines are produced: Memorias and El Principal. Memorias is made from younger vines, usually around two-thirds Cabernet Sauvignon and one-third Carmenère. Grapes are hand-picked and the wine is aged for more than twelve months in French oak before being bottled without filtration. Memorias has a thick, juicy texture, its mentholated black fruit becoming more prominent after decanting. The top wine, El Principal, is made from Cabernet Sauvignon alone, using similar techniques to Memorias. Its black fruit is even more concentrated than Memorias.

Valle Andino *See* TerraNoble

Valle Frío (B75)

Providencia, Santiago de Chile
Tel: (+56) 02 634 6778
Valle Frío ("cold valley") owns three vineyards called Los Pocillos, Santa Elena, and Ranquimili located near San Clemente, in the Maule Valley. Since 2000, Valle Frío's modernized winery has produced clean, elegant wine under the Los Pocillos and Don Sebastien labels. Red wines from

Merlot and Cabernet Sauvignon show particularly well-balanced, light textures and appealing fruit flavours augmented by ageing in French oak. White wines from Chardonnay and Sauvignon Blanc are clean, chalky examples for early drinking.

Ventisquero (B30)

Punta de Cortés, Rancagua
ventisquero@agrosuper.com
AgroSuper, the leading producer of fresh food and meat in Chile, entered the wine business by founding Ventisquero in 1996. Initially, the winery was called Vial, after Gonzalo Vial, the owner of AgroSuper. Vial's SuperPollo and SuperCerdo chicken and pork brands have made AgroSuper one of Chile's ten largest agro-industrial groups. AgroSuper's immense purchasing power allowed it to buy or plant extensive vineyards in Chile's leading wine valleys, including Casablanca, mainly for white wines, and Maipo and Rapel's fashionable Apalta Valley area for reds. A modern, gravity-fed winery has been built in the coastal hills southwest of Maipo Valley. Dry red and white wines, under the Yali and Chileno labels, are competently made in a light, clean, fruity style aimed at early drinking. Yali is named after the river valley in which the winery is located, and is also the name of a finch-like bird which breeds in a UNESCO-protected reserve on the nearby Pacific coast. Ventisquero is launching one of Chile's largest organic vineyard projects.

Veramonte (A10)

Ruta 68, Casablanca
www.veramonte.com
Veramonte's motto could well be "if at first you don't succeed, try, try again." Agustín Huneeus developed Veramonte in Casablanca Valley in the 1990s. Huneeus is also the man behind California's successful Franciscan Winery. In keeping with its California roots, Veramonte's Casablanca winery is tourist-friendly, incorporating a French château design, including a visitor centre and a shop. It is the first winery one sees travelling to Viña del Mar and the coast from Santiago. Agustín Huneeus' first venture in Chile was Caliterra, with Errázuriz in the late 1980s. Even though this partnership did not last, the Caliterra wines from that period were critically acclaimed for their exceptional value and vibrant fruit. They proved that Chile could provide fruit-packed wines as good as those from Australia for everyday drinking, while offering even better value for money. Errázuriz has since found another Californian partner for Caliterra, but with a few exceptions, the current crop of wines do not compare to those produced by the Franciscan and Errázuriz partnership. Señor Huneeus moved on from Caliterra and founded Veramonte with his son, Agustín Francisco Huneeus, in association with America's second-largest wine company (and the fourth largest wine company in the world), Constellation Brands. The obvious question is, if Franciscan made such good Chilean wines with

Errázuriz, is it repeating the feat with Veramonte? The answer is yes, more or less, the key limitation being that the grapes Veramonte use at present generally come from vines with a lower average age compared to those it worked with on the Caliterra project more than a decade ago. Veramonte's own vineyard in Casablanca was only planted from 1991, and produced its first vintage in 1995. However, Veramonte's winemaking is consistent and takes account of the fact that a good proportion of the grapes it works with are far from being blockbuster material. The wines are styled for the USA market, where 80% of Veramonte wine is sold. This means that white wines such as Sauvignon Blanc and Chardonnay exude overtly tropical flavours and have a hint of sweetness on the palate. Early vintages of the Chardonnay were barrel-fermented but, as the wood tended to dominate the delicate peach and mango fruit from the young vines, the oak influence was toned down. The asparagus aromas that dominate some examples of Sauvignon Blanc from New Zealand mark wines made from that grape here, too. Veramonte's two main red wines are made from Merlot and Cabernet Sauvignon. Both are stylish, confident examples with integrated oak flavours, for immediate drinking. Veramonte's top wine, Primus, is a blend of Carmenère, Cabernet Sauvignon, and Merlot, which is aged in oak barrels for around one year. Perhaps it is sheer coincidence that it has a similar price to

Caliterra's Arboleda range of oak-aged red wines. In terms of styling, it has that overt ripeness, a chewy quality that Caliterra seems to have lost since Huneeus was last involved in its production. Perhaps, after all, it is Caliterra and its new Californian partner, not Veramonte that needs to "try, try, try again."

VIA Group
Fundo Las Chilcas, Talca
www.viawines.cl
VIA Group is a partnership involving Jorge Coderch and members of his family, who part-own Valdivieso (*see* above) and who have also created San Rafael (*see* above), and four other Chilean wineries, of which the best-known is La Fortuna (*see* above). Michel Laroche, Coderch's partner in the Laroche & Coderch joint venture, is also a partner in VIA. VIA's flagship is the San Rafael vineyard and winery, but other joint venture wineries are in Casablanca Valley and in the Curicó Valley. The challenge for all the partners involved in VIA will be to transform the potential for quality from so many diverse sources into consistent and interesting wines. Early results are extremely promising. VIA's wines are produced under a number of labels including Cascada, Chilcas, and Chilensis (the latter range comes from from Casablanca Valley).

Vial *See* Ventisquero

Villard Estate (A11)
Ruta 68, Casablanca
www.villard.cl

French winemaker Thierry Villard and Santa Emiliana (*see* above) founded Villard Estate in 1989. Several years later, in 1996, Villard built its own winery in Casablanca Valley, and now produces around 3.5 million bottles annually from vineyards in Maipo and Casablanca Valleys. Villard Estate's Expresión label includes unoaked Sauvignon Blanc for immediate drinking; oak-aged Cabernet Sauvignon and Merlot, which show discreet flavours of older wood; and a decent, partially oak-fermented Chardonnay. Villard's Expresión Pinot Noir is his most subtle red wine. Villard Estate's Esencia range includes crisp, oak-fermented Chardonnay and a light, oak-aged Pinot Noir with more concentrated flavours than the Villard Expresión label. Villard Estate's Equis is a lean, Bordeaux-style red made from Maipo Valley Cabernet Sauvignon and Merlot aged in 300-litre hogsheads (rather than the usual 225-litre barrels) to minimize the risk of excess oak flavour. Villard Estate's El Noble Sauvignon Blanc is a barrel-fermented late-picked white with balanced sweetness and oak.

Viña Casablanca (A8)
Santiago de Chile
Tel: (+56) 02 410 3000;
www.santacarolina.com
Santa Carolina set up Viña Casablanca in 1990. Initially, the winery was to make white wines sourced from Casablanca Valley, at that time an exciting, emerging region with potential. Today, both Casablanca Valley and Viña

Casablanca are firmly part of Chile's wine establishment. Santa Carolina's success with its Casablanca project led many other Chilean wineries to invest in the region. Meanwhile, Viña Casablanca has also made wines from Chilean regions outside Casablanca Valley. The first Casablanca wines to gain worldwide critical acclaim were made by Ignacio Recabarren (*see* Quebrada de Macul and Concha y Toro, above), but after he left in the mid-1990s standards slipped. Today, just over one million bottles are produced annually. The basic Viña Casablanca White Label range includes a rich, tropical Chardonnay and a more subdued Sauvignon Blanc, both sourced from Casablanca Valley. White Label Pinot Noir, Merlot, and Cabernet Sauvignon reds come from Maipo and Rapel Valleys; some carry a vineyard name, such as Miraflores. They show good colour, but lighter fruit flavours. The Viña Casablanca El Bosque range (Cabernet Sauvignon and Carmenère) have shown greater consistency since 1999. Ageing in French oak accentuates the density provided by Maipo and Rapel Valley grapes. Viña Casablanca's Santa Isabel and Santa Isabel Barrel Fermented ranges are sourced from Santa Carolina's Santa Isabel Estate in Casablanca Valley. The Chardonnay, Sauvignon Blanc, and Gewurztraminer wines are overtly tropical, but appealingly restrained on the palate. Grapes are picked at three different ripeness levels: slightly underripe grapes provide crispness; ripe grapes give

above Preparing a "starter" – a mix of yeast and grape juice – to kickstart the fermentation.

the key flavours; and overripe grapes add breadth. Cabernet Sauvignon and Merlot grapes are picked more conventionally, and the wines lack the texture of the white wines. The top red wine, Neblus, which is blended from Cabernet Sauvignon, Merlot, and Carmenère and is aged in new and second-use French oak, is one of Chile's less generously flavoured "icon" reds.

Viña de Larose (B44)

Fundo Santa Anita de Totihué, Rengo
Tel: (+56) 72 551197;
castoqui@entelchile.net
Viña de Larose is majority-owned by the French insurance company Assurances Générales de France (AGF), which also owns other wine interests, such as Château Larose-Trintaudon in Bordeaux's Médoc region. The Chilean Granella family own the minority shareholding, and it is from their vineyards in the Rapel Valley's Totihue area that the wines are made. Insurance companies tend to survive by avoiding undue risk, so it is no surprise to learn that the wines

produced here are rather mundane, with Cabernet Sauvignon especially tame. Chardonnay and Semillon wines are pleasant but light on flavour. Semillon is also used to produce a late-harvest sweet white wine with a high-toned, varnish-like texture. Other labels used here include Leyenda and Las Casas del Toquí.

Viña Leyda (A15)

www.leyda.cl;
gllona@ffv.cl
Viña Leyda is currently the only vineyard and winery venture in the newly developed cool Leyda area of the Aconcagua region, although there are other vineyards there, too. Pinot Noir, Chardonnay, and Sauvignon Blanc were planted in the coastal hills from 1997. Early releases of Chardonnay have produced a promising barrel-fermented wine with excellent balance; Sauvignon Blanc is similar in style and equally subtle. Pinot Noir shows good levels

of ripeness and flavour. Viña Leyda also releases high-quality wines made from grapes purchased from Maipo and Rapel Valleys. Highlights include a rich Colchagua Valley Carmenère with a Bordeaux-like character; a lighter Maipo Valley Cabernet Sauvignon; and a Rapel Valley Syrah/Cabernet Sauvignon blend with elegant flavours.

Viñas Viejas *See* Lomas de Cauquenes

Vitisterra *See* Morandé

Vistamar *See* Morandé

Viu Manent (B50)

Santa Cruz, Colchagua
www.viumanent.cl
This family owned winery is based at Cunaco, near Santa Cruz de Colchagua, in the Rapel Valley. Unusually for Chile, Viu Manent's main focus is on wines made from Malbec, a variety that seems to adapt well to the Mediterranean climatic conditions of this part of Rapel. Viu Manent has three vineyards. The oldest, called San Carlos de Cunaco (or Hacienda Cunaco), also contains the Viu family's winery. In 1990, when the Viu family decided to move away from making bulk wine for the Chilean market in favour of bottled wine for export, they acquired the La Capilla estate in Peralillo. Another estate near Peralillo (called El Olivar), located on more steeply sloping ground, has recently been planted. All three Viu vineyards contain Malbec, and three wines are made, according to the age of the vines. Viu

Manent is made from younger vines, Viu Manent Reserva from mature vines (more than ten years old), and Viu Manent Special Selection is made from vines aged between fifty and one hundred years old. In addition, Viu Manent's top red wine, called Viu 1, is made mainly from old-vine Malbec, rounded out with Cabernet Sauvignon. Malbec not only ripens well in this part of Chile, but it also reacts well to barrel-ageing, which, in Viu Manent's case takes place in French oak (in Argentina Malbec is often aged in American oak barrels). Malbec's naturally lush, juicy, tar-like texture seems to combine well with the firm oak notes brought by French-oak ageing, and it accentuates Malbec's black cherry character. Viu Manent's Malbecs show appealing ripeness and flavour, with wines from the oldest vineyards showing a degree of complexity. The Viu family is also starting to make good use of other varieties that, like Malbec, need Mediterranean climatic conditions to ripen fully: Sangiovese, Syrah, and Carmenère. As the new vines from El Olivar vineyard come on stream, Viu Manent's production is set to jump from 2.4 million bottles to nearly four million annually. Judicious blending will be needed to ensure that dilution does not occur among the wines in Viu Manent's oak-aged Reserva and Special Selection ranges.

VOE

Las Condes, Santiago de Chile
Tel: (+56) 02 235 7715
VOE is an organic/biodynamic

vineyard and winery project run by Santa Emiliana (*see* above). The initials stand for Viñedos Orgánicos Emiliana ("Emiliana Organic Vineyards"). The winery is based at a vineyard in the coastal hills near Nancagua in the Colchagua Valley called Los Robles ("the oak trees") (NB: This Los Robles vineyard is not to be confused with the Los Robles cooperative, *see* above, in Curicó). Only red wine grapes are planted, with Carmenère dominating on flatter ground, and Syrah on the slopes. Cabernet Sauvignon, Tempranillo, Malbec, and Mourvèdre are also planted. Alvaro Espinoza (*see* Antiyal and Geo Wines, above) was hired in 1997 to begin an organic programme here. Since 2000, a more radical organic method called biodynamics has been adopted. Biodynamics attempts to make the vineyard like a traditional farm, and as self-sufficient as possible. To this end, habitat corridors have been landscaped into the vineyard. The flowers and plants within these habitat corridors grow from seeds collected from wild vegetation surrounding the vineyard. The aim is to create biodiversity and attract beneficial predator insects that naturally control vineyard pests. Such habitat breaks help minimize the destabilizing effect that a vineyard monoculture has on the local environment. Certain plants in the habitat break are used to make extremely dilute but highly effective homeopathic infusions, which are sprayed onto the vines. Such sprays do not kill diseases in the way that conventional pesticides do but,

wines of south america

instead, spur the vine's own impulses to resist disease. All infusions are made at Los Robles rather than transported in from outside. The biodynamic form of organics encourages certain annual vineyard tasks to be performed according to planetary positions and to the phases of the moon and the sun. For instance, the vines are not pruned in late autumn as is usual. Instead, the workers wait for the sap in the vines to be drawn up from the roots in spring, when the sun starts to rise higher in the sky each day. Pruning the vine as it is still drawing sap down towards its roots in late autumn risks drawing in fungal infections and bacteria through open pruning wounds. Also, if vine-wood is pruned off before the sap reaches the roots, the nutrients contained in the sap, which the vine needs to survive winter, are lost. This starves the vine of energy, and makes it more susceptible to disease the following season. Santa Emiliana built the gravity-fed Los Robles winery in 2001. It is made of natural materials such as wood and adobe, which blend in with the Nancagua landscape. The winery has a village feel to it, with corridors on the outside of the buildings rather than on the inside. VOE make red wines in the style of Mediterranean France, with plenty of ripe fruit, and natural freshness. The winemaking team incorporate biodynamic ideas in the winery, too. Wines are racked off the sediment that settles at the bottom of the barrels only when the moon is falling. This way, the sediment is

more compact, and the wine is less cloudy and tastes cleaner. The first vintage to be fermented in the new winery was 2002. The red is blended from Carmenère, Syrah, Cabernet Sauvignon, and Mourvèdre. It has incredible purity, clarity, ripeness, depth, and freshness. The quality is down to three things. First, Santa Emiliana has nearly a dozen vineyards, and Los Robles consistently produced good wines before organic practices began, so the vineyard site happens to be a good one. Second, the organic and biodynamic management practices have made the vines stronger, and more expressive. Finally, yields have been cut dramatically, which helps the vines stay strong and means that the grapes are more likely to be fully ripe in the autumn. Sceptics of organics or biodynamics should compare this wine to Seña, Chadwick Estate, and Almaviva, all of which are more expensive, and then consider where the future of Chilean wine lies.

VSC *See* Santa Carolina

Walnut Crest *See* Santa Emiliana

Wild Ferment *See* Errázuriz

White Label *See* Viña Casablanca

William Cole (A13)
Casablanca Valley
Tel: (+56) 02 206 5995
William Cole is an American who, following on from a successful business career, founded a vineyard and winery project in Casablanca Valley in 2000. This will almost

certainly be among the last new vineyard projects in Casablanca. There is plenty of spare land in the valley, but water for irrigation and for cleaning winemaking facilities is scarce, and the Casablanca Valley authorities are under pressure from existing vineyard and winery owners not to grant planning permission for any new projects. William Cole's Pinot Noir wines are adequate, but lack the depth or complexity of comparable examples from Cono Sur or Errázuriz. Other red wines made from Merlot, Cabernet Sauvignon, and Carmenère show light fruit. White wines are made from Sauvignon Blanc and Chardonnay, and from the 2002 vintage these wines showed superior texture and elegance in the aftertaste. As well as selling wine under his own name, William Cole also uses two other labels, Albamar and Quinteros.

Yali *See* Ventisquero

ARGENTINA

argentina

Argentina is the only major wine-producing country yet to be discovered by a world audience. California made it in the 1970s, Australia in the 1980s, and New Zealand, South Africa, and Chile emerged in the 1990s. Now it's Argentina's turn. The country is the largest wine producer in South America and the fifth-largest in the world. Only France, Italy, Spain, and the USA produce more than Argentina.

Argentina's wines have remained undiscovered outside South America for two reasons. First, Argentina is the only South American country with a long-standing culture of wine drinking. It has a population of around thirty-seven million, and the average annual per capita consumption of wine is more than forty-five bottles. To compare, Chile averages twenty-five, the UK twenty, and the USA, ten bottles per capita. With an annual production of over two billion bottles, this means that what wine Argentina has produced, historically, she has drunk, with any surplus being sold to other South American countries. The need to export to the USA or Europe was never vital to the survival of Argentina's wine industry.

Second, Argentine wine has been a prisoner of national politics since the end of the Second World War when, under a succession of military governments, Argentina became isolated from the world community. Corruption, bureaucracy, and chaotic centralized planning, coupled with localized anarchy, saw the wine industry revert to producing huge volumes of low-quality, cheap wine for the local market. Political corruption and economic mismanagement remained rife even after the return of civilian government in the late 1980s under elected presidents such as Carlos Menem (now a wine producer at Saúl Menem, *see* p.143).

But civilian rule did finally open Argentina up to world markets and the possibility of exportation. An export drive became a priority because wine consumption within Argentina was falling, even though drinkers were trading up from cheap basic table wines to more expensive "fine" wines. This change made Argentina's wine industry potentially more profitable, but producers needed to find the money to invest in better winemaking equipment. They also needed to grub up bulk wine grapes such as Criolla and Cereza in favour quality ones such as Chardonnay and Cabernet Sauvignon. The weakness of the Argentine currency (the peso) made exporting to the USA and Europe a financial necessity. At the same time, civilian rule, coupled with Argentina's cheap currency, encouraged dollar-rich foreign interests to invest in the country's wine industry. Investors included high-profile winemakers such as Michel Rolland and the Lurton brothers from Bordeaux, as well as multinational drinks corporations such as Pernod Ricard (Etchart), Allied Domecq (Balbi and Santiago Graffigna), wine producers such as Portugal's Sogrape (Finca Flichman), Spain's Codorníu (Séptima), California's Kendall-Jackson (Tapiz), Chile's Concha y Toro (Trivento), and Champagne house Moët & Chandon (Chandon Argentina).

Better wines with clearer labels and cleaner flavours were the result, and the wines are still

key facts about argentina

Argentina's vineyards experience **desert conditions** because they lie in the rainshadow of the Andes; Malbec reds are **rich, soft, and easy to drink**, while unique whites are made from the spicy Torrontés; the wealth of wine grapes is **unmatched in South America**; wine regions stretch from the cool lowlands of Patagonia in the south to the **high altitude** Calchaquíes Valley in the far north; Argentina's political isolation and a **thriving domestic wine market** kept her wines hidden until recently.

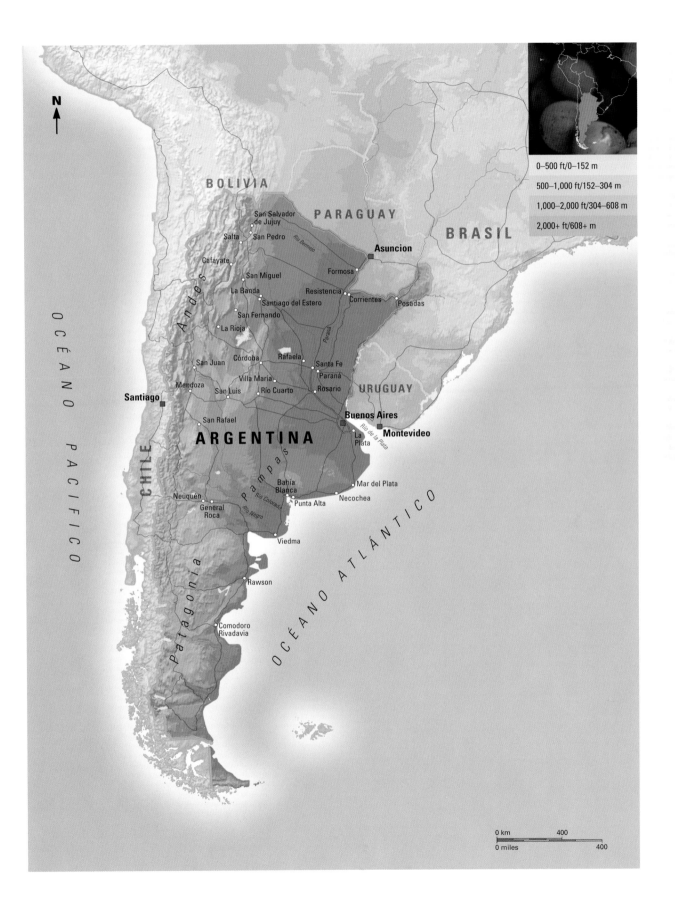

N

BOLIVIA

PARAGUAY

BRASIL

San Salvador
de Jujuy

Salta   San Pedro

Cafayate   Río Bermejo   Asuncion

San Miguel   Formosa

La Banda   Resistencia

Santiago del Estero   Corrientes   Posadas

San Fernando

La Rioja

San Juan   Córdoba   Rafaela   Santa Fe

Villa María   Paraná

Mendoza   San Luis   Río Cuarto   Rosario   URUGUAY

Santiago   San Rafael   Buenos Aires   Montevideo

ARGENTINA   La   Río de la Plata
Plata

Andes

P a m p a s

Bahía   Mar del Plata
Blanca
Neuquén   Río Colorado   Punta Alta   Necochea

General   Río Negro
Roca

Viedma

CHILE

P a t a g o n i a

Rawson

Comodoro
Rivadavia

OCÉANO PACIFICO

OCÉANO ATLÁNTICO

Paraná

0–500 ft/0–152 m

500–1,000 ft/152–304 m

1,000–2,000 ft/304–608 m

2,000+ ft/608+ m

0 km   400
0 miles   400

improving. But Argentina still only exports ten per cent of the wine produced within its borders. As wine quality improves, prices will need to be reassessed, too. Production costs are higher in Argentina than in Chile, Argentina's strongest direct wine competitor. Consequently, Argentine wine can seem poorer value in comparison. However, the collapse in December 2001 of Argentina's currency made the country's wines much better value, and should add impetus to wine exports.

Argentina is entering a world wine market just as its Southern Hemisphere competitors – Australia, Chile, and New Zealand – are wondering how to sell the extra wine coming from the huge, super-productive new vineyards they planted in the 1990s. Incidentally, Argentina's total vineyard area decreased during the same period. Savvy wine drinkers may note that, for the first time in its wine history, Argentina

has a clear conscience when everyone else is talking of an excess of cheap wine made from grapes grown in immature vineyards.

Argentine Wine Label Terms

DOC (DENOMINACIÓN DE ORIGEN CONTROLADA) This term signifies that the wine has come from a "controlled region of origin," a concept that was invented in Europe to stop fraud. Argentina is negotiating with European officials to put an end to the use of names of European controlled regions of origin (Chablis) or wine styles (Champagne/*Champaña*) on wines sold within Argentina. In return, European governments would allow easier access to the European market. Argentina's own DOC system is still being developed. At present, only Luján de Cuyo, San Rafael, and the Famatina Valley in La Rioja are officially covered.

left Chilli peppers drying under the early February sun in the Calchaquíes Valley, Argentina. "Chilli con carne" is Spanish for minced beef and bean stew spiced with chilli powder.

Argentine Wine Styles – Introduction

Argentina is moving away from the soft, slightly "baked" wines beloved by the huge (if declining) domestic market, in favour of fresher wines with the clean fruit flavours preferred by drinkers in Europe and the USA. Overall, Argentine wine is to Chilean wine what Australian wine is to New Zealand wine: more obviously fruity, fuller in body, and much softer in the mouth. The difference is the result of the climate; Argentina and Australia are hotter and drier. Grapes grown in hot climates produce more sugar and retain less acidity than those grown in cooler ones; hence, the wines have more alcohol and taste rounder and less crisp. Argentine wines, especially reds, can reach nearly fifteen per cent alcohol, whereas 13.5 per cent is more normal in Chile and 12.5 per cent is standard in Bordeaux.

Higher alcohol levels appeal to some drinkers, but most people find that wines are easier to digest, and taste more balanced, when they have fourteen per cent alcohol or less. Harvesting the grapes a week or so earlier than usual, before sugar levels get too high, can be an effective means of reducing excess alcohol – but doing so may also mean that the grapes lack flavour. The best way to obtain grapes with balanced sugar ripeness and balanced flavour ripeness in hotter regions is to have balanced vines.

What does "balanced vines" mean? It means getting the vine to grow steadily throughout the season, from when the tiny grapes first form in spring to when the swollen bunches are ready for harvesting about three months later. Pedro Marchevsky, formerly of the Catena Group (*see* pp.125–126) and now with Vintage (*see* p.148) is one of Argentina's most respected viticulturalists. Marchevsky likes each vine to grow ten grape-bearing shoots with a maximum of two grape bunches per shoot. The shoots are allowed to grow 1.3 m (4.3 ft) high before they are trimmed, allowing each shoot fourteen "working" leaves.

A working leaf traps sunlight and carbon dioxide and converts these to sugar (in the grapes) and oxygen. If you think this is a dogmatic approach you're right, but vines are predictable plants. They'll try to produce three bunches per shoot rather than two in order to increase the chance of attracting birds. The birds digest and then excrete the grape seeds (pips) onto the ground where they have a chance of growing into vines, thus helping the vine to fulfill its instinct to reproduce. Curbing the vine's capacity to overproduce is vital. Wine made from two good bunches is better than wine made from three moderate ones.

A further important factor is that vines are perennial plants: the same vine produces a crop of grapes for each of its thirty to one hundred years of life. In contrast, annual cropping plants such as wheat or carrots have to be re-sown every year. It stands to reason that a vine occupying the same piece of ground for decades needs good soil that is nurtured properly.

Finding a good piece of ground is no problem in Argentina, which has a wide range of soil types: volcanic soil in Mendoza's San Rafael region, sandy soil in East Mendoza, river-borne alluvial soil in Central Mendoza and any mix of gravel, clay, limestone, sand and loam you care to name elsewhere. Ninety-five per cent of Argentina's vines are ungrafted (*i.e.* grow on their own rootstocks).

For balanced vines, it is also important that the ground remains fertile and is not impoverished by, for example, overirrigation. An excess of irrigation (*el riego*) will dilute the flavour in the grapes. It will also dilute the minerals in the soil that the vine needs to produce grapes with ripe flavours and the right balance of alcohol (for body) and acidity (for crispness) in the wine later on. Like Chile, Argentina is changing from flood to drip irrigation.

Drip irrigation is more precise than flood irrigation. The winegrower can control to the nearest

below Cooking fruit, "ranch-style", is a popular way of serving, and preserving, perishables.

drop how much water each vine receives, and when. In the early 1990s, Argentine vineyards would receive 600 mm (twenty-three inches) of irrigation in winter and another 600 mm between spring bud-break and autumn picking (in late February to mid-April). With annual average rainfall levels in Argentina of 200 mm (7.8 inches) this equates to a total of 1,400 mm (fifty-five inches) of water per vine per year.

This total is now being reduced by around thirty per cent between bud-break and picking. Argentina's vines are better balanced as a result, producing fewer "water shoots" in the spring. Water shoots carry no grapes but take energy and sunlight away from other shoots, preventing flavour ripeness.

Reducing irrigation in the final weeks before ripening produces grapes with better balance. By late summer (January) Argentine grapes have reached full size and are changing from green to gold (for white wine grapes) or purple (for red wine grapes). Historically, Argentine growers would, at this point, carry on irrigating, which would confuse the vine. The vine would think that it was being asked to produce a second crop and start trying to produce more shoots, taking energy and nutrients away from what should be its prime task – ripening its existing grapes. Stopping irrigation in the weeks after the grapes change colour gives the grapes the opportunity to ripen both their grape sugars and their flavours completely by harvest-time, without lowering acidity levels. Changes in vine and water management explain why Argentine wines are starting to show balanced alcohol, increased levels of natural crispness, and riper-tasting fruit flavours.

When acidification in the winery is required (grapes can lose their acidity quickly in very warm climates), producers are learning to use lower levels of acid by using it more efficiently. Foreign winemakers such as Alberto Antonini (*see* Altos Las Hormigas, Tittarelli, and Vintage) have encouraged local winemakers to add acidity as soon as the grapes arrive at the winery.

Adding acid is standard practice in warm-climate wine regions such as California, Australia, South Africa, and Argentina. However, if acid is added too late during winemaking, the wines lose freshness more quickly in bottle than they should. Antonini prefers to acidify the grape juice before the fermentation begins (rather like adding lemon juice to an apple pie before it goes into the oven). Antonini's approach may come from his Italian background: Italian grapes generally have enough natural acidity for the wines to keep their freshness without any intervention by the winemaker.

Argentine Blended Wine Styles (By Colour)

RED WINE BLENDS

With such a wealth of grape varieties to choose from, Argentina has unlimited potential to create wines blended from two or more grape varieties. For red wines, Malbec forms the backbone of many blends, offering a thick texture without potentially off-putting blockbuster tannins. Bordeaux-style blends made with Malbec, Cabernet Sauvignon, Merlot, Cabernet Franc (sometimes called Bouchet), and Petit Verdot provide some of Argentina's leading red wines. *See* Achával Ferrer (Achával Ferrer and Quimera), Alta Vista (Alto), Amalia (Dos Fincas), Bacchus (Terruño 27), CA-RO, Catena Zapata (Nicolás Catena Zapata), Domaine St Diego (Pura Sangre), Fabre-Montmayou (Grand Vin), Felipe Rutini (Apartado), Humberto Canale (Canale Black River Reserve Cabernets), Luigi Bosca (Leoncio Arizu) (Finca Los Nobles), Norton (Privada Estate Reserve), Trapiche (Astica and Iscay), Vintage (Brioso), and Weinert (Cavas de Weinert).

Three Calchaquíes Valley producers – Etchart (Arnaldo B. Etchart Cafayate), Mounier, and San Pedro de Yacochuya – are broadening the Bordeaux mix with Tannat, while Bright Brothers Argentina (Elementos), Escorihuela Gascon (Candela President's Blend), Infinitus, Luigi Bosca (Leoncio Arizu) (Finca Los Nobles), Medrano Estate (Filos and Lazos), and

Michel Torino (Altimus) are using Syrah to create wines with spicy, sometimes animal, notes.

Blends influenced by Spanish grapes such as Tempranillo are being made by Alta Vista (Premium), O. Fournier (A Crux, B Crux and Urban Oak), Zuccardi (Santa Julia Magna and Santa Julia Fuzion), while Italian grapes such as Bonarda, Greco Nero, and Sangiovese feature at Alta Vista (Cosecha), Finca Las Moras, Vintage (Anubis, Susana Balbo BenMarco VMS), and Zuccardi (Santa Julia Reserva).

WHITE WINE BLENDS

Blended white wines usually include Chardonnay, paired with either Chenin Blanc for freshness or texture, Torrontés for aroma, or Viognier for flavour. Alta Vista's Cosecha blends Chardonnay with both Chenin *and* Torrontés. Chardonnay/Chenin Blanc blends include Esmeralda (Malambo), Finca Las Moras, and Zuccardi (Santa Julia Fuzion). Chardonnay/Torrontés blends include Medrano Estate (Casaterra) while Chardonnay/Viognier blends include Bright Brothers Argentina (Elementos). Chardonnay's solid texture is also lightened by pairing it with Sauvignon Blanc, as in Felipe Rutini's Destino, or it can be made creamier with the addition of Semillon, as Finca La Anita (Finca, de Finca La Anita), Infinitus, and Valentín Bianchi (Bianchi) show.

Argentine Wine Styles (By Grape Variety)

Argentina grows a wider range of grape varieties than any other wine-producing country in South America does. This diversity reflects the backgrounds of the immigrant wine-growers who arrived from France, Spain, Italy, and other Mediterranean countries from the mid-nineteenth century onward. Often, different grape varieties would be planted together in the vineyards, sometimes along with other crops such as olives and fruit trees. Only recently have grapevine experts (called ampelographers) begun to make sense of Argentina's often confusing grape-variety mix.

As various grape varieties ripen at different times, the aim is to pick each variety at its optimum ripeness. The Zorzetto vineyard in Río Negro province, which sells organic grapes to producer Humberto Canale, has painted white marks on the vine trunks to distinguish one vine type from another; this way, all the grapes can be picked at the correct moment, even if ripeness occurs weeks apart. As Argentina begins to exploit the diversity brought by its immigrant wine-growers, the quality of its wines can only improve.

BARBERA (RED)

This productive grape is often confused with another variety called Bonarda. The confusion arose because both vines were brought from northern Italy in the late-nineteenth century and were often planted together in the same vineyard. Barbera wines are full-bodied (alcohol rich), have a deep ruby-red colour and a crisp taste of wild black or red fruit. *See* La Riojana (La Nature), Lavaque, and Valentín Bianchi.

BONARDA (RED)

Bonarda is Argentina's most widely planted red wine grape after Malbec. It gives refreshing red wines with a bitter cherry twist in the aftertaste, generally for drinking young. It is underrated both in its Italian homeland and in Argentina, especially in East Mendoza where the bulk of Argentina's old-vine Bonarda is found. *See* Cabernet de Los Andes (Vicien), Catena Zapata (Alamos), Esmeralda (Malambo and Argento), Finca Alma (Alhue), Finca Las Moras, Mayol, Michel Torino, Nieto y Senetiner, Santa Faustina, Santiago Graffigna, Saúl Menem, Tittarelli, Sendero Alto, Vintage, and Zuccardi.

CABERNET FRANC (RED)

This underused French grape variety has one supreme advantage: it ripens after Merlot but before Cabernet Sauvignon. As a result, it avoids Merlot's tendency to taste "baked" and overripe and Cabernet Sauvignon's tendency to taste green and underripe. The best Cabernet Francs smell of raspberry, violets and, in Argentina, show less of the vegetal, herbaceous aromas common in the cooler Bordeaux or Loire regions of France. *See* Cheval des Andes and Finca Las Moras.

CABERNET SAUVIGNON (RED)

Cabernet Sauvignon is undoubtedly one of the world's top wine grapes, but it has yet really to excel in Argentina. Patagonia can be too cool and La Rioja province too hot. In Central Mendoza and in Salta and Catamarca provinces, Cabernet Sauvignon can easily match Malbec for elegance and complexity, as long as it is encouraged to ripen with sensible yields. Not all of the buds on a Cabernet will necessarily grow, so growers play safe by pruning long, leaving extra fruiting buds to cover any potential shortfall in yield. If spring is warm and all the buds are fertilized the result can be a big, unripe crop. At its best, Argentine Cabernet Sauvignon smells of cassis, strawberry, and liquorice. It retains its elegance in bottle longer than Malbec. *See* Amalia, Bacchus (Ruca Malen and Ruca Malen Grand Cru), Cabernet de Los Andes (Vicien), Cabrini, Catena Zapata (Catena Alta), Dolium (Reserve), Esmeralda (Argento), Fabre-Montmayou, Finca Alma (Alhue), Finca La Anita, Finca La Celia (La Celia), J.&F. Lurton, La Riojana (La Nature), Lavaque, López López, Luigi Bosca (Leoncio Arizu), Medrano Estate (Medrano Altos), Michel Torino, Norton, Pascual Toso, Terrazas de Los Andes (Gran Terrazas), Tittarelli, Trapiche, Valentín Bianchi, Vintage, and Weinert.

CEREZA (RED)

This widely planted, poor-quality grape produces huge yields of grapes with a light red skin. *See* Criolla, below.

CHARDONNAY (WHITE)

Chardonnay is so ubiquitous that it comes as a surprise to learn that Argentina has only half as much land planted to Chardonnay as Chile has. However, Chardonnay has become the must-plant grape in newly developed areas like Mendoza's Uco Valley, and in the equally cool but lower-lying Patagonia, where Chardonnay grapes are gradually taking the place of fruit orchards. Chardonnay in Argentina produces rich-tasting, dry white wines which are easier to drink than to describe in words, for the variety tends to have a subdued character (of cantaloupe, grapefruit, or light tropical fruit) in Argentina. *See* Alta Vista (Premium), Amalia, Cabrini, Catena Zapata (Catena Alta), Dolium, Doña Paula (Los Cardos), Etchart (Etchart Cafayate), Esmeralda (Argento), Fabre-Montmayou (Cuvée Diane), Finca Alma (Alhue), Finca La Anita, Hispano-Argentinas, J.&F. Lurton, La Riojana (La Nature), Lavaque, Luigi Bosca (Leoncio Arizu), Medrano Estate (Medrano Altos), Michel Torino, Norton (Reserva), Salentein (Estate Pr1mus), Santiago Graffigna, Saúl Menem, Terrazas de Los Andes (Reserva), Tittarelli, Trapiche (Astica), Valentín Bianchi, and Vintage.

CHENIN BLANC (WHITE)

Chenin Blanc is considered to be one of the world's nine classic grape varieties; it is also the most widely planted, classic white grape in Argentina. So far, so good, you may think. But Argentina produces no outstanding Chenin Blanc white wines to rival great French examples like Vouvray. At its best, Chenin Blanc wines exude quince, cinnamon, and hazelnut flavours. In Argentina, Chenin's potential for high-acid, high-alcohol wines means it is used mostly as a component for dull blends (it often fulfills the same role in California's Central Valley and in South Africa). *See* Hispano-Argentinas.

CRIOLLA (RED)

Criolla is believed to have been brought to South America by the Spanish conquistadors in the sixteenth century. It produces high yields of rather austere wine. The variety thrived in East Mendoza in the 1960s, when government tax breaks encouraged its replanting at a time of increased domestic wine consumption. It is now slowly being grubbed up or regrafted to better-quality varieties, but Criolla, and the similar Cereza, still account for around thirty per cent of the Argentine vineyard. *See* Colomé.

GRECO NERO (RED)

The "black Greek" variety probably has southern Italian rather than Greek origins, and adapts well to the hot climate of San Juan province, where it produces deeply coloured wines of good structure, tasting of black chocolate. *See* Santiago Graffigna.

MALBEC (RED)

Malbec (sometimes spelled "Malbeck") is Argentina's most-adaptable and most-planted, fine red wine grape, and is successfully grown in all regions. There are revealing contrasts in style between Malbec red wines made in the north by Tacuil, those from various parts of Central Mendoza and the Uco Valley bottled under single-vineyard names by Catena Zapata, and the Noemía Malbec from Patagonia. Yet all share a common theme: deep, purple-hued wines which taste of black cherry, damson, raspberry, mulberry, and blackcurrant when young, with anise, violet, and truffle flavours emerging with age. Like Tannat in Uruguay, Malbec performs better in South America than in its French homeland. In France, Malbec is grown in Bordeaux's Bourg and Blaye subregions and in Cahors in South West France. Unlike Tannat in Uruguay, Malbec has soft tannins, making the wines more easily approachable immediately after bottling. Malbec wines are generally best enjoyed within five years of the harvest, before the fruit flavours dry out. When barrel-aged, it responds well to both French and American oak, making it extremely versatile in the winery. Argentina is finally becoming a serious player on the world wine stage, and its Malbec red wines are the main reason why. *See* Achával Ferrer (Single Vineyard), Alta Vista (Premium and Grande Reserve), Altos Las Hormigas (Reserve), Amalia, Bacchus (Ruca Malen), Cabrini (Don Leandro Cabrini), Cassone, Catena Zapata (Catena Alta and Single Vineyard range), Cobos, Dolium, Doña Paula (Estate and

Selección de Bodega), Esmeralda (Argento), Etchart (Etchart Cafayate), Fabre-Montmayou (Cuvée Diane), Fabril Alto Verde (Buenas Ondas), Felipe Rutini, Finca Alma (Alhue), Finca La Anita, Finca La Celia (La Celia Reserve), Finca Las Moras, Hispano-Argentinas, Humberto Canale (Reserve), J.&F. Lurton, La Riojana (La Nature), Lagarde, Lavaque, Luigi Bosca (Leoncio Arizu), Mayol, Medrano Estate (Medrano Altos), Michel Torino, Noemí, Norton (Reserva), Pascual Toso, San Pedro de Yacochuya (Yacochuya de Michel Rolland), Santa Faustina, Saúl Menem, Sendero Alto, Terrazas de Los Andes (Gran Terrazas), Tittarelli, Trapiche, Valentín Bianchi, Viniterra, Vintage, Weinert, and Zuccardi (Familia Zuccardi and Terra Orgánica).

MERLOT (RED)

The Merlot grape is highly favoured in Bordeaux regions such as St-Emilion and Pomerol for its ability to ripen early, before equinox rains arrive. But in the Argentine heat, Merlot can ripen *too* quickly losing its structure and seeing its plump red-fruit flavours turn unattractively fat. Hence, the best examples come from cooler regions such as Patagonia, Mendoza's Uco Valley, or in the best parts of Central and Eastern Mendoza where quality-conscious producers limit Merlot's capacity to self-destruct by restricting its yield. *See* Cabrini, Esmeralda (Argento), Fabre-Montmayou, Felipe Rutini, Finca Alma (Alhue), Finca La Anita, Humberto Canale (Canale Estate and Black River), Infinitus, Lavaque, López López, Luigi Bosca (Leoncio Arizu), Medrano Estate (Medrano Altos), Michel Torino, Norton (White Label), Salentein (Estate), Saúl Menem, Sendero Alto, Valentín Bianchi, Villa Atuel, Vintage, and Weinert.

PINOT GRIS OR PINOT GRIGIO (WHITE)

This Italian grape has great potential in Argentina to produce nutty, oily, dry white wines that age well, thanks in part to their naturally high acidity levels. *See* J.&F. Lurton, Santiago Graffigna, and Viniterra.

above Adobe houses, and a communal wood-fired oven, near Salta.

PINOT NOIR (RED)

Argentine Pinot Noir remains a work in progress, largely because producers have no long-term experience of working with this, one of the world's most difficult grape varieties. It tends to be light and fruity in Argentina, but lacks even a hint of its Burgundian counterpart's complexity. *See* Esmeralda (Argento), Luigi Bosca (Leoncio Arizu), and Salentein (Estate Pr1mus).

RIESLING (WHITE)

Riesling's naturally high level of acidity – and inherent complexity – is currently underexploited by Argentine wine producers, whether it is used to make blended or varietal wines. Luigi Bosca (Leoncio Arizu) is a welcome exception to the rule.

SANGIOVESE (RED)

Sangiovese, a mainstay of Italian Chianti, is often referred to as "Lambrusco" here because it can be used to make lightly sparkling, sweetish rosé wines. Argentina's best Sangiovese red wines come from hotter areas such as East Mendoza and San Juan province, where this late-ripening grape produces attractively bitter, black-cherry flavours. *See* Norton (White Label), Tittarelli, and Zuccardi.

SAUVIGNON BLANC (WHITE)

Sauvignon Blanc wines are often lambasted for smelling of cat's pee and gooseberry. Argentine examples generally avoid this caricature. The best examples combine fresh green fruit with an unusually lush mouthfeel. *See* Cabrini, Doña Paula (Los Cardos), Esmeralda (Argento), Finca Alma (Alhue), Finca La Celia (Angaro), Luigi Bosca (Leoncio Arizu), Michel

Torino, Norton (White Label), Pascual Toso, Sendero Alto, Trapiche, and Valentín Bianchi.

SAUVIGNON GRIS (WHITE)

This rare grape variety was resurrected in Bordeaux in the 1990s and has emerged in Argentina, where it produces musky, forceful wines, used as part of a blend. *See* Cabrini.

SEMILLON (WHITE)

Semillon, despite its vast potential, is underused and underrated in Argentina. Growers who shun the variety say it produces flabby wines – which is true only if the vines are overirrigated and overcropped. Good examples show delicate flavours of lime and acacia. *See* Finca La Anita, Humberto Canale (Canale Organic), and Chandon Argentina.

SYRAH OR SHIRAZ (RED)

Syrah/Shiraz could be Argentina's secret red wine weapon. It has the ability to ripen both tannin and sugar without losing its acidity, which keeps the wine from turning flabby. There are plenty of good Argentine Syrahs, but you'd struggle to find one that is world-class. But with lower yields (and lower irrigation levels) expect Argentine Syrah to lose its occasionally stretched character and to challenge the world's best. *See* Balbi, Bright Brothers Argentina, Cabernet de Los Andes (Vicien), Finca La Celia (La Consulta), Finca Las Moras, La Riojana (La Nature), Mayol, Medrano Estate (Medrano Altos), Michel Torino, Norton (Reserva), Santa Faustina, Santiago Graffigna, Saúl Menem, Tittarelli, Sendero Alto, and Villa Atuel.

TANNAT (RED)

South America's best Tannat wines may come from Uruguay (*see* p.162) but Argentina is starting to stake its own claim. Tannat's thick skin seems perfectly adapted to the high-altitude areas of Salta and Catamarca, as well as to the heat of San Juan province, producing thick, chewy wines with incredible colour and a constitution hardy enough for barrel-ageing. *See* Lavaque, Michel Torino, and Santiago Graffigna.

TEMPRANILLO (RED)

Tempranillo is Spain's equivalent of Merlot, producing juicy wines from early ripening grapes. The difference is that Tempranillo seems better adapted to extreme heat than Merlot does. "Spanish-Argentine" wineries such as Hispano-Argentinas (in Central Mendoza) and O. Fournier (in Mendoza's Uco Valley) set great store by this grape, while Santa Faustina and Tittarelli, in East Mendoza, are trying to locate the oldest, slowest-ripening plots of Argentine Tempranillo. *See* also Trapiche (Astica), Viniterra, Vintage, and Zuccardi (Familia Zuccardi and Terra Orgánica).

TOCAI FRIULANO (WHITE)

Tocai Friulano produces firm white wines usually made for early drinking. *See* Finca La Anita, Roca.

TORRONTÉS (WHITE)

No one is really sure how Torrontés arrived in

Argentina, nor exactly when. It is the only white grape variety well adapted to all of Argentina's wine regions, possibly due to the fact that there are at least three substrains of the variety, probably descended originally from the Torrontés from Galicia in Spain. The Torrontés Riojano strain is supposed to have the most refined flavours, and is found in the northern provinces of Salta and Catamarca; the Torrontés Mendocino (from Mendoza) strain is somewhat neutral tasting, and Torrontés San Juánico (from San Juan province) is only lightly flavoured. Most wine critics believe that Torrontés (of whatever strain) produces distinctive, peach and musk-scented white wines that may lack subtlety or class, but which are distinctive. The variety can be the best-value introduction to Argentina's rapidly improving white wines. Salta usually provides the most critically

acclaimed Argentine Torrontés, with Etchart (Etchart Cafayate), Michel Torino, and San Pedro de Yacochuya often cited. *See* also Alta Vista (Premium), Cabrini, Infinitus, J.&F. Lurton, La Riojana (La Nature), Norton (White Label), Saúl Menem, Tittarelli, and Zuccardi (Terra Orgánica).

TREBBIANO (WHITE)

This grape produces crisp, neutral white wines, useful for blending, at Santiago Graffigna.

VIOGNIER (WHITE)

Viognier could equal the quality of its Rhône counterpart, Shiraz/Syrah, if the wines produced from it so far in Argentina are anything to go by. It seems ideally suited to the heat of Mendoza and San Juan provinces, and is being planted farther south in

below Hail nets protecting grapes in Valentín Bianchi's vineyards in Mendoza's San Rafael region.

Patagonia and to the north in Salta and Catamarca. Wines made from Viognier have a slightly oily, or fat, texture and distinctive, exotic aromas of peach blossom and honeysuckle. Most of Argentina's Viognier vines are less than ten years old, so the wines should be drunk very young. *See* Escorihuela Gascon, Finca Las Moras, J.&F. Lurton, and Viniterra.

Argentine Wine Styles (Other)

ORGANIC WINE

Argentina, in common with the rest of the world, has less than one per cent of its vineyard certified organic. The number of organic producers in Argentina is increasing, however, not only because world demand for organic wine is increasing, but also because conditions within Argentina suit organic grape growing, for two main reasons. The first is that the dry climate and lack of humidity mean that vine fungal diseases, which cause problems in other parts of the world, are more easily controlled here.

Second, common airborne vine pests, such as sharp-shooters and leaf-hoppers, prefer to operate at altitudes below 500 m (1,640 ft); in Argentina the majority of vineyards are above this level. The hardest thing for would-be organic growers is to accept that it is much easier to make the change to organic conversion with lower grape yields. Argentina's culture of overproduction, not its climate, is the biggest obstacle to what could easily be an organic grape growing revolution here. *See* Cabernet de Los Andes, Fabril Alto Verde, Fapes, Humberto Canale, La Riojana, López López, Nanni, Punte del Monte, Zorzetto, and Zuccardi.

SPARKLING WINE

Visitors to Argentina will find some extremely good sparkling wines available in shops and restaurants. Sparkling wines are viewed in Argentina as they are in Italy – as something to be enjoyed and consumed, usually at the start of a family meal, rather than as something to be revered and opened only on high days and holidays. Both tank-fermented and the more expensive, bottle-fermented styles are produced. *See* Cavas de Zonda, Chandon Argentina, Domaine St Diego, Luigi Bosca (Leoncio Arizu), Rosell Boher, and Valentín Bianchi.

Argentine Wine Producers

Argentina has more than 1,800 registered wine producers, from unimaginably large wine cooperatives with wine vats the size of Olympic swimming pools to small-scale, family owned and run wineries making enough wine to fill a few goatskins. True, the majority of the best Argentine wine producers are large, professionally run and often foreign-owned wineries whose production can be counted in the tens of millions of bottles, as in Chile. But while Chile's winemaking facilities are almost entirely housed in modern, prefabricated buildings with no sense of wine history, Argentina's are rich in wine heritage.

The Michel Torino and Goyenechea wineries follow the Spanish colonial style, with high ceilings supported by whitewashed columns. Mendoza has ninety per cent of Argentina's wineries and these are dominated by historic, Italian-style designs. Impoverished immigrants from phylloxera-struck European wine regions were encouraged to settle in Argentina in the late-nineteenth century with promises of land. Italians outnumbered all other ethnic groups, and they built their wine cellars along Italian architectural lines. As the cellar often doubled as the family home, no separation existed between work and leisure. Today, however, modern winery offices are deserted at night, except at harvest-time.

The style favoured by the Italians was often a long, rectangular structure with a slanted roof and windows at either end to allow ventilation and light. On the outside they resembled a railway station and, within, a cathedral nave. As the family wine business expanded, extra "naves" could be built alongside with no disruption to the existing business. The idea of light being allowed to penetrate the wine cellar fulfilled a practical need to make conditions safer for the workers, but it also demonstrated the importance of religion in people's thinking: light, after all, comes from above and allowing light in meant the winery was connected, practically and spiritually, to God.

Wineries were being built at the time of the Industrial Revolution, and the arrival of the railway in Mendoza in 1885 not only gave wineries the opportunity to exploit new markets in Buenos Aires and abroad (see Norton below), but it also allowed them to import heavier raw materials. So, as family wineries became more profitable, the materials used in winery construction changed from adobe (earthen, sun-dried bricks made locally by hand) to imported metal and wood, requiring a degree of mechanization.

Central Mendoza wineries such as La Superiora in Russell, and the Tonelli and Los Tonneles wineries in Guaymallén (now defunct) embraced the new style. The Escorihuela winery in Godoy Cruz and Weinert's winery in Luján de Cuyo, also established at that time, are still in use today. French consultants who brought architectural knowledge about the construction of the winery shell also brought their expertise in what to construct inside: hence wine vats and wine presses became more sophisticated.

From 1900 onwards, square-shaped wine vats made of concrete became widespread, replacing circular wooden vats. A fashion spread for wineries to take on a fortress-like appearance, inspired by the buidings around Milan, the Veneto, and Tuscany. Wineries were consciously designed to look different from each other, and this individuality survives today, as the new wineries constructed at the start of the twenty-first century show. Salentein's "church," Catena Zapata's Mayan-inspired form, and Séptima's homage to Native American culture all look totally different, yet they retain that common thread: the idea that the winery is a kind of temple that serves both its local environment and the one above.

Argentine Wine Regions

Potential vineyard owners in Argentina are faced with an awesome choice. Do they choose a vineyard by its latitude or by its altitude? Vineyards cross nearly twenty degrees of latitude and 1,700 km (1,056 miles) over ten of Argentina's twenty-four provinces, and range from under 500 m to nearly 3,000 m (1,640–9,840 ft) in altitude. All the vineyards lie in the west of the country, more than 1,600 km (1,000 miles) from the Atlantic and the capital, Buenos Aires. They are sheltered by the Andes mountain range, on the other side of which lies Chile and the Pacific Ocean beyond.

The Argentine vineyards enjoy a dry, sunny climate because clouds coming off the Pacific cross Chile but shed their rain as snow on the mountains before they reach Argentina. When the snow melts, it provides the irrigation water without which winegrowing or any other type of farming would be impossible in Argentina. The importance of the Andes to the Argentine economy is reflected in the national flag, the colours of which show the blue and white of the Andean skyline with the sun in between.

Argentina has more than 200,000 ha (494,200 acres) of vineyards. However, just under half is planted with vines producing grapes for grape juice or concentrate. The 110,000 ha (272,000 acres) remaining is used for wine production. This figure makes Argentina's wine vineyard about the same size as that of Bordeaux, France's largest fine wine region.

Around 60,000 ha (148,260 acres) of Argentina's wine vineyard is planted to white wine grapes, the rest to red. In Bordeaux, by comparison, eighty per cent of the vineyards are planted to red varieties. However, while Argentina's red wine vineyards are dominated by internationally recognized quality grape varieties such as Malbec (12,000 ha/29,652 acres), Cabernet Sauvignon (6,500 ha/16,062 acres), Syrah (4,500 ha/11,120 acres) and Merlot (3,500 ha/8,650 acres); Argentina's white wine vineyards contain only relatively small quantities of international stars such as

above An Argentine vineyard worker, and friend, contemplate a day's pruning in the Calchaquíes Valley.

Chardonnay (4,700 ha/11,600 acres), Viognier (1,600 ha/3,950 acres), Riesling (170 ha/420 acres), Semillon (1,300 ha/3,210 acres), and Sauvignon Blanc (900 ha/2,225 acres), but these acreages are increasing. The wine vineyards are officially located in the following regions:

NORTH WEST Covers Jujuy, Salta, Tucumán, Catamarca and La Rioja provinces and produces around five per cent of all Argentine wine.

CENTRE-WEST Covers San Juan and Mendoza provinces; it produces more than ninety per cent of Argentine wine. The Centre-West is also sometimes referred to as The Cuyo. It only became part of Argentina in 1776, more than a century after Mendoza City was founded.

PATAGONIA (SOUTH) Covers Río Negro, Neuquén and Chabut provinces and produces less than three percent of all Argentine wine.

The most important province for wine production is Mendoza, which contributes around seventy per cent of the national total, followed by San Juan, with more than twenty per cent. The rest is shared between the North West, followed by Patagonia.

All regions receive at least 300 days of sunshine per year, so the major differences between the regions are linked to altitude. The difference between wine-growing at 500 m (1,640 ft) in East Mendoza and 1,500 m (4,920 ft) in Mendoza's Uco Valley, less than one hundred kilometres (sixty-two miles) away is enormous; it's like moving from the Mediterranean heat of, say, Sicily to the coldest French wine region, Champagne – the equivalent of a distance of more than 1,500 km (930 miles)!

All Argentine wine regions suffer from hail, which regularly devastates the country's vineyards and other key crops, such as sunflowers, soy beans, wheat and tobacco. Nets are installed to protect the vines' leaves, shoots, and grape bunches from being shattered by the falling hailstones. In the case of vines trained to vertical hedges, on the northern European model, the nets cling along the sides of the vines, touching the leaves and sometimes cramping the grapes as they swell near ripening.

In response to this problem, Valentín Bianchi in Mendoza's San Rafael region has developed new, looser netting, which allows better air circulation, vital for preventing vine fungal diseases from taking hold. For vines trained to the more widespread overhanging "pergola" system, which originated in the Mediterranean, the nets must be sited well above the horizontal vine canopy, on stilts. The nets must be emptied after hailstorms; otherwise they sag and burst under the weight.

The Mediterranean pergola system of vine training (here called "*parral*" or "*parron*") remains popular in Argentina (and Chile) because it gives high yields. This is because all of the vine leaves in a horizontal pergola receive full, direct sunlight all day long, like grass on a lawn. In contrast, one side of vertically hedged vines is slightly shaded for part of the day according to the sun's movement across the sky.

The vine leaf can be thought of as the sugar factory of the vine, converting sunlight to sugar in the grapes via photosynthesis. With proportionately more leaves exposed to the sun, vines grown on the pergola system can produce more grape sugar than hedge-trained vines can. But, because pergola-trained grapes must hang beneath the leaf canopy, they are shaded from direct sunlight. This means that, although they develop high sugars, they can fail to develop ripe flavours in the grape skins. However, it is possible to overcome this problem, as demonstrated by producers such as Norton, Finca La Anita, and

Zuccardi, whose vineyards are dominated by pergola-trained vines. They get around the problem by removing some of the leaves in the pergola canopy during the growing season, allowing more sunlight to get to the grape bunches.

Grapes grown on well-managed pergola vines also seem capable of retaining their naturally present acids. This is because the slight shade provided by the pergola keeps the grapes cool in Argentina's desert conditions, and cool grapes retain more acidity than hot ones do. Acidity is necessary if the finished wine is to taste fresh and have the ability to age well. Grapes that retain natural acids are less likely to need to have acidity (in powdered form) added during winemaking (a practice that is allowed under winemaking rules).

Another benefit of pergola vineyards is that they are generally flood irrigated, which may help discourage the dreaded vine disease phylloxera. Phylloxera is a root louse that kills vines by infecting their roots with its saliva. The louse is drowned or washed away by flood irrigation. Even without flood irrigation, though, experts believe that the strain of phylloxera present in Argentina is less virulent than that found in California or Australia, for example, where the disease has wreaked havoc. This may be because phylloxera prefers quite heavy soils and may find it difficult to reproduce in the light, easy texture of Argentine soils.

The low phylloxera risk means that ninety-five per cent of Argentina's vines are grown on their own roots, rather than on rootstocks from other vine species that are tolerant to phylloxera (the norm in most other wine-producing countries). The ability to plant vines on their own roots is one of Argentina's great viticultural gifts. On the negative side, Argentina is so dry and hot that the wines must routinely be acidified. So unless measures are taken on an industry-wide basis to get around this problem, Argentina's claim to be a "wine paradise" will lack resonance.

salta, tucumán, catamarca, & jujuy

These four provinces in the North West region of Argentina are home to the country's highest-altitude and northern-most vineyards. Of the four, Salta is the most important for wine-growing, while Jujuy is a relatively minor player. The total vineyard area represents about 4,000 ha (9,885 acres), or just under two per cent of Argentina's total.

As in Patagonia, in the far south, the first commercial vineyards here were developed relatively late, from the nineteenth century onwards, by wealthy entrepreneurs. They occupy the breathtaking Calchaquíes Valley that the Incas briefly occupied before the Spanish arrived (despite frequent earthquakes here, this is one of the few places in Argentina where Spanish colonial buildings have survived). Spanish Jesuits planted their first vines in the Calchaquíes Valley in a town now called La Viña ("the vineyard").

The Calchaquíes Valley runs south from Salta province for 200 km (125 miles), through Tucumán province and into Catamarca. Most of the vineyards are found around the beautiful towns of Cafayate and Molinos in Salta province, and in Chañar Punco in Catamarca. Tucumán province is better known for its vast lemon orchards and sugar-cane plantations than for wine grapes. The vineyards enjoy an incredible 340 days of sunshine per year. Vines are prevented from overheating partly through irrigation drawn from underground springs; cool night-time temperatures, owing to the high altitude, also temper the heat. On summer nights, temperatures can drop by up to 26°C (104°F) to below 10°C (50°F).

These are Argentina's highest commercial vineyards, planted at 1,500–3,000 m (4,900–9,800 ft). Some individual vineyards are planted at even higher altitudes than those of Bolivia, although the average altitude of Bolivia's vineyards is higher. The combination of constant daytime sunshine and cool nights produces wines with astonishingly deep, bright colours and explosive fruit flavours. These fruit flavours are best captured by drinking the wines as

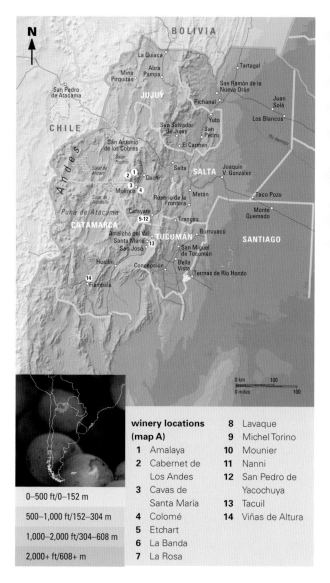

winery locations (map A)	8	Lavaque
1 Amalaya	9	Michel Torino
2 Cabernet de Los Andes	10	Mounier
	11	Nanni
3 Cavas de Santa María	12	San Pedro de Yacochuya
4 Colomé	13	Tacuil
5 Etchart	14	Viñas de Altura
6 La Banda		
7 La Rosa		

0–500 ft/0–152 m	
500–1,000 ft/152–304 m	
1,000–2,000 ft/304–608 m	
2,000+ ft/608+ m	

young as possible (the sandy soils here mean that the wines tend to age quite quickly).

White wines are made from Torrontés, Chardonnay, and Sauvignon Blanc; reds from Barbera, Bonarda, Cabernet Sauvignon, Malbec, Merlot, Tannat, and Syrah. Recent plantings of red varieties such as Barbera, Bonarda, Tannat and Syrah show great potential. *See* Amalaya, Cabernet de los Andes, Cavas de Santa María, Colomé, Etchart, La Banda, La Rosa, Lavaque, Michel Torino, Mounier, Nanni, N. Valentín Ramiréz, San Pedro de Yacochuya, Tacuil, and Viñas de Altura.

La Rioja province in the North West region of Argentina has around 7,500 ha (18,500 acres) of vineyards, or 3.5 per cent of the Argentine total. It was here that the first Argentine vineyards were planted by Spanish conquistadors coming south from Peru in the sixteenth century. The vineyards lie at around 1,000 m (3,300 ft) in dark, barren, mountainous terrain.

The land here proved a rich source of income for miners, notably in the early twentieth century, when Chileans flocked east across the Andes to mine the gold deposits. The mines they worked closed in 1926, as did the thirty-three kilometre-long (twenty-one-mile) cable-car that the miners built near the town of Chilecito, or "little Chile," also established by the miners. It is in this town that the La Riojana cooperative and the smaller Valle de la Puerta are based. In general, though, La Rioja's isolation, its extreme desert conditions and a lack of ready water for irrigation (growers here must rely on underground springs rather than snow-melt from the Andes) have seen the region superseded by Mendoza province as Argentina's wine heartland.

Nevertheless, some of Argentina's best-value everyday drinking wine is emerging from La Rioja province and its main winegrowing area, the Famatina Valley. This valley runs between two chains of hills, the Sierra de Velazco to the east and the Sierra de Famatina to the west. The climate here is regular and predictable, producing good yields of superripe grapes each year. Summers are dry and hot enough to encourage ripening, while short, cold winters allow a vital period of dormancy.

Foreign winemaking consultants keen to develop La Rioja's undoubted potential began arriving here in the mid-1990s, notably at the huge, but well-run, La Riojana cooperative. As well as its beneficial climate, another advantage of the province's isolation is that few local winegrowers have easy access to pesticides – nor do they need them. The local vineyards are fairly isolated from pests, owing to

the altitude, and the desert climate means that fungal diseases such as rot and mildew are minimal. High-quality organic projects are emerging, notably among small vineyard owners who send their grapes to the La Riojana cooperative.

The majority of La Rioja's vineyards are planted to white varieties such as Torrontés and Chardonnay, which produce intense, full-bodied wines. For reds, Bonarda, Cabernet Sauvignon, Malbec, Merlot, and Syrah are the mainstays, making deeply-coloured, soft, ripe reds. *See* La Riojana, Saúl Menem, and Valle de Puerta.

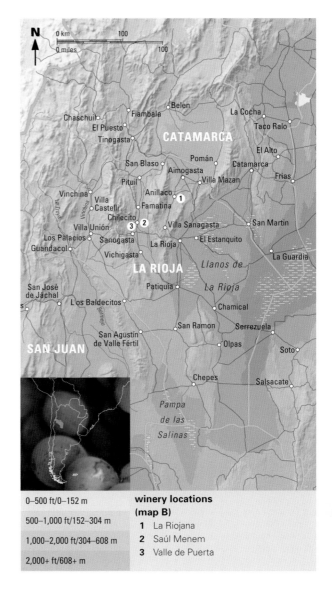

0–500 ft/0–152 m	**winery locations**
500–1,000 ft/152–304 m	**(map B)**
1,000–2,000 ft/304–608 m	1 La Riojana
2,000+ ft/608+ m	2 Saúl Menem
	3 Valle de Puerta

san juan

San Juan province lies between Mendoza to the south and La Rioja to the north. To the west are the Andes and, to the east, a range of hills called the Sierra de Pie de Palo. San Juan is Argentina's viticultural workhorse, producing more than thirty per cent of the country's wine from only twenty-three per cent of its vineyards (around 48,000 ha/119,000 acres). Yields are high here, owing to the hot climate, high-yielding, pergola-trained vines and generous irrigation. Many grapes are low-quality, suited only to the production of vermouths, sherry-style wines, grape juice, or juice concentrate. In recent years, however, San Juan has begun to shake off its "quantity, not quality" image. Leading the charge is Peñaflor, with its new Finca Las Moras venture, and Santiago Graffigna.

For the first time, these producers are separating out vineyard areas with the potential to make fine, rather than bulk, wine. New areas such as the low-lying Tulum Valley (630 m/2,065 ft) and the higher, cooler El Pedernal Valley (1,350 m/4,430 ft) are gaining recognition. The recently planted Finca Durazno ("peach vineyard") in the El Pedernal Valley is geared to quality fruit. Although it makes no wine itself, in 2002 it sold its grapes to Nieto y Senetiner, Santiago Graffigna, the Catena Group, Escorihuela Gascon, and Finca La Celia, among others. The vines are vertically trained and drip-irrigated. El Pedernal's cool night-time temperatures allow the grapes to retain their flavours.

In the region's hot climate, red wines stand out, producing juicy, rich wines for early drinking. Bonarda, Cabernet Franc, Greco Nero, Syrah, and Tannat can reach near-perfect levels of ripeness. *See* Bright Bothers Argentina, Cavas de Santa María, Cavas de Zonda, Fabril Alto Verde, Finca Las Moras, Peñaflor, Punte del Monte, and Santiago Graffigna.

Mendoza is the most important wine-producing province in Argentina, with 140,000 ha (346,000 acres) of vines – about seventy per cent of the country's total. About ninety per cent of all Argentine wine exports come from Mendoza. Jesuit priests planted the province's first vineyards in the sixteenth century, but quality winegrowing wasn't established until the mid-nineteenth century. Then, as Europe fought the devastating effects of phylloxera, a French botanist called Pouget came to Mendoza to see if French grapes could prosper here. They did, and it only took investment from powerful local figures like Tiburcio Benegas, founder of Trapiche, for the vineyards to expand.

The arrival of the railway in 1885 provided the first direct link from Mendoza to Buenos Aires,

below Flood irrigation is a popular, if haphazard, way of ensuring vines have enough water.

1,000 km (620 miles) to the east, and the fledgling wine industry was born. Mendoza province is divided into the following wine subregions:

North Mendoza

North Mendoza is a warm area producing soft wines for early drinking. Soils are light-textured and altitude varies from 750 m (2,460 ft) in the west to 500 m (1,640 ft) in the east. North Mendoza covers four departments: Guaymallén, Las Heras, Lavalle, and San Martín. West of Mendoza city is Las Heras, where Mendoza airport and the González Videla winery are located. The northern suburbs of Mendoza city cover the Guaymallén area where Santa Ana and Urquiza wineries are based. A few vineyards have survived the suburban sprawl, but the most important crops now grown in Guaymallén are lettuce, garlic, and tomatoes. Guaymallén is named after a canal built by an Inca chief of the same name; it brought – and still brings – melted snow from the Andes. The city becomes less built-up in the suburb of Lavalle, where Sendero Alto and Viñas Argentinas are based. The San Martín department east of Mendoza city marks the transition from North to East Mendoza.

Central Mendoza

Central Mendoza is the most highly regarded wine-producing area in Argentina, and is home to virtually all of Argentina's most famous wine names. It contains around 30,000 ha (74,000 acres) of vineyards, running

mendoza: points of interest

Argentina's wine heartland; the main city of Mendoza is subject to **frequent earthquakes**; the subregions of Luján de Cuyo and Maipù produce Argentina's **finest Malbec** reds; cooler, **higher altitude vineyards** are being developed in the Uco Valley for Malbec and Chardonnay; warm East Mendoza is home to (often **old vine**) Bonarda, Barbera, Syrah, Sangiovese, and Tempranillo; the sandier, flatter soils in the south generally suit wines for **early drinking**.

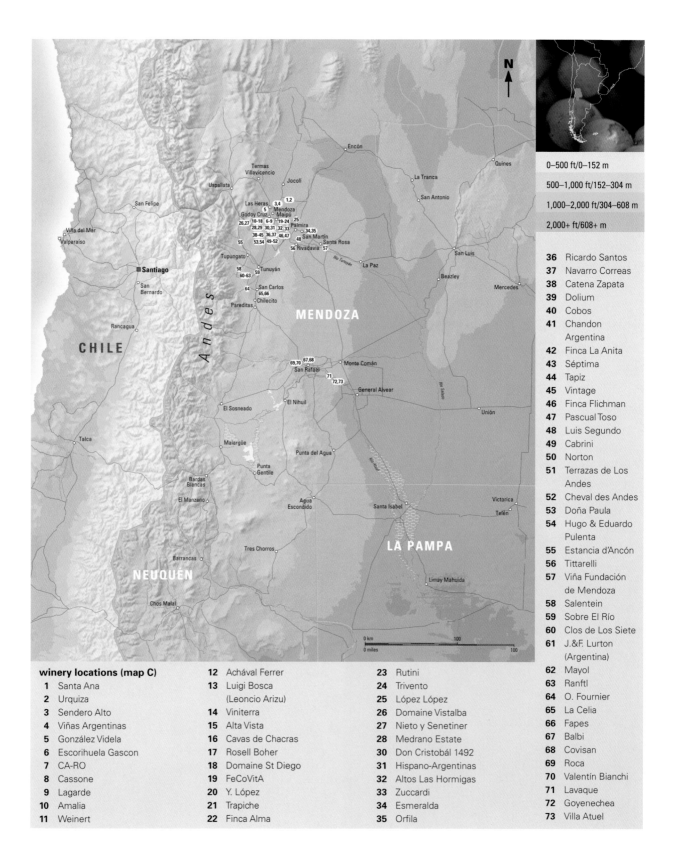

N

0–500 ft/0–152 m

500–1,000 ft/152–304 m

1,000–2,000 ft/304–608 m

2,000+ ft/608+ m

Encón

La Tranca

Quines

Termas
Villavicencio

Jocolí

San Antonio

Uspallata

Las Heras **3,4**
5 Mendoza
Godoy Cruz Maipú
26,27 **10-18** **6-9** **19-24** **25**
28,29 **30,31** **32** **33** Palmira
38-45 **36,37** **46,47** **34,35**
55 **53,54** **49-52** **48** San Martín
56 Rivadavia Santa Rosa
57

1,2

San Felipe

Viña del Mar

Valparaíso

Río Tunuyán

La Paz

San Luis

Tupungato

■ **Santiago**

58 **59**
60-63 Tunuyán

San Bernardo

Beazley

Mercedes

Andes

64 San Carlos
65,66 Chilecito
Pareditas

Rancagua

MENDOZA

CHILE

67,68
69,70 San Rafael
71
72,73

Monte Comán

General Alvear

Unión

Talca

El Sosneado

El Nihuil

Río Salado

Malargüe

Punta del Agua

Bardas
Blancas

Punta
Gentile

El Manzano

Agua
Escondido

Santa Isabel

Victorica

Tefén

Río Atuel

Barrancas

Tres Chorros

LA PAMPA

NEUQUÉN

Limay Mahuida

Chos Malal

0 km | 100
0 miles | 100

36	Ricardo Santos
37	Navarro Correas
38	Catena Zapata
39	Dolium
40	Cobos
41	Chandon Argentina
42	Finca La Anita
43	Séptima
44	Tapiz
45	Vintage
46	Finca Flichman
47	Pascual Toso
48	Luis Segundo
49	Cabrini
50	Norton
51	Terrazas de Los Andes
52	Cheval des Andes
53	Doña Paula
54	Hugo & Eduardo Pulenta
55	Estancia d'Ancón
56	Tittarelli
57	Viña Fundación de Mendoza
58	Salentein
59	Sobre El Río
60	Clos de Los Siete
61	J.&F. Lurton (Argentina)
62	Mayol
63	Ranftl
64	O. Fournier
65	La Celia
66	Fapes
67	Balbi
68	Covisan
69	Roca
70	Valentín Bianchi
71	Lavaque
72	Goyenechea
73	Villa Atuel

winery locations (map C)

1	Santa Ana	12	Achával Ferrer	23	Rutini
2	Urquiza	13	Luigi Bosca (Leoncio Arizu)	24	Trivento
3	Sendero Alto	14	Viniterra	25	López López
4	Viñas Argentinas	15	Alta Vista	26	Domaine Vistalba
5	González Videla	16	Cavas de Chacras	27	Nieto y Senetiner
6	Escorihuela Gascon	17	Rosell Boher	28	Medrano Estate
7	CA-RO	18	Domaine St Diego	30	Don Cristobál 1492
8	Cassone	19	FeCoVitA	31	Hispano-Argentinas
9	Lagarde	20	Y. López	32	Altos Las Hormigas
10	Amalia	21	Trapiche	33	Zuccardi
11	Weinert	22	Finca Alma	34	Esmeralda
				35	Orfila

south and west of Mendoza city on either side of the River Mendoza towards the Andes and Mount Aconcagua (*See also* Chile's Aconcagua Valley, p.23). At 6,959 m (22,826 ft) this is the highest peak in the Americas. Central Mendoza is sometimes called Upper or High Mendoza because most of the vineyards are at an altitude of 1,000 m (3,280 ft) and above.

The city of Mendoza has a population of nearly 750,000 making it the largest city in western Argentina. Located 1,000 km (620 miles) from the capital Buenos Aires, it lies on a geological fault line and has been hit by severe earthquakes (in 1861 and 1985). Mendoza was founded in 1561 by Spanish soldiers on their way across the Andes from Chile. They found in Mendoza easily workable, fertile soils and plentiful irrigation. The population of the city has expanded rapidly over the last century; much of the best potential vineyard land is now given over to housing. The city is rapidly spreading south and east; the Chacras de Coria area is the latest area where vineyard land is being sold for real estate.

The main subregions within Central Mendoza are the departments of Maipù in the southeast and Luján de Cuyo in the southwest.

LUJÁN DE CUYO DEPARTMENT

The first Malbec vines arrived in Luján de Cuyo in 1861, and the area is now considered the best for this variety in Argentina – some would say in the world. The variety responds to the loose-textured soils, cool nights and long warm days. Merlot ripens here one week before Malbec, and is also among Argentina's most refined. Syrah, too, is establishing an excellent reputation. Luján de Cuyo's key subregions here are:

AGRELO Agrelo is thirty-five kilometres (twenty-two miles) south of Mendoza city, and directly south of Perdriel. Agrelo's vineyards produce some of Argentina's best Malbec, particularly from the highest part of Agrelo (called Alto Agrelo), which has an altitude of 1,000 m (3,280 ft). The area around the Séptima vineyard and winery is drip-irrigated from

underground wells. Flood irrigation from the Río Mendoza is used on the lower-lying ground to the east. Alta Vista, Escorihuela Gascon, Finca La Anita, Nieto y Senetiner, Norton, and Viniterra all have vineyards in Agrelo. Catena Zapata, Chandon Argentina, Dolium, Séptima, Tapiz, and Vintage are Agrelo-based and also own vineyards here.

CARRODILLA Carrodilla lies in the northern part of Luján de Cuyo where the Mendoza city suburb of Godoy Cruz gives way to open country. It is another outstanding area for Malbec, because the topsoils are fine and contain lots of small stones, aiding drainage. Days here are slightly warmer and nights are slightly cooler than in other Luján de Cuyo areas, and this gives the Malbec powerful aromas and deep colour. Amalia, Luigi Bosca (Leoncio Arizu), and Nieto y Senetiner have vineyards here. Weinert's historic winery is in Carrodilla town centre.

CHACRAS DE CORIA Chacras de Coria means "Coria's Farms," named after an Italian immigrant called Coria who developed it as an agricultural centre in the nineteenth century. This farmland and its vineyards are now being sold off to wealthy Mendoza city dwellers keen to build second homes. The fine, clay-rich soil gets sandier and stonier nearer the Río Mendoza which flows to the south, producing a distinct, spicy character in the Malbec grown here.

Chacras de Coria's finest Malbec vineyards contain a good mix of what vine experts (ampelographers) call "mother vine" material. In other words, the vine cuttings used to propagate these vineyards by Italian immigrants like Coria in the nineteenth century were of excellent provenance. The lack of phylloxera meant that vines could be propagated without the need for grafting onto a phylloxera-tolerant rootstock (as is the case in most wine-growing regions in the world). Propagation was done by "layering" or directing a living vine shoot into the ground at an angle. When the shoot reappears above ground it can be trained into a new vine. Layering allowed gaps in the vineyard to be filled as vines died, and meant that the original vinestocks never had to be replaced by modern vines from Europe. Amalia and Dolium source grapes from Chacras de Coria. Cavas de Chacras has vineyards and its winery here, while Alta Vista and Rosell Boher have their wineries here.

COLONIA LOS AMIGOS This isolated area in western Luján de Cuyo is home to the first vineyard planted by Altos Las Hormigas – and also to an infestation of ants (*las hormigas*) that gave this producer its name.

GODOY CRUZ This is now a built-up area in Mendoza city where Escorihuela Gascon's historic winery and the associated CA-RO project are located.

LA PUNTILLA This area is very close to Chacras de Coria but few vineyards remain; Luigi Bosca (Leoncio Arizu) has a vineyard here for white wine.

LAS COMPUERTAS The name Las Compuertas refers to an irrigation gate that controls the flow of water from the River Mendoza via a canal running south of the adjacent town of Vistalba. Alta Vista and Fabre-Montmayou, Chandon Argentina, Cavas de Chacras and Luigi Bosca (Leoncio Arizu) source some of their best grapes from their own vineyards in Las Compuertas. The soils are stony, similar to those in Perdriel on the other (south) side of the Río Mendoza.

LUJAN DE CUYO TOWN The Luján de Cuyo department centres on the town of the same name sixteen kilometres (ten miles) due south of Mendoza city. Achával Ferrer, Lagarde, Luigi Bosca (Leoncio Arizu), and Viniterra have vineyards or wineries here. Note: Luján de Cuyo is not to be confused with "The Cuyo", a term sometimes used to refer to San Juan and Mendoza provinces or the Centre West region (*see* above).

LUNLUNTA Lunlunta is divided between Luján de Cuyo and Maipù departments, with the best part in the higher Luján de Cuyo side to the west. Lunlunta benefits from deep, stony soils rich in minerals brought down from the Andes over time by the Río Mendoza, which flows close by. Day-night temperature differences are lower here than in Agrelo, which seems

to suit Malbec, for which Lunlunta, especially the higher area in the west, is renowned. Cassone, Catena Zapata, Domaine St Diego, Medrano Estate, Norton, Santa Faustina, and Weinert all source grapes from here, either from their own vineyards or from growers under contract.

PERDRIEL Perdriel lies between the south bank of the Río Mendoza and Agrelo, with the Andes to the west and the Lunlunta Hills to the east. Its name is sometimes written "Pedriel". Soils are similar to those of Las Compuertas north of the Mendoza River. Malbec, Cabernet, Merlot and Bonarda thrive here. Many of the Malbec vineyards are of considerable age and pedigree. Sauvignon works well as far as the white wine varieties are concerned, and is quite widely grown. The equally successful Semillon, however, has fallen victim to the fashion for red wine; many of Perdriel's

old Semillon vineyards have been grubbed up over the last fifteen years. Cabrini, Cheval des Andes, Norton, and Terrazas de Los Andes have vineyards and wineries here, while Achával Ferrer, Chandon Argentina, Cavas de Chacras, Cobos, Etchart, Medrano Estate, and Viniterra have vineyards or grape suppliers here.

UGARTECHE Ugarteche is the most southerly part of the Luján de Cuyo department. It lies south of Agrelo at the point where the soil becomes sandier, allowing grapes to ripen more quickly. Those with vineyards here, such as Don Cristobál and Trapiche, pick relatively early to avoid overripeness. Merlot, Malbec, and Cabernet all perform well. Doña Paula and Hugo and Eduardo Pulenta also have vineyards, and their wineries, here.

below Traditional singers celebrate a religious festival near the old mining town of Chilecito, La Rioja.

VISTALBA Vistalba means "View of the sunrise over the Andes." It is the vineyard area closest to the Andes in Luján de Cuyo, which gives it a natural slope, affording good drainage, air circulation and sun exposure. In fact, drainage here is so rapid as to make flood irrigation problematic so, historically, local vineyards would be ploughed frequently. This cut the vine's surface roots, forcing them deep into the ground to find water. Deep-rooting vines tend to produce long-lived, complex wines.

Chardonnay and Malbec thrive here, with the oldest Malbec vines producing larger than usual berries, possibly due to the presence of an old substrain brought from France. Luigi Bosca (Leoncio Arizu) and Trapiche have excellent vineyards here, while Domaine Vistalba and Nieto y Senetiner have vineyards and wineries here.

MAIPÙ

The Maipù department is the warmest area in Central Mendoza. It begins twenty-five kilometres (15.5 miles) southeast of Mendoza city, due east of the slightly cooler, higher Luján de Cuyo department. Maipù's loamy clay soil produces renowned Syrah, Cabernet Sauvignon, and Malbec, similar to the wines of Luján de Cuyo, if slightly broader-textured and less intense. The main areas within Maipù include:

BARRANCAS Barrancas lies south of the Río Mendoza and is named after the riverbanks (*barrancas*) upon which it sits. J.&F. Lurton and Fabre-Montmayou have vineyards here, while Finca Flichman and Pascual Toso have vineyards and wineries here.

COQUIMBITO Coquimbito, Maipù town's eastern suburb, took off as a wine area with the arrival of the railway in Mendoza in 1885, which encouraged Italian immigrants such as Rutini to establish businesses here. Rutini has a Cabernet Sauvignon vineyard here that was planted in 1885. Finca Alma is based here, too, while Peñaflor and Trapiche each have a large winery on a shared site.

CRUZ DE PIEDRA This town lies between Russell and the north bank of the Río Mendoza. Don Cristobál 1492 and Hispano-Argentinas are based here, Y. López has one of its oldest vineyards here, and Chandon Argentina has a large Cabernet Sauvignon vineyard here.

FRAY LUIS BELTRÁN Fray Luis Beltrán has a high water table. The advantage of this is that Sangiovese and Tempranillo grapes, when yields are kept sensible, can take on an appealing mint character. Tittarelli and Medrano Estate have vineyards here and next to its vineyard is Zuccardi's main winery.

LUNLUNTA Lunlunta is divided between Luján de Cuyo and Maipù departments. *See* Luján de Cuyo department (above).

MAIPÙ TOWN Maipù town lies twenty-four kilometres (fifteen miles) southeast of Mendoza city, midway between the city and the Mendoza River. Y. López and FeCoVitA are based here.

MAYOR DRUMMOND "Drummond" (as it is referred to locally) is situated between Carrodilla and Maipù town. Chandon Argentina and Etchart have vineyards here, while Cassone and Lagarde have wineries here.

RUSSELL Russell is a flat area where Luigi Bosca (Leoncio Arizu), Ricardo Santos, Navarro Correas, and Trivento have vineyards.

VILLA SECA Villa Seca in eastern Maipù is where the organic producer López López is based. The town lies next to the main irrigation canal, so the water is clean and nutrient rich.

East Mendoza

East Mendoza is the largest subregion in Mendoza province, but the least highly regarded. Its 60,000 ha (150,000 acres) of vineyards account for more than forty per cent of Mendoza's total production (and thirty per cent of the national total). East Mendoza's climate is much hotter than that of any other Mendoza wine region, being further from the night-cooling influence of the Andes. Also, East Mendoza's vines grow between 550–750 m (1,800–2,460 ft) on much lower, warmer (and flatter) ground than Mendoza's cool, mountainous Uco Valley (*see* below). East Mendoza's vines will give grapes rich in sugar (and thus potential alcohol) even when yields are pushed to the limit with irrigation. Dull but high-yielding grape varieties such as Criolla were planted here in the 1960s, during Argentina's domestic wine boom.

Plenty of high quality, old vineyards remain, though. Warm to hot-climate grape varieties such as Bonarda, Syrah, Malbec, Sangiovese, Tempranillo, and Torrontés are naturally suited to the conditions. The best dark-skinned grapes produce superripe, deeply coloured wines with lush, soft textures reminiscent of Australian wines. The pity is that many of these grapes are still trundled into wine cooperatives, their unique flavours blended away with dilute grapes suitable only for jug-wine blends. Santa Faustina, Tittarelli and Esmeralda, however, are actively searching out these

above The Tacuil vineyard near Molinos in the Calchaquíes Valley, is Argentina's highest commercially productive vineyard.

old vines, while Zuccardi is showing how well-suited East Mendoza's warm climate is to organic methods.

East Mendoza's best producers are also regrafting Bonarda, Syrah, and Tempranillo buds onto old (but healthy) Criolla vines left over from the 1960s planting boom. Criolla may produce dull wine but it puts down a strong root system. Within six to eighteen months the regrafted vine can produce wine from the new variety with outstanding results, at a much cheaper cost than grubbing up vines and replanting from scratch. With a few more similarly minded wineries committed to detective work and hard graft, East Mendoza can justifiably expect its reputation to be re-examined. *See* Esmeralda, Orfila, Santa Faustina, Segundo Correas, Tittarelli, Viña Fundación de Mendoza, and Zuccardi.

Mendoza's Uco Valley

In the 1920s, when the first would-be vineyard owners such as Enrique Fallardi (*see* Fapes) settled here, the Uco Valley was considered isolated and difficult to farm – but the land was cheap. Over the last fifteen years the Uco Valley has become the most sought-after vineyard area in Argentina. It possesses Mendoza's highest-altitude vineyards, many of which were used as orchards (apple, cherry, and apricot) until a vine-planting boom began in the late 1980s.

At that time, foreign investors were finding that land near Mendoza City in Central Mendoza was becoming too expensive, owing to its worth as real estate for homes. So the likes of Salentein (The Netherlands), J.&F. Lurton (Bordeaux), O. Fournier (Spain), Finca La Celia (Chile), and the Clos de Los Siete (France) have invested tens of millions of dollars here, in wineries, vineyards and wine-related tourism. Argentine-owned producers such as Amalia and Catena Zapata have also planted large estates here.

The Uco Valley is as far from Mendoza City as Napa is from San Francisco and investors hope that Uco Valley will become the Napa Valley of South America, renowned for its wine as well as for its tourism. But whereas many vineyards in the Napa Valley occupy the low-altitude valley floor, vineyards in the Uco Valley lie on uneven, mountainous terrain at 900–1,500 m (3,000–4,900 ft). And the Uco Valley has the Andes as a dramatic backdrop.

The Uco Valley has 10,000 ha (24,700 acres) of vineyards, or seven percent of Mendoza province's total. They are the only vineyards in Mendoza province to grow directly beneath the Andes mountain range (*La Cordillera*). All other Mendoza vineyards grow in the foothills of the Andes. Because of its altitude and proximity to the high mountains, Uco Valley is considered a cool area in Argentine wine terms. The climate suits Chardonnay, Semillon, and Sauvignon Blanc for white wines and Merlot, Pinot Noir, Malbec, and Tempranillo for reds.

Uco Valley wines are characterized by their firm, crisp mouthfeel and forceful aromas; they are quite distinct from other Mendoza wines, which tend to be rounder and less aromatic. Uco Valley is too cool for late-ripening grape varieties such as Bonarda and Cabernet Sauvignon to mature fully every year.

Uco Valley is subdivided into the three departments which, from north to south, are:

TUPUNGATO Areas to look for in Tupungato include: Cordón del Plata, where Cabrini and Doña Paula have vineyards; Gualtallary, where Catena Zapata has its highest vineyard, Adrianna; San José, where the picturesque Estancia d'Ancón is based; and the area around Tupungato town where Salentein and the smaller Mayol are based, and where Achával Ferrer, Chandon Argentina (for sparkling wine), Finca Flichman, Trapiche, Trivento, and Viniterra own vineyards. Bear in mind some commentators loosely refer to the entire Uco Valley as "Tupungato".

TUNUYÁN Areas to look for in Tunuyán include: Los Árboles, from where the reliable Amalia, Medrano Estate and Tapiz all source grapes; and Vistaflores, which is now almost a French colony, thanks to the arrival of some of France's most famous wine names (J.&F. Lurton and the ambitious French investors at Clos de Los Siete). Argentine producers such as Ranftl are also expanding their interests here.

SAN CARLOS Areas to look for in San Carlos include: Altamira, where Amalia has vineyards, as do Chandon Argentina for the Terrazas de Los Andes wines; San Carlos town, where Finca La Celia is based, and La Consulta, which produces some of Argentina's most appetising, black-cherry-scented Malbec and Tempranillo wines from the likes of O. Fournier, Altos Las Hormigas, Achával Ferrer, and Catena Zapata.

Mendoza's San Rafael Region

The San Rafael region is the most southerly Mendoza province and is sometimes referred to as South Mendoza. The main town of San Rafael is two hours' drive from Mendoza's Uco Valley and three hours by car from Mendoza city about 240 km (150 miles) to the northwest. San Rafael's isolation means its wines are often unfairly ignored, even though the region has 30,000 ha (74,000 acres) of vineyards, fifteen per cent of the national total. San Rafael is frequently struck by hail, leading some to question the region's reliability. In response, producers such as Valentín Bianchi have pioneered new types of hail netting, which shield the grapes from the hail but allow sunlight through.

San Rafael's vineyards are irrigated by the Diamante and Atuel rivers. The soils are generally light in texture and easy to work. Vines in the best sites, away from the water table, can put down deep roots which draw minerals into the grapes, giving the wines complex aromas and flavours. White wines from Sauvignon Blanc, Chardonnay and Semillon are especially good, as are reds from Bonarda, Cabernet Franc, Cabernet Sauvignon, Malbec, Merlot, and Syrah. *See* Arizu, Balbi, Covisan, Goyenechea, Lavaque, Roca, Valentín Bianchi, and Villa Atuel.

Patagonia is one of those places that everyone has heard of but few know much about. A tableland of mountains, deserts, pampas, glaciers, fjords and lakes, it encompasses a small part of southern Chile and all of southern Argentina. Vineyards are found in three provinces, Neuquén, Río Negro ("black river") and Chabut. Combined, these account for a mere 6,000 ha (15,000 acres), less than three percent of Argentina's vineyard. Town names have historical associations. Darwin is named after the English naturalist whose trip to Patagonia from 1831 presaged his seminal work, *The Origin of Species*. Roca, Belislel, and Fernández are named after the generals who, by 1910, had brutally removed the indigenous peoples Darwin had studied.

Patagonia's vineyards are some of the most southerly in the world. They are unusual in Argentina for three reasons. First, the Andes are too far away to have any direct effect on wine-growing. Second, the vineyards are relatively low-lying, at 200–350 m (655–1,150 ft). And, third, their distance from the Equator means that, compared with other Argentine regions, they enjoy a relatively cool climate.

Patagonia's cool climate suits apple, pear and quince growing and it is here that some of Argentina's most highly charged dry white wines are made. Chardonnay, Semillon, Viognier, and Torrontés show fantastic balance; the cool climate gives the fruit flavours freshness and balance and keeps alcohol levels relatively low. Reds from Merlot, Pinot Noir, Cabernet Franc, Cabernet Sauvignon, and even Syrah (which generally prefers hotter climates) show great subtlety and elegance of texture – if the tannins are fully ripe. When they are, the wines can develop in bottle for two to five years. *See* Humberto Canale, Infinitus, Noemí, Weinert, and Zorzetto.

The one Patagonian grapegrower mentioned here, Zorzetto, is somewhat isolated from Humberto Canale, Infinitus, and Noemí, all of which have wineries near the town of Roca in Patagonia's main wine-growing area, the Río Negro valley. The Río Negro crosses Neuquén and Río Negro provinces and provides water for irrigation. A fourth producer, Weinert, is developing vineyards much further south, in Chabut province.

0–500 ft/0–152 m

500–1,000 ft/152–304 m

1,000–2,000 ft/304–608 m

2,000+ ft/608+ m

winery locations (map D)
1 Humberto Canale
2 Infinitus
3 Noemí
4 Weinert
5 Zorzetto

notable producers

Achával Ferrer (C12)

Luján de Cuyo, Mendoza
www.achaval-ferrer.com;
ventas@achaval-ferrer.com
This excellent venture has worked
from a rented winery in Luján de
Cuyo city, Central Mendoza, since
its foundation in 1998. Its founding
owners are Tuscan wine producer
Roberto Cipresso, an Argentine
businessman called Santiago
Achával, and a cousin of Achával's
wife, Manuel Ferrer. Achával Ferrer
produces around 60,000 bottles
of concentrated, refined, Malbec-
dominated red wines from
contracted growers working old
Mendoza vines. Achával Ferrer is
also developing its own, carefully
sited, low-yield vineyards. The wines
include Achával Ferrer, a blend of
Malbec, Merlot, and Cabernet
Sauvignon. Its ripe, elegant tannins
and concentrated fruit flavours are
reminiscent of top red Bordeaux.
Achával Ferrer Single Vineyard
Malbec is a wild-tasting red Malbec
from select vineyard plots such as
Finca Altamira in the La Consulta
area of Mendoza's Uco Valley. This
vineyard was abandoned until 1999,
although the vines were still alive.
They give extremely small, ultra-
concentrated yields of grapes. The
top wine, Achával Ferrer Quimera,
is a strongly oak-influenced,
complex, age-worthy, multilayered
blend of Cabernet Sauvignon,
Malbec, and Merlot.

Alamos *See* Catena Zapata

Alhue *See* Finca Alma

Allied Domecq Argentina

Ciudad, Buenos Aires
Tel: (+54) 11 4313 4800;
ada@adsw.com
This multinational drinks firm owns
Balbi and Santiago Graffigna.

Alta Vista (C15)

Luján de Cuyo, Mendoza
Tel: (+54) 0261 4964;
www.altavistawines.com.ar
Alta Vista is based in a beautiful,
tastefully renovated winery with
extensive, cool, underground cellars.
It was built in 1890 in Chacras de
Coria, in the Luján de Cuyo
department of Central Mendoza.
Alta Vista's vineyards, near the winery
in the excellent areas of Las
Compuertas and Agrelo, contain high
percentages of old vines. The French
d'Aulan family founded Alta Vista in
1996. Modern winemaking equipment
was installed in the winery, but its
historic shell was restored. Both the
d'Aulans and their winemaking
partner, Michel Rolland, are involved
in Clos de Los Siete (*see* below).
Rolland famously pioneered a new,
much riper-tasting style of red
Bordeaux wine in the 1980s. Rolland's
critics say all his wines taste the
same, because he favours long
ageing in new oak barrels that impart
fairly standard vanilla flavours. They
also criticize his "extractive"
winemaking, which produces deeply
coloured, thick-textured reds. Rolland
achieves this by leaving the grape
solids in contact with the newly
fermented wine in vat for up to six
weeks (two to three is usual). If the
grape skins and seeds are not fully
ripe, "extractive" wines can end
up tasting too dry, like tea left too
long in the pot. However, Rolland's
style seems more consistent in
Argentina where the ripeness is
more regular than it is in Bordeaux.
(Rolland's other Argentine projects
are San Pedro de Yacochuya, and
"Iscay" at Trapiche, but *see also*
Salentein, below.) Alta Vista produces
around 700,000 bottles.
The basic Alta Vista Cosecha range
includes an appealing, generous
unoaked blend of Chardonnay,
Chenin Blanc, and Torrontés (one-
third each), and an attractively bitter-
cherry-flavoured, unoaked blend
of Malbec, Bonarda, Cabernet
Sauvignon, Merlot, and Tempranillo.
The Alta Vista Premium range
includes a competent, unoaked
Chardonnay and a diverting oak-aged
dry Torrontés, plus sound reds made
from Malbec and an especially
characterful Malbec/Tempranillo
blend. Alta Vista Grande Reserve is a
100% Malbec red aged in new French
oak barrels combining juicy grape
tannins with firm oak tannins. It
benefits from early drinking (within
five years of the vintage). The top red
wine, called Alta Vista Alto, has a
dense but elegant fruit core leading to
a decisive aftertaste of black cherry
and blackcurrant. It is blended from
Malbec (80%) and Cabernet
Sauvignon (20%) vines averaging fifty
years of age.

Altimus *See* Michel Torino

Altos de Temporada *See*
Temporada

Altos Las Hormigas (C32)

Cuidad Mendoza

Tel: (+54) 0261 298186;

info@altoslashormigas.com

This Italian-Swiss-Argentine venture dates from 1995 and enjoys considerable (and justified) critical acclaim for red wines made from Malbec. The company's first vineyard, planted in Colonia Los Amigos in Central Mendoza's Luján de Cuyo department, was attacked by ants (*las hormigas*), hence the name. While the new Malbec vines planted here become established, grapes are purchased from small growers in La Consulta, an outstanding area for intense Malbec in Mendoza's Uco Valley to the south. Around 120,000 bottles are produced annually. The basic Altos Las Hormigas Malbec has easy-drinking texture and clear black plum flavours and an elegant, uplifting aftertaste. The Altos Las Hormigas Reserve has a thicker fruit texture softened and refined by ageing in new French oak barrels. Winemaker and co-partner is the talented Italian Alberto Antonini, who has also consulted to other Argentine wineries such as Tittarelli and Vintage, *see* below. (*See also* Argentine Wine Styles – Introduction, p.97.)

Amalaya (A1)

Molinos, Salta

Tel: (+54) 03868 494044;

www.hesscollection.com

Hess Collection Winery owns this estate averaging 2,450 m (8,036 ft)

above Raúl Dávalos sold Colomé vineyard to Hess Collection (California) but retained Tacuil.

in altitude in the Cachi area of Salta province's Calchaquíes Valley, as well as the nearby Colomé estate. Hess planted Malbec, Cabernet Sauvignon, Tannat, and Sauvignon Blanc on Amalaya's 300 ha (741 acres); although the project is still at experimental stage, a winery will follow if the wines are deemed good enough. *See also* Viñas de Altura.

Amalia (C10)

Luján de Cuyo, Mendoza

Tel: (+54) 0261 436 0677;

www.vinamalia.com.ar

The Basso family produces clean, elegant, sometimes rich Cabernet

Sauvignon, Malbec, and Chardonnay wines from its winery in Carrodilla, in the Luján de Cuyo area of Central Mendoza. Grapes are sourced from quality-oriented Mendoza growers, and from Amalia's own vineyards, Finca Los Montes Negros and Finca La Amalia, in Mendoza's Uco Valley. The wines are labelled Villar Cortes and Viña Amalia. Viña Amalia Dos Fincas is a blend of Cabernet Sauvignon and Malbec with ripe flavours of dark fruit; the fine tannins are seasoned by oak ageing. The Amalia wines show welcome subtlety and elegance and provide very pleasurable drinking.

Ancón See Estancia d'Ancón

Andean See Finca Las Moras

Andes Sur See Viñas Argentinas

Angaro See Finca La Celia

Anubis See Vintage

Apartado See Rutini

Argento See Bodegas Esmeralda

Arizu
This famous but now defunct Argentine wine name once owned the world's most extensive vineyards, in Villa Atuel in Mendoza's San Rafael region. Arizu planted these using tax concessions on new vineyards granted when Argentine wine consumption was rising (in the 1960s). The boom did not last and the Arizu vineyards have mostly been replanted with olives (a vineyard that survived is used by Bodega Villa Atuel, see below). One Arizu family member has re-emerged in northern Argentina's Catamarca province at Cabernet de los Andes.

Arriero See Viñas Argentinas

Astica See Trapiche

Bacchus
Capital Federal, Buenos Aires
Tel: (+54) 11 4331 1131;
juan.thibaud@lomanegra.com.ar
This Mendoza-based, French-owned venture makes crisp, stylish red wines from purchased grapes. The Terruño 27 red, blended from Malbec and Cabernet Sauvignon, is most refreshing if served slightly chilled. The Ruca Malen range includes lightly oak-aged Cabernet Sauvignon and Malbec reds showing attractively spicy fruit. The Ruca Malen Grand Cru Cabernet Sauvignon is aged in French and American oak barrels and shows ripe blackcurrant fruit and an agreeably fresh aftertaste.

Balbi (C67)
San Rafael, Mendoza
Tel: (+54) 11 4313 4800;
ada@adsw.com
Balbi is one of Allied Domecq Argentina's two Argentine wineries (see also Santiago Graffigna). Based in the town of Las Paredes in Mendoza's San Rafael region, Balbi produces around 2.5 million bottles annually of reasonably priced still and sparkling wines made in a traditional, old French style. The most attractive wine made without oak influence is an off-dry Syrah rosé. Where oak is used, on the Barrel Select or Reserve ranges, it is used sensitively. Balbi Barbaro, its top oak-aged red, shows thick, peppery tannins and is made from mainly Cabernet Sauvignon with Merlot, Syrah, and Malbec.

Baron B See Chandon Argentina

Black River See Humberto Canale

Bodega del Novecientos (Bodega del 900) See Tittarelli

Bodegas y Viñedos Andinos
This is part of Peñaflor and includes Michel Torino and Santa Ana. See also Lavaque.

Bohème See Luigi Bosca (Leoncio Arizu)

Bramare See Cobos

Bright Brothers Argentina
www.brightbrothers.pt
The Australian Bright Brothers produce their range of Argentine wines at Peñaflor's facilities in San Juan province. The top range, called Elementos, includes a barrel-aged Malbec/Shiraz with lively, peppery fruit and excellent ripeness, and a Chardonnay/Viognier white with a fine, creamy core of citrus fruit leading to a rich, tropical-fruit aftertaste. Bright Brothers also make wine in Chile (see p.51) and Uruguay (see p.165).

Brioso See Vintage

Brut Xerox See Domaine St Diego

Buenas Ondas *See* Fabril Alto Verde

Bykos *See* Viniterra

Caballero de la Cepa *See* Finca Flichman

Cabernet de los Andes (A2)
Buenos Aires
Tel: (+54) 11 4433 0824
Carlos Arizu is descended from the family that founded Arizu (*see* above). He learned his winemaking style in California and returned to Argentina to found Cabernet de los Andes in 2001. Bonarda, Cabernet Sauvignon, and Syrah reds under the Vicien brand are softcentred and puretasting, with vibrant primary fruit aromas mixing with flavours of menthol and chocolate. The grapes are organically grown at 1,800 m (5,904 ft) in the Fiambala Valley in Catamarca province.

Cabernet Sauvignon de las Reinas *See* Orfila

Cabrini (C49)
Luján de Cuyo, Mendoza
Tel: (+54) 0261488 0218;
ivgcabri@infovia.com.ar
Since 1997 this fourth-generation family winery has benefited from the winemaking expertise of Patrick Campbell from California's Laurel Glen. Since then, Cabrini reds from Cabernet Sauvignon, Malbec, and Merlot, plus whites from Chardonnay, Torrontés, and Sauvignon Blanc (the latter blended with 15% Sauvignon Gris) under the Cabrini label have displayed more dense, more

complex flavours, as well as greater balance and clarity. The top red wine, Don Leandro Cabrini, shows rich Malbec flavours of anise and violets. Grapes come from vineyards in Central Mendoza's Luján de Cuyo department planted in 1918 by the original Cabrini.

Cadus *See* Nieto y Senetiner

Canale Estate *See* Humberto Canale

Candela *See* Escorihuela Gascon

CA-RO Catena/Rothschild (C7)
Godoy Cruz, Mendoza
Tel: (+54) 0261 424 6477;
gerencia@bodegascaro.com.ar
CA-RO is an alliance between the Catena Group and Domaines Barons de Rothschild (Lafite), owner of Château Lafite-Rothschild in Bordeaux and other wineries in Portugal and Hungary, as well as a part-share in Los Vascos in Chile (*see* p.70). The aim is to produce around 360,000 bottles of top red wine at Escorihuela Gascon's winery (*see* below). The first wine, produced in 2000, was 30% Malbec and 70% Cabernet Sauvignon, but Malbec should gain a 40% share of the blend in the future. The wine is already more flavourful and riper-tasting than the Los Vascos wines from Lafite-Rothschild's venture in Chile, and should improve further once the owners fine-tune the blend.

Carrascal *See* Weinert

Casa Nieto Senetiner *See* Nieto y Senetiner

Casaterra *See* Medrano Estate

Cassone (C8)
Luján de Cuyo, Mendoza
Tel: (+54) 0261 423 3203;
www.familiacassone.com.ar
This emerging fourth generation, family owned, grape-grower-turned-winemaker is based in Mayor Drummond, in the Luján de Cuyo area of Central Mendoza, but draws grapes from vineyards in various parts of Mendoza province. Cassone's well-styled Malbec reds have improved steadily since 1998. They are aged in older oak barrels to soften firm fruit tannins without imparting excess oak flavour.

Catena Group
Dr Nicolás Catena and his family control the Catena Group. This holding company owns a number of wineries, of which the most important are Esmeralda and Catena Zapata (*see* below). They are acknowledged to produce Argentina's most complete range of quality wines, at both the everyday drinking level in the case of Esmeralda, and at the more serious, high-quality level in the case of Catena Zapata. Nicolás Catena's grandfather Nicola left Italy for Argentina in the late nineteenth century and laid the foundations for the family's wine business. Nicola's son Domingo was highly successful in the bulk wine market that thrived in Argentina until the mid-1960s. When Nicolás Catena took over from his father Domingo, he decided to use the family's Esmeralda winery to

develop quality wine to be sold in bottle. Within ten years, Nicolás Catena had control of 40% of the Argentine-bottled wine market. Time spent visiting California's leading wineries gave Nicolás Catena the blueprint for the style of wine he wanted: clean, fruit-driven and expressive. Former vineyard manager Pedro Marchevsky (*see* Vintage, below) reduced irrigation to produce healthier, more concentrated grapes. Catena maximized the new potential by hiring Californian Paul Hobbs (*see* Cobos), the first foreign winemaking consultant to work in Argentina, and then Bordeaux winemaker Jacques Lurton of J.&F. Lurton (*see* below). In 1999 the Catena group's flagship Catena Zapata winery in Agrelo (*see* below) opened, and a separate joint-venture agreement was signed with the French Domaines Barons de Rothschild (Lafite) to produce a top Argentine wine range called CA-RO (*see* above). Catena Group has also acquired more wine interests in Argentina with Cavas de Santa María (*see* below), while Dr Catena has also personally invested in the La Rural/Escorihuela Group (run separately from Catena Group but with the same attention to detail).

Catena Zapata (C38)

Agrelo, Luján de Cuyo, Mendoza
Tel: (+54) 0261 490 0214;
catenazapata@nysnet.com.ar
Catena Zapata, located in Agrelo in Central Mendoza's Luján de Cuyo area, is the Catena Group's flagship winery. The design was inspired by

the Mayan civilization that once populated Central America. Red wine vats are short and squat to allow better extraction of colour and tannin. White grapes arrive as whole grape clusters, to prevent any risk of oxidation or spoilage. The common-sense procedures are adopted in the Catena Zapata vineyards, too. Former head viticulturalist Pedro Marchevsky, now with Vintage (*see* below), aimed at growing balanced vines. Early in 2003, Marchevsky left Catena Zapata, and was replaced by Alejandro Sejanovich, who was Catena Zapata's assistant vineyard manager from 1995 to 1999, before becoming winemaker at Luca and Tikal winereies (owned by Nicolás Catena's children, respectively, Laura and Ernesto). The consistent quality of Catena Zapata's range of Bonarda, Cabernet Sauvignon, and Malbec reds shows the benefit of balanced vines. Alamos Chardonnay is among Argentina's most reliable, and enjoyable, white wines. It is part-aged in second- and third-use oak barrels and has a golden colour, with ripe tropical-fruit flavours and a citrus twist. The Catena label range is more complex than Alamos. Catena Cabernet Sauvignon has small amounts of Merlot and Cabernet Franc blended in for extra texture. Catena Malbec shows benchmark blackberry and cassis flavours and soft, ripe tannins. Catena Chardonnay has the rich tones sought by the winemaking team. The Catena Alta range of Cabernet Sauvignon, Malbec, and

Chardonnay is sourced from the best-sited blocks of the Catena Zapata vineyards and is aged in new French oak barrels.

All three wines show concentrated, elegant fruit flavours. The top wine, Nicolás Catena Zapata, is mainly Cabernet Sauvignon with less than 10% Malbec. It is aged for almost two years in new French oak barrels and is not fined or filtered at bottling. It is Argentina's most expensive wine. Catena Zapata is developing a more affordable range of single-vineyard Malbecs. The Adrianna Vineyard in Gualtallary, in Mendoza's Uco Valley, was only planted in 1997, but the wine has deep colour, expressive floral aromas and vibrant texture. Angélica Vineyard is in Lunlunta, Central Mendoza. Its Malbec vines, planted in the 1930s, produce Catena Zapata's most consistent, complex, and piercing Malbec. Nicasia Vineyard in La Consulta, in Mendoza's Uco Valley, produces predictably soft, open-textured wine for early drinking. Uxmal Vineyard was planted in 1983 in Agrelo in front of where the Catena Zapata winery now stands. It produces soft Malbecs with fruit and structure.

Cavas de Chacras (C16)

Luján de Cuyo, Mendoza
ecesa@slatinos.com.ar
The Festa family came to Argentina from Italy in 1888. Their small winery in Chacras de Coria, in Central Mendoza's Luján de Cuyo department, works on a gravity system, with two levels of concrete

tanks, ideally suited to red wines made using minimal pumping. Various members of the Festa family provide grapes from excellently sited and often old vines. Reds from Cabernet Sauvignon, Malbec, Merlot, and Tempranillo, and whites from Chardonnay show increasing texture, clarity and balance since the 2001 vintage, when advice was sought from foreign consultants.

Cavas de Santa María (A3)

Punta Arenas, Buenos Aires
Tel: (+54) 11 4854 8300;
info@cavas-sa.con.ar
Cavas de Santa María was founded in 1892 as Abel Michel Torino, after a card-game between a big landowner and a Señor Michel. Sr Michel won and later married a lady with the surname Torino. Their descendants eventually founded Michel Torino (*see* below), while Abel Michel Torino eventually became Cavas de Santa María. Cavas de Santa María, which also owns vineyards and wineries in San Juan province, is one of the three biggest suppliers of wine within Argentina. The wines are sold under the Secreto de los Andes and Sucesión Michel Abel Torino labels. As the Catena Group (*see* above) recently purchased Cavas de Santa María, wine quality should improve.

Cavas de Weinert *See* Weinert

Cavas de Zonda

Rivadavia, San Juan
www.cavasdezonda.com.ar
This solid-quality sparkling wine

producer has cellars cut into the Zonda hills sixteen kilometres (ten miles) from San Juan city in San Juan province. Yugoslav immigrants originally dug the cellars in the 1930s as an underground road. They offer a cool storage area for Cavas de Zonda's rich and overtly fruity sparkling wines.

Cayenne *See* Hugo and Eduardo Pulenta

Chandon Argentina (C41)

Luján de Cuyo, Mendoza
Tel: (+54) 0261 490 9900;
visitorcentre@chandon.com.ar
Champagne giant Moët & Chandon's Argentine sparkling wine arm in Agrelo, Central Mendoza, is the largest producer of good quality, fully sparkling wine in Argentina. These are increasingly made using the traditional (bottle-fermented) method rather than the cheaper tank method. Chandon Argentina also produces a slightly fizzy, sparkling red sweet wine called Oxygen aimed at female drinkers. Still wines under a variety of French-sounding names are also produced for local sale. In the mid-1990s Chandon Argentina created a range of still wines for international sales called Terrazas de los Andes (*see* below), while keeping its prime vineyards for sparkling wines. *See* Chandon do Brasil (p.184).

Cheval des Andes (C52)

c/o Terrazas de Los Andes
Luján de Cuyo, Mendoza;
www.terrazas de los andes.com
This jointventure between Château

Cheval-Blanc, one of Bordeaux's best wineries, and Champagne Moët & Chandon's Argentine subsidiary, Terrazas de Los Andes, was still being planned as this book went to press. Cheval-Blanc is best known for its use of the dark-skinned Cabernet Franc; in Argentina this Bordeaux grape has largely been ignored, even though it has more chance than Cabernet Sauvignon of ripening at the high altitudes at which Terrazas de Los Andes grows most of its grapes.

Clos de Los Siete (C60)

Tunuyán, Mendoza
Tel: (+54) 0261 423 4230
A group of French investors from Bordeaux created Clos de Los Siete ("The Club of Seven") vineyard in Vistaflores, in Mendoza's Uco Valley. The investors are the Dassault family of Château Dassault in St-Emilion (*see also* Viña Totihue in Chile, p.85), Benjamin de Rothschild of Château Clarke in the Médoc, Didier Cuvelier of Château Léoville-Poyferré in St-Julien; Michel Rolland of Château Le Bon Pasteur in Pomerol (*see* also Alta Vista, above, and San Pedro de Yacochuya and Trapiche, below); Catherine Péré-Vergé of Château Montviel in Pomerol and Cristal d'Arques glassware, and the d'Aulan family which owns vineyards in Bordeaux, Champagne, Hungary, Argentina (Alta Vista, *see* above) and two of Clos de Los Siete's seven shares. Each investor will build their own winery on the site: Altamira, Mariflor, Los Dassos, Rocaflor, Lindaflor,

Monteviejo, and Primaflor. The first winery established, Bodega Monteviejo, belongs to Michel Rolland. Its 2002 red wines showed typically deep colours and concentrated textures.

Cobos (C40)

Central Mendoza
phobbs@paulhobbs.com
Paul Hobbs, a California resident but New York State-born apple farmer's son with immense experience of Argentine wine, became a winemaker despite the antipathy of a teetotal parent. His wines show elegance and individuality. He played a key role in the Catena Group's transition from bulk winery to, arguably, Argentina's leading source of premium wine, and has consulted to Valentín Bianchi, Dolium, and Pascual Toso, and other wineries. His Cobos project is named after a road in Perdriel in Central Mendoza adjoining the vineyard that provides the old-vine Malbec grapes for Cobos. This red wine is a benchmark Argentine Malbec for its deep purple colour and rich, nuanced damson fruit. A second label is Bramare ("to yearn for" in Italian).

Coleccíon Privada *See* Navarro Correas

Colomé (A4)

Molinos, Salta
Tel: (+54) 03868 494044;
www.hesscollection.com
In 2001, Raúl Dávalos (and his family) sold Colomé to Donald Hess, the Swiss-born owner of the Hess

Collection winery in California. Colomé is a vast estate near the town of Molinos in Salta province's Calchaquíes Valley. At 2,380 m (7,806 ft) it is one of the world's highest vineyards. Dávalos kept part of the land (*see* Tacuil, below) but the remaining part of Colomé is being transformed. Extensive new vineyards will be added to existing ones containing unidentified grape varieties dating from the nineteenth century. Sustainable farming methods will be used. The production of herbs, cereals, fruit, dairy products, meat, nuts, flowers, and medicinal plants will make Colomé more self-sufficient. The workers have been given their own church, school, and health-care facilities. The 2002 Colomé wines included Torrontés, Sauvignon Blanc, Cabernet Sauvignon, and Criolla reds. A Malbec red showed bright, clean, intense, fruit flavours. As the nearest large town is four hours' drive away, across deserted and difficult terrain, the logistics of the Colomé project are daunting. So, the food served in the small, luxury hotel and restaurant opened at Colomé in 2003 will be grown at Colomé. Other Hess projects in this part of Argentina include Viñas de Altura (*see* below) and Amalaya (*see* above).

Compañía Vitivinícola San Rafael *See* Covisan

Cooperativa Vitivini Frutícola de la Rioja Ltda *See* La Riojana

Cosecha de Otoño *See* Weinert

Covisan (Compañía Vitivinícola San Rafael) (C68)

San Rafael, Mendoza
covisan@satlink.com
Covisan controls 40% of the grape supply in Mendoza's San Rafael region, and supplies nearly 10% of Argentina's domestic wine demand. It also owns the Suter winery in San Rafael. Wine quality improved at Covisan at the end of the 1990s when foreign winemaking consultants had some influence here, but since their departure, quality has been rather inconsistent.

Cuatro Ríos *See* Segundo Correas

Dedicado *See* Finca Flichman

Destino *See* Rutini

Dolium (C39)

Agrelo, Mendoza
Tel: (+54) 0261 490 0200;
dolium@dolium.com
Dolium is a Latin term for a sealed wine amphora that can be buried underground to keep it at a constant temperature. Hence Dolium's winery is – unusually for Argentina – also underground. Mario Giadorou, Dolium's founder and owner, built and designed the winery, in Agrelo in Central Mendoza's Luján de Cuyo area, while in his seventies. After a career spent designing oil refineries, getting Dolium ready was "not such a big task". Grapes come from Giadorou's own vines or from quality local growers. Dolium makes a direct style of Malbec, an understated

Chardonnay, and an oak-aged Reserva Cabernet Sauvignon with a vibrant blackcurrant flavour. It is one of Argentina's more elegant Cabernet Sauvignons, thanks to ripe tannins and a well-judged level of alcohol. Paul Hobbs (*see* Cobos) consults to Dolium's winemakers.

Domaine Don Carlos *See* Saúl Menem

Domaine St Diego (C18)
Lunlunta, Luján de Cuyo
Tel: (+54) 261 499 0414;
juanmmendoza@sinectis.com.ar
Angél Mendoza, the talented, conscientious former Trapiche winemaker, produces two excellent wines from a boutique winery in Lunlunta, in the Maipù area of Luján de Cuyo in Central Mendoza. A dry white sparkling wine called Brut Xerox is made from Chardonnay (70%) and Malbec (30%), which is pressed as a white wine. The Pura Sangre ("pure blood") still red is made from Malbec (70%) and Cabernet Sauvignon (30%).

Domaine Vistalba (C26)
Luján de Cuyo, Mendoza
Tel: (+54) 0261 498 2330;
domvistalba@infovia.com.ar
Domaine Vistalba is owned by a French consortium including a former Bordeaux wine merchant, Hervé Joyaux-Fabre, and his wife Diane. It produces Fabre-Montmayou (*see* below), Temporada (*see* below), and Infinitus (*see* below) from its own vineyards and wineries, and is also involved in the production of the Fébus brand (*see* below).

Dominio de Agrelo *See* Hispano-Argentinas

Don Carlos *See* Saúl Menem

Don Cristobál 1492 (C30)
Maipù, Mendoza
Tel: (+54) 0261 499 0003;
infobodega@doncristobal.com.ar
Argentine businessman Eduardo Lapania founded this well laid-out winery in Cruz de Piedra, Maipù department, in Central Mendoza, in 1997. Lapania produces clean, fruity, well-made wines in an understated style under the Don Cristobál and Don Cristobál 1492 labels.

Don David *See* Michel Torino

Don Enrique Fallardi *See* Fapes

Don Leandro Cabrini *See* Cabrini

Don Luis *See* Segundo Correas

Don Matías *See* Nieto y Senetiner

Don Miguel Escorihuela Gascon *See* Escorihuela Gascon

Don Nicanor *See* Nieto y Senetiner

Doña Paula (C53)
Luján de Cuyo, Mendoza
Tel: (+54) 0261 498 4410;
donapaula@arnet.com.ar
This venture, begun in 1997 by Chile's Santa Rita, comprises a winery and vineyard in Ugarteche in Central Mendoza's Luján de Cuyo area. Grapes are also sourced from a Doña Paula vineyard in Cordón del Plata in Mendoza's Uco Valley. The basic range is called Los Cardos, or ("the thistles") and includes clean, crisp, dry Chardonnay with a mouthwatering aftertaste of lime and citrus, and one of the few Argentine Sauvignon Blancs with a pronounced gooseberry aroma. The Doña Paula Estate Malbec is distinctive for its dry, peppery tannins and forthright black fruit. The top of the range, an old-vine Malbec called Doña Paula Selección de Bodega, has pin-point balance between fruit and oak, allied to generous concentration.

Dos Fincas *See* Viña Amalia

Duarte *See* Hispano-Argentinas

El Malbec de Ricardo Santos
See Ricardo Santos

Elementos *See* Bright Brothers Argentina

Elsa's Vineyard *See* Valentín Bianchi

Escorihuela Gascon (C6)
Godoy Cruz, Mendoza
Tel: (+54) 0261 424 2282
The Gascon family built Escorihuela's beautiful, cathedral-like winery from 1884. Escorihuela's accessible location in the Godoy Cruz suburb of Mendoza city has helped it become one of Mendoza's leading wine tourist attractions. Winery tours are available, and there's a souvenir shop and tasting room; one of Mendoza's leading restaurants, the "1884," is sited within the winery complex. The La Rural/Escorihuela Group (*see* below) acquired

wines of south america

left Federico Cassone checking Malbec pomace before deciding whether to press.

Escorihuela in 1992 and produce ultra-clean, fruit-filled wines under a variety of labels including One Bunch, High Altitude, Escorihuela Gascon, and Don Miguel Escorihuela Gascon. The Candela (or Gascon) range includes one of Argentina's most characterful Viognier wines. The top red wine, Candela President's Blend, comprises 85% rich Malbec, with Cabernet Sauvignon and a seasoning of Syrah for aromatic complexity.

Esmeralda (C34)

Distrito Algarrobo, Mendoza
bod.esmeralda@interlink.com.ar
The Catena family acquired the Esmeralda winery in Junín, East Mendoza, in 1966 and it is now part of the Catena Group. Export brands such as Malambo and Argento offer high-quality fruit flavours for immediate drinking at competitive prices. Malambo red is a crisp, approachable wine with bright red-cherry fruit made from Bonarda. Malambo white blends Chenin Blanc, which gives full, crisp, lime fruit textures, with Chardonnay, which provides the elegance for a mouthwatering, refreshing wine. The Argento range, and its more heavily oak-aged Reserva counterpart, is becoming one of Argentina's most heavily promoted and recognised brands abroad, and is helping to raise the country's international wine profile. Argento Cabernet Sauvignon shows notably ripe black fruit.

Argento Chardonnay is a crisp, floral dry white combining ripe fruit and soft oak flavours. Argento Malbec has a deep colour and concentrated, ripe blackberry and bramble flavours. Recent additions to the Argento range include Bonarda, Merlot, Pinot Noir, and Sauvignon Blanc.

Estancia Ancón (C55)

Tupungato, Mendoza
Tel: (+54) 02622 488 245;
estanciancon@yahoo.com.ar
Estancia Ancón occupies a stunning plateau beneath Mount Tupungato near San José, in Mendoza's Uco Valley. The vineyards reach 1,450 m (4,756 ft) and are surrounded by a mixed farm. The owners, the Bombal family, produce small amounts of distinctive wine and sell any unused grapes. The age and location of the vines mean these grapes are eagerly sought by other wineries. Estancia Ancón is also a peaceful, twelve-bedroom hotel offering authentic Argentine cuisine.

Estrella *See* Weinert

Etchart (A5)

Capital Federal, Buenos Aires
Tel: (+54) 11 4382 6923;
www.prargentina.com.ar
This winery belongs to Pernod Ricard, who bought it from the Etchart family (*see* San Pedro de Yacochuya, below) in 1996. Etchart has extensive, excellently sited vineyards in both Mendoza province and also way to the north in Salta province, where the firm was

originally established in the 1850s (and from where its best wines are still sourced). These are labelled "Etchart Cafayate;" Cabernet Sauvignon, Malbec, and Torrontés are the grape varieties to look for (*see also* Mounier). The Etchart Río de Plata range from Mendoza includes the popular white Torrontés/Chardonnay blend. The Chardonnay element subdues the sometimes excessively "grapey" aroma of Torrontés. The top Etchart red, Arnaldo B. Etchart, from Cafayate, is an often sturdy, sometimes stylish blend of Malbec, Cabernet Sauvignon, Merlot, and Tannat.

Fabre-Montmayou

Luján de Cuyo, Mendoza
Tel: (+54) 0261 498 2330;
domvistalba@infovia.com.ar
Domaine Vistalba (*see* above) founded Fabre-Montmayou in 1992. Contracts were struck with grapegrowers, and vineyards were acquired, then renovated in Las Compuertas, Vistalba, and Barrancas in Central Mendoza. Fabre-Montmayou's French winemaking team works from a renovated winery in Vistalba. The wines show clean, rich fruit flavours and textures and subtle oak flavours. Cabernet Sauvignon reds have a fine black-fruit aftertaste, while Malbec is more wildly flavoured. A mouthfilling dry Merlot has a gentler texture and longer, less clinical aftertastes compared to the Merlots made by the French-inspired winemaking teams at Salentein or Alta Vista, for example. A lush Chardonnay for

early drinking is also made. The Fabre-Montmayou Cuvée Diane includes a Malbec and a Chardonnay from older vines. The Fabre-Montmayou Grand Vin is the top red wine. It is a blend of 80% Malbec with 10% each of Cabernet Sauvignon and Merlot. Its flavours are mouthfilling and ripe, without being jammy.

Fabril Alto Verde

Pocito, San Juan
altoverde@arnet.com.ar
This family owned producer in San Juan province farms its vineyards organically, but until 2000, struggled to convert excellent grapes into excellent wines. Since then, with the help of foreign organic wine specialists, Fabril Alto Verde has hit stride, in particular with Malbec red wines under the Buenas Ondas label. The wines show a mix of loganberry and spiced cherry fruit, with ripe tannins tasting of dark chocolate in the aftertaste.

Falling Star *See* Trapiche

Famiglia Bianchi *See* Valentín Bianchi

Fapes (C66)

San Carlos, Mendoza
bodegafapes@hotmail.com
This emerging family owned winery has excellent vineyards, some of which are organically farmed, in La Consulta, in Mendoza's Uco Valley. Their top wine, Don Enrique Fallardi, is named after the founder, who left his native Italy for Mendoza in 1922.

Fébus

Luján de Cuyo, Mendoza
Tel: (+54) 0261 498 2330;
domvistalba@infovia.com.ar
Fébus is a well-made, value-for-
money range of Chardonnay,
Malbec, and Tempranillo wines
produced in Mendoza by local
investors and vineyard owners in
association with Domaine Vistalba.

FeCoVitA (C19)

Maipù, Mendoza
Tel: (+54) 0261 497 3400
fecomext@nysnet.com.ar
FeCoVitA stands for Federación de
Cooperativas Vinícolas Argentinas, a
group of thirty-two cooperative
wineries drawing on 30,000 ha
(74,130 acres) of vineyards across
Mendoza province from 5,000 grape-
growers. An increasing percentage
of the vineyards contain quality
grape varieties such as Bonarda,
Cabernet Sauvignon, Chardonnay,
Malbec, Merlot, Shiraz, and
Torrontés, which are suitable for
export. FeCoVitA's wines offer value
and reasonable quality, but are often
sold under supermarket or wine
merchant own-labels. Its best-known
export labels include Llewellyn and
MarcusJames (*sic*) which are
prominent in the USA.

Federación de Cooperativas Vinícolas Argentinas *See* FeCoVitA

Felipe Rutini *See* Rutini

Felix Lavaque *See* Lavaque

Filos *See* Medrano Estate

Finca Alma (C22)

Maipù, Mendoza
Tel: (+54) 11 4661 2574;
www.fincaalma.com
Winemaker Alejandra Lozano and
former wine salesman Marcelo
Manghi founded Finca Alma in 1998
in Coquimbito, in Maipù, Central
Mendoza. The couple use their
contacts in the industry to source
quality grapes from well-sited
vineyards across Mendoza province.
They produce around 200,000 bottles
annually. Their Alhue label is named
after a Mapuche word meaning
"soul" or "inner light". It includes
well-made, clean-tasting red wines
characterized by generous black fruit
flavours, made from Bonarda,
Cabernet Sauvignon, Malbec, and
Merlot, and well-crafted whites from
Chardonnay and Sauvignon Blanc.

Finca Altamira *See* Achával Ferrer

Finca de Altura *See* Lavaque

Finca Durazno *See* introduction to San Juan province, p.112

Finca, de Finca La Anita *See* Finca La Anita

Finca El Portillo *See* Salentein

Finca El Retiro *See* Tittarelli

Finca Flichman (C46)

Maipù, Mendoza
Tel: (+54) 11 4326 7300;
international@flichman.com.ar
This historic Argentine wine
producer is now owned by Sogrape,
Portugal's largest wine company.

Finca Flichman's main vineyards,
as well as the winery, are located in
the town of Barrancas, in the
Maipù area of Central Mendoza.
The wines made under the Finca
Flichman and Caballero de la Cepa
("knight of the vine") labels age
quite quickly once bottled. Malbec
and Chardonnay are the most
consistent varieties in a large but
commercially successful range.
Oak-aged Reserve wines have
more substance, especially in the
case of reds. Dedicado, the top red
wine, is a soft-centred blend of
Cabernet Sauvignon, Syrah, Merlot,
and Malbec, with distinctive baked-
fruit flavours.

Finca La Anita (C42)

Luján de Cuyo, Mendoza
fincalaanita@infovia.com.ar
Finca La Anita's owner, Antonio Mas,
is a vineyard consultant who decided
in 1992 to make his own wine from
family vineyards in the best part of
Agrelo, in the Luján de Cuyo area of
Central Mendoza. The concentrated
character of the wines is achieved
mainly by allowing the vines only
minimal irrigation during summer.
The Finca La Anita range includes
a rich Cabernet Sauvignon, which
smells of roasted meat, as well as
(more typically) of blackcurrant;
a partially oak-aged Chardonnay
smelling of wild fruit and jam; a
Malbec with harmonious black-
cherry and eucalyptus flavours; a
Merlot which remains refreshing to
drink despite a high alcohol level; a
barrel-fermented Semillon from old
vines smelling of acacia blossom

(and which ages incredibly well); a Syrah which needs early drinking; and a dry Tocai Friulano, which has lovely balance. The top label Finca, de Finca La Anita, includes a blend of Chardonnay and Semillon (50% each) showing rich, interesting flavours.

Finca La Celia (C65)
San Carlos, Mendoza
Tel: (+54) 0261 425 9459;
fincalacelia@ccu.com.ar
Finca La Celia is named after the daughter of the man who first planted the vines at San Carlos in Mendoza's Uco Valley in 1880. Most of the current 600 ha (1,500 acres) of vineyard is made up of young vines. Chile's San Pedro acquired La Celia in 2000 and produces light, well-made, reasonably priced wines. The Angaro range includes a Sauvignon Blanc with a tropical richness. The La Consulta range, La Celia's best-value and most consistent, includes a Syrah with soft, Mediterranean flavours. The La Celia range includes an attractive Cabernet Sauvignon with black fruit overlaid by oak, and La Celia Reserve, an oak-aged range, of which the most balanced red is made from Malbec.

Finca La Linda *See* Luigi Bosca (Leoncio Arizu)

Finca La Merced *See* Medrano Estate

Finca La Pampa *See* Salentein

Finca Las Moras
San Martín, San Juan
Tel: (+54) 0261 497 4002;
lasmoras@fincalasmora.com
This Peñaflor (*see* below) subsidiary produces refined wines from desert vineyards in the Tulum Valley, San Juan province. The main wine labels are Finca Las Moras, Finca Las Moras Reserve and Andean. Another label, Intis, is named after the sun god worshipped by the Inca and Huarpe Native American people who ran the first irrigation canals from the Andes to San Juan. The best reds include a blackberry and apple-flavoured Bonarda; a blend of Bonarda and Greco Nero (Italian grapes which complement each other well in San Juan); a Cabernet Franc with bright menthol and violet flavours; a refreshing Malbec made from grapes grown in hills above the heat of the San Juan Valley floor; and a Syrah with wild, expressive fruit flavours. Among the whites are a simple, good-value and amazingly (given San Juan's heat) crisp blend of Chardonnay and Chenin Blanc, and a Viognier with characteristic exotic peach-blossom aromas.

Finca Los Nobles *See* Luigi Bosca (Leoncio Arizu)

Finca San Pablo *See* Salentein

Finca Urquiza *See* Urquiza

Fond de Cave *See* Trapiche

Fresco *See* Chandon Argentina

Fuzion *See* Zuccardi

Gascon *See* Escorihuela Gascon

González Videla (C5)
Las Heras, Mendoza
Tel: (+54) 0261 448 2261;
info@gonzalesvidela.com
González Videla claims that its winery in the Las Heras area of North Mendoza is Argentina's oldest, dating from 1826. A González family ancestor is also said to have brought the first French Malbec vines to Argentina in the early nineteenth century. Malbec, Merlot, and Tempranillo reds are this winery's best.

Goyenechea (C72)
Villa Atuel, Mendoza
Tel: (+54) 11 4952 0269;
goyenechea@infovia.com.ar
This fifth-generation, family owned winery has extensive vineyards on gently sloping land around Villa Atuel, in Mendoza's San Rafael region. The winery, called La Vasconia after the founding family's Basque origins, has high, atmospheric wooden ceilings and square, concrete vats. The best wines are the Goyenechea Centenario and the oak-aged Goyenechea Quinta Generación ("fifth generation") Cabernet Sauvignon reds for their soft, pleasant texture and light blackcurrant flavours.

Graffigna *See* Santiago Graffigna

Gran Lurton *See* J.&F. Lurton Argentina

Gran Terrazas *See* Terrazas de los Andes

Hess Collection Winery See Colomé, Viñas de Altura, and Amalaya

High Altitude See Escorihuela Gascon

Hispano-Argentinas (C31)

Maipù, Mendoza
Tel: (+54) 0261 499 0365;
bha@impsat1.com.ar
The giant Spanish wine concern Bodegas Unidas acquired mature vineyards and a winery in one of the best areas of Cruz de Piedra, in the Maipù department of Central Mendoza, in 1998. Bodegas Unidas is known for Rioja wines under the Berberana, Marqués de Griñon, Marqués de Monistrol, and Lagunilla brand names. The group's Argentine wines are sold under the Dominio de Agrelo, Duarte, Marqués de Griñon Argentina, and Martins labels. They taste remarkably like the group's Spanish wines. One of Spanish Rioja's defining characteristics is a vanilla aroma that comes from ageing the wine in barrels made of American oak. This vanilla element is very noticeable in the wines of Hispano-Argentinas. Dry Chenin Blanc and Chardonnay whites are full-bodied but elegant. Of the red wines, those made from Malbec and Tempranillo show especially good balance between soft, ripe fruit tannins and the more forceful wood tannins from oak-ageing.

Hugo and Eduardo Pulenta (C54)

Ciudad, Mendoza
Tel: (+54) 0261 420 0800;
vinedosdonantonio@infovia.com.ar

The Pulenta family is known in Argentina for its involvement at Peñaflor (*see* below). Two family members, Hugo and Eduardo Pulenta, planted their own vineyard in 1992 in Ugarteche in Central Mendoza's Luján de Cuyo area. The first wines, under the Cayenne label, were made in 2002, comprising clean-tasting whites made from Chardonnay and Sauvignon Blanc, and round, simple reds with good colour made from Merlot, Cabernet Franc, and Malbec.

Humberto Canale (D1)

General Roca, Río Negro
Tel: (+54) 11 4307 7990;
www.bodegahcanale.com
This family owned producer near General Roca, in Patagonia's Río Negro province, once produced biscuits and fruit for panettone (Italy's famous fruitcake). Since 1991, Humberto Canale began converting its orchards to vineyards. The best wines have a silky texture and understated, clear, firm, fruit flavours that are quite distinct from those made further north in warmer Mendoza. The most consistent grape varieties are Chardonnay, Sauvignon Blanc, Semillon, and Viognier for white wines, and Cabernet Franc, Cabernet Sauvignon, Merlot, Malbec, and Pinot Noir for reds. Since 1999 Hans Vinding-Diers (*see* Noemí, below) has been winemaking consultant. He likes each vat to be fermented at exactly the correct temperature because wine yeasts have a preferred temperature for fermentation. If the yeast is happy

with the temperature it is working at, then fewer off-flavours are produced. An example is the Canale Estate Merlot, one of Argentina's most distinctive Merlots for its refinement and clarity of fruit, and its texture. The Humberto Canale Reserve range includes a classy Malbec with subtle oak influence. The Canale Black River range includes a brightly flavoured organic Merlot and the subdued, Canale organic Semillon made from estate grapes and grapes purchased from local growers such as Zorzetto (*see* below). The Canale Black River Reserve range includes Humberto Canale's most age-worthy, complex wine, the rich-tasting "Cabernets," a blend of 60% Cabernet Franc with 40% Cabernet Sauvignon.

Infinitus (D2)

Allen, Río Negro
Tel: (+54) 0261 498 2330;
domvistalba@infovia.com.ar
The Infinitus winery in General Roca, in Patagonia's Río Negro province, was abandoned until the Mendoza-based Domaine Vistalba (*see* above) purchased it in 1996, and renovated it. The Infinitus label includes: a Cabernet Sauvignon/Merlot blend which has Bordeaux-style aromas of cedar and lead pencils; a rich, almost heavy, peach-scented Chardonnay/ Semillon; a balanced Malbec/Syrah blend in which the Malbec provides the backbone and the Syrah provides the flesh; a concentrated Merlot with the tannic elegance and weight of fruit one would expect from vines planted in the 1960s, and a Torrontés with understated fruit (compared to

the more exuberant examples of this grape made in hotter regions to the north, such as Salta province's Calchaquíes Valley).

Intis *See* Finca Las Moras

Iscay *See* Trapiche

J.&F. Lurton Argentina (C61)
Godoy Cruz, Mendoza
Tel: (+54) 0261 421 8400;
bodegalurton@bodegalurton.com
The Bordeaux-based Lurton brothers, winemaker Jacques and brand manager François, produce their finest South American wines in Argentina (*see also* J.&F. Lurton Chile and J.&F. Lurton Uruguay). Jacques Lurton is one of Argentina's most experienced winemakers, having played a key role in developing the Catena Group's wines (*see* above) under Nicolás Catena in the early 1990s (*see also* San Pedro in Chile). The Lurtons' Argentine vineyards are in the hot, low-lying Barrancas area in Central Mendoza, and at Vistaflores in Mendoza's cooler, more mountainous Uco Valley. The winery at Vistaflores lies along the Camino Manzano Historico ("apple tree pass"), site of the apple tree under which a key, troop-rallying speech was made by General San Martín, who facilitated Argentina's (and Chile's) liberation from Spain in the early 1800s (*see* Rapel Valley, Chile, p.34). Its concrete fermentation tanks have so far survived cracking brought about by frequent tremors in the region. Generously flavoured Chardonnay, Pinot Gris, Torrontés,

and Viognier white wines are made in an ultra-clean, creamy style that is highly distinctive. Gran Lurton is an elegant blend of Cabernet Sauvignon and Malbec, combining a firm core of Bordeaux-like cedar flavours with juicier Argentine fruit. Piedra Negra is a firm Malbec aged in new French oak barrels that develops generous, supple flavours of mint and fig in bottle. Other labels include Tierra del Fuego ("land of fire").

Jubileus *See* Viniterra

La Banda (A6)
Tel: (+54) 387 421 7716;
www.vasijasecreta.com
This family owned producer in Cafayate town, Calchaquíes Valley (Salta province) obtains good-quality grapes from its vineyards, but produces only average wines under the Vasija Secreta and Viñas de Salta labels.

La Boca *See* Medrano Estate

La Celia *See* Finca La Celia

La Consulta *See* Finca La Celia

La Nature *See* La Riojana

La Riojana (Cooperativa Vitivini Frutícola de la Rioja Ltda) (B1)
Chilecito, La Rioja
finos@lariojana.com.ar
This cooperative in La Rioja province's Famatina Valley claims to be the largest wine cooperative in the Southern Hemisphere, with an annual wine production of forty

million bottles. There are 900 vineyard owners in La Rioja province, and more than 650 of them supply La Riojana with wine grapes. Since 1995, when La Riojana hired Californian, Spanish, and Australian winemakers, it has become one of Argentina's top five wine exporters. La Riojana is set to become one of the world's largest producers of wine from organically grown grapes. These sell under the La Nature or Pircas Negras ("black stones") brands, and offer very good value for money. They include vibrant, ripe-tasting red wines smelling of burnt tar (in the case of Barbera and Syrah) and of dried fig and blueberry (in the case of Malbec and Cabernet Sauvignon). Elegant, early drinking whites include one of Argentina's most appealing, accessible examples of Torrontés. La Nature Chardonnay has freshness and intensity.

La Rosa (A7)
Santa María, Catamarca
Tel: (+54) 03838 423 292;
larosa@cosama.com.ar
Lavaque & Bodegas y Viñedos Andinos (BVA) founded La Rosa in 1994 in a joint-venture. BVA is also the owner of Michel Torino in Cafayate, some seventy kilometres (forty-five miles) to the north of La Rosa's vineyard and new winery. La Rosa produces ten million bottles annually. La Rosa's vineyard in the beautiful, broad Chañar Punco Valley in Catamarca province covers 500 ha (1,125 acres). What look like gentle, arid slopes create floods during torrentially wet winter weather;

drystone walls are used as dams to divert the flow. During the building of these dams, three cemeteries containing Inca remains dating from the fifteenth century were unearthed; these are being preserved in a museum. When the vineyard was being created, cactus plants, some of which are more than 200 years old and several metres high, were left untouched (cactus grown here produces the red pigment cochineal used for food colouring). The wines produced from La Rosa's vineyard are shared between Michel Torino and Lavaque, who use them in wines sold under their own names.

La Rural *See* Rutini

La Rural/Escorihuela Group

This consortium involves Nicolás Catena of the Catena Group (*see* above) and owns Escorihuela Gascon and Rutini, *see* above, (formerly La Rural).

Lagarde (C9)

Luján de Cuyo, Mendoza
info@lagarde.com.ar
One of Argentina's leading families of industrialists, the Pescarmonas, own this Mayor Drummond winery. One of the vineyards dates from 1903. The historic winery has begun a process of modernization, and the wines are gaining in clarity and freshness. Old-vine, oak-aged Malbec is the most consistent.

Lavaque (A8 & C71)

Capital Federal, Buenos Aires
Tel: (+54) 11 4771 9113;
www.lavaque.com

This is one of Argentina's most famous wine names. Today the Lavaque family owns vineyards in three Argentine provinces. Its vineyards in Salta province lie just outside Cafayate town, in the Calchaquíes Valley. Here they produce the Finca de Altura and Peñalva Frías ranges. Lavaque's vineyards in Catamarca province, in the southern part of the Calchaquíes Valley, were developed in partnership with Bodega y Viñedos Andinos (*see* separate entry for La Rosa, above). Its vineyards in Mendoza are in the San Rafael region; these supply the grapes for the Lavaque and Felix Lavaque ranges, the latter named after the company's founder. Winemaking is remarkably consistent considering the huge distances between its vineyards and wineries. The Peñalva Frías wines are reliable examples of what the Calchaquíes Valley can produce, with red wines from Barbera, Cabernet Sauvignon, Malbec, Merlot, Syrah, and Tannat all capable of bright, deep colours and exuberant fruit, for early drinking.

Lazos *See* Medrano Estate

Leoncio Arizu *See* Luigi Bosca (Leoncio Arizu)

Llewellyn *See* FeCoVitA

López López (C25)

Belgrano y Juan Vargas, Villa Seca
Tel: (+54) 261 497 3283
In 1978 Manuel López López left his native Spain to play hockey. Within

two years he had settled here, buying the Finca El Zorzal vineyard on the outskirts of Villa Seca, in the Maipù area of Central Mendoza. The vines are grown organically, on two-metre-high (6.6 ft) pergolas with weed growth beneath controlled by grazing sheep. The Cabernet Sauvignon and Merlot red wines are called Villa Seca, and López López Patrón Santiago (after Mendoza's Patron Saint). They have bright, ripe flavours and intriguing flavours, including refreshing mineral tones driven by the high level of natural acidity in these wines.

Los Cardos *See* Doña Paula

Luigi Bosca (Leoncio Arizu) (C13)

Luján de Cuyo, Mendoza
Tel: (+54) 11 4331 2206;
luigibosca@luigibosca.com.ar
This family owned producer is based in the town of Luján de Cuyo and owns several excellent vineyards elsewhere in Central Mendoza. Some of these contain vines that were inter-planted with olive trees in the 1920s. The names of these vineyards, such as Finca La Linda ("the beautiful farm"), Finca Los Nobles, and Paraíso ("paradise") sometimes appear on Luigi Bosca's labels. The wines are made in a clean, modern style, retaining a definite Argentine character. The basic Luigi Bosca range includes Cabernet Sauvignon with refreshing black fruit, and good Merlot and Malbec made in a tight, withdrawn style. A Pinot Noir retains its

freshness despite the hot Argentine climate. Luigi Bosca's dry white Riesling, Chardonnay, and Sauvignon Blanc wines are made in an ultra-crisp, almost green style. Attractive sparkling wines, made using the traditional method and sold as Bohème, are arguably Luigi Bosca's most dynamic white wines. Luigi Bosca's top red wines, called Finca Los Nobles, include a blend of Malbec and Petit Verdot, and a fruitier-tasting Cabernet Sauvignon and Cabernet Franc (called "Bouchet" here) blend from vines that were field blended (planted together) in the Finca Los Nobles vineyard in the 1930s. In 1997 the Los Nobles vines were grubbed up, but cuttings were taken from the oldest vines and these were then replanted, this time in separate plots rather than mixed together. In the future this will allow the two Cabernet varieties to be picked at different times and thus riper. Cabernet Sauvignon ripens ten to fourteen days after the Cabernet Franc; if it is picked too early the wine tastes of green pepper (capsicum). Note that Luigi Bosca (Leoncio Arizu) is distinct from Arizu.

Luis Segundo Correas (C48)

Medrano, Mendoza
Tel: (+54) 0261 423 0604;
lscorreassa@lanet.com.ar
The Correas family trace their arrival in Argentina from Spain to the era of the conquistadors, and have been producing wine in East Mendoza since 1860. Some of their best vineyards are found in the warm Maipú area where North and East

Mendoza meet. Their wines under the Cuatro Ríos ("Four Rivers"), Don Luis, and Luis Correas labels generally offer light, clean fruit flavours.

Magna *See* Zuccardi

Malambo *See* Bodegas Esmeralda

MarcusJames (*sic*) *See* FeCoVitA

Medalla *See* Trapiche

Marilen (olive oil) *See* Y. López

Mariposa *See* Tapiz

Martins *See* Hispano-Argentinas

Mayol (C62)

Tupungato, Mendoza
Tel: (+54) 0261 449 9919;
www.bodegamayol.com
The Mayol family has vineyards in both Central Mendoza and farther south in Mendoza's Uco Valley, but only began making its own wine in a rented winery in 2000. Bonarda, Malbec, and Syrah (which come from Mayol's oldest vines) are especially promising for their clean, deep fruit and well-managed tannins, thanks in part to advice gained by Australian winemaker and South American resident David Kingsbury, who happened to be sharing the same rented winery at the time.

Medrano Altos

See Medrano Estate

Medrano Estate (C28)

Ciudad, Mendoza
Tel: (+54) 0261 429 1752;
www.medranowine.com

Medrano Estate was founded in 1997 by Gustavo Capone and Ambrosio Di Leo, two of the most influential shippers of bulk wines in South America. Medrano Estate's wines are produced in a winery in Lunlunta in Central Mendoza. The Casaterra and La Boca ranges of Bonarda, Malbec, Syrah, Tempranillo, and Torrontés/ Chardonnay wines show clean ripe fruit flavours allied to subtle oak. Filos is a concentrated blend of Syrah and Malbec grown in the vineyard opposite Medrano Estate's Lunlunta winery. Yields have been lowered here and a greater effort made to increase ripeness by leaf plucking around grape bunches in the run-up to harvest. The varietal wines in the Medrano Altos range come from different soil types within Mendoza, and show clearly defined grape flavours in Cabernet Sauvignon (blueberry), Chardonnay (pineapple), Malbec (sour-cherry), Merlot (strawberry), and Syrah (raspberry). Lazos, Medrano Estate's top red wine, is a blend of the company's best Syrah and Malbec grapes and is aged for twelve months in French oak barrels. Medrano Estate's wines sell under the Montmedra name in some foreign markets for copyright reasons.

Michel Torino (A9)

Cafayate, Salta
Tel: (+54) 03868 421139
Michel Torino's origins lie with Cavas de Santa María (*see* above). Now Michel Torino is part of

Peñaflor's Bodegas y Viñedos Andinos group. The atmospheric, whitewashed, Spanish colonial-style winery and luxury hotel in Cafayate, in Salta province's Calchaquíes Valley, attract more than 50,000 visitors annually. The "zero farming" approach to agriculture, incorporating minimal spraying techniques, is used in the vineyards. Michel Torino's basic range of Chardonnay, Sauvignon Blanc, Torrontés, Bonarda, Cabernet Sauvignon, Malbec, Merlot, Syrah, and Tannat show clean fruit and moderately intense flavour; since the 2001 vintage they have shown appreciably greater freshness and ageing potential. The Michel Torino Colección range sees some oak, while the Don David range has more overt oak influence, but deeper, more concentrated fruit to match; the Don David Cabernet Sauvignon is a particularly appealing example. First produced in 2001, the top wine, Altimus, is a solid red blended from Malbec, Cabernet Sauvignon, and Syrah, aged in a combination of French and American oak barrels.

Miscelánea *See* Weinert

Montfleury *See* Weinert

Montemedra *See* Medrano Estate

Mounier (A10)
Tel: (+54) 387 15 582 9533;
japmounier@yahoo.com.ar
José-Luis Mounier has been winemaker at Etchart's Cafayate winery since 1986. In 2000 he also founded his own boutique vineyard

and winery outside Cafayate town in Salta province's Calchaquíes Valley. Mounier has French grandparents (his surname is French for "miller") but it was pure chance that the land he purchased for his small vineyard contained an ancient milling stone for grinding wheat, maize, and fruit from the *algarrobo*, a tree prevalent in Argentina's mountain deserts. Mounier makes a single red wine, a subtly oak-aged blend of Malbec, Cabernet Sauvignon, and Tannat with well-defined fruit flavours.

N. Valentín Ramiréz
This now-retired, one-man band sold his vineyards near Molinos in Salta province's Calchaquíes Valley in 2001. Considering that the N. Valentín Ramiréz wines were made in a very antiquated winery, the wines produced were quite remarkable. They included a red with real brightness and depth, blended from Malbec, Cabernet Sauvignon, and some unidentified grapes, as well as a Torrontés with incredible intensity.

Nanni (A11)
Valle de Cafayate, Salta
Tel: (+54) 03868 421028;
bodegananni@hotmail.com
Nanni produces modest-quality wines from estate-grown organic and conventionally farmed grapes in Cafayate town, in Salta province's Calchaquíes Valley. The organic vines are grown on a windy, and thus difficult, site with unusual red soils that may help to create distinctively flavoured wines

(Cafayate soils are generally lighter in colour).

Navarro Correas (C37)
Ciudad, Buenos Aires
www.ncorreas.com
This unspectacular producer in the Maipù area of Central Mendoza has geared its elegantly labelled wines to the USA market, although Navarro Correas is owned by the British-based multinational drinks group Diageo. Wines under the Navarro Correas, Navarro Correas Coleccíon Privada, and Navarro Correas Gran Reserva are good, rather than great, and lack the balance and elegance of wines from Norton, Catena Zapata, or Trapiche, for example, particularly with regard to the oak-influenced styles.

New Age *See* Valentín Bianchi

Nicolás Catena Zapata *See* Catena Zapata

Nieto y Senetiner (C27)
Capital Federal, Buenos Aires
Tel: (+54) 11 4833 2065;
www.nietosenetiner.com
Nieto y Senetiner began life in 1969, when Nicanor Nieto and Adriano Senetiner bought a winery in Carrodilla, in the Luján de Cuyo area of Central Mendoza. Over time other vineyards and wineries were acquired and Nieto y Senetiner developed strong wine sales within Argentina. However, in 1998 the founders sold Nieto y Senetiner. Adriano Senetiner then invested in his son Flavio's new wine venture,

Viniterra (*see* below). Nieto y
Senetiner's vineyards in Luján de
Cuyo, Central Mendoza, are
extensive and generally well sited.
The wines are steady rather than
spectacular, with Bonarda reds
consistently the most ripe and
typically flavoured; a Malbec called
Cadus is notable for its baked-fruit
and brawny oak flavours.

Noemí (D3)

General Roca, Río Negro
hansvinding@hotmail.com
Noemí is a source of revelatory,
single-vineyard, old-vine Malbec,
handmade in tiny quantities in a
fruit-packing warehouse in General

Roca, in Patagonia's Río Negro
province. Hans Vinding-Diers,
a Danish winemaker, and Noemí
Cinzano of the eponymous Italian
Vermouth family, are Noemí's
founding owners. Vinding-Diers
came to this part of Argentina as
winemaking consultant to Humberto
Canale (*see* above) and discovered
a Malbec vineyard in the area last
replanted in the 1930s. It contained
a unique mix of genetic material
because the "Malbec" vines were
actually Cot, the name given to
Malbec in South West France, where
this variety originates. Modern
vineyards are planted with a single
genetic strain (or clone) of Malbec,

whereas the Noemí vineyard
contains 10,000 individual Malbec
vines, each of which is genetically
distinct from any of its neighbours.
The wine produced is called Noemía.
It has a deep mulberry colour, and
multifaceted Malbec flavours
including anise, plum, black-cherry,
and damson. The brilliance and
clarity of these flavours is preserved
by Vinding-Diers, who makes the
wines (about 10,000 bottles annually)
by hand, with no mechanical aids.
Vinding-Diers has also worked as
winemaking consultant to Pisano in
Uruguay (*see* p.171).

below Connie Aldao, the manager of "1884"
restaurant at Escorihuela, riding with a friend.

Noemía *See* Noemí

Norton (C50)

Luján de Cuyo, Mendoza

Tel: (+54) 0261 488 0480/1;

www.norton.com.ar

Norton produces eight million bottles annually from its Perdriel winery in Luján de Cuyo, Central Mendoza. Sir Edmund (Edmundo) James Palmer Norton, a British railway engineer, founded Norton in 1895. Norton is now owned and run by the Austrian Swarovski family of glassmakers. Since 1989 they have improved consistency in both Norton's unoaked White Label and more expensive, lightly oak-aged Barrel Select ranges. The grapes to look for include Merlot and Sangiovese, for the vibrancy and lightness of their tannins, and Sauvignon Blanc and Torrontés, for their expressive and intense aromas. Randle Johnson of California's Hess Collection Winery (*see* Colomé) has been influential in helping to improve Norton's barrel arrangements and blending. In particular, Norton Reserva, a fully oak-aged range including Cabernet Sauvignon, Malbec, Syrah, and Chardonnay, has improved dramatically since the mid-1990s; the oak flavours are combined in a much cleaner, more direct and refreshing way with the grape flavours. The dry red Norton Privada Estate Reserve is an unfiltered French oak-aged blend of Cabernet Sauvignon, Malbec, and Merlot, with well-defined fruit flavours, and a soft oakiness. Norton seems to have a much smaller promotional budget than some of its rivals (notably Catena Zapata) but its wines are some of Argentina's most enjoyable and easy to appreciate. *See also* Ricardo Santos (below).

Nuestra Esencia *See* Fabril Alto Verde

O. Fournier (C64)

La Consulta, Mendoza

www.bodegasofournier.com

Four hundred and fifty years after the Spanish conquest of Argentina, a new one has begun. The Spanish Ortega Gil-Fournier family is adopting Spain's low "bush" system of training for its newly planted vines in La Consulta, in Mendoza's Uco Valley. The bush system has a proven track record in Spain, but is uncommon in South America. The French system of a vertically trained hedge (*see* Uruguay, p.154) and the overhanging "*parral*" system (*see* Introduction to Argentine Wines, p.109) dominate in South America but invariably require irrigation. The low bush system does not use support posts or wires because the wines are freestanding. By being so low to the ground, the bush vine's leaves shade the soil and the grapes, minimizing moisture loss. It remains to be seen how the bush vines react to Argentine conditions, so in the meantime O. Fournier is sourcing grapes from growers in La Consulta. Most of these vines are more than thirty years old, and deliver grapes with enough concentration and flavour to withstand ageing in new oak barrels. In order of ascending price the wines are: Urban Oak, a red blend made from younger vines; B Crux, a red blend of 85% Tempranillo, 10% Merlot, and 5% Malbec, aged in new oak barrels made of French (80%) and American (20%) oak, and showing a dense colour and even denser texture, and A Crux, the top wine, in 2001 a blend of 70% Tempranillo, 20% Malbec, and 10% Merlot with more elegant texture than the B Crux and more pronounced Tempranillo characteristics of red and black soft-fruits. Fournier named its A Crux and B Crux wines after the stars in the Southern Cross constellation.

Omnium *See* Viniterra

One Bunch *See* Escorihuela Gascon

Orfila (C35)

Junín, Mendoza

info@orfila.com.ar

This fifth generation, family winery in San Martín, East Mendoza, produces a wine called Cabernet Sauvignon de las Reinas ("Cabernet of the Queens") red. The wine is partly foot-trodden by young beauty queens at Mendoza's Harvest Festival (a street event held during the first weekend in March, which attracts over 100,000 people to the city of Mendoza). Foreign winemaking consultants have helped Orfila develop clean, fruity, uncomplicated Cabernet Sauvignon, Tempranillo, Shiraz, Chardonnay, and Chenin Blanc wines for everyday drinking.

Oxygen *See* Bodegas Chandon Argentina

Paraíso *See* Luigi Bosca (Leoncio Arizu)

Pascual Toso (C47)
Guaymallén, Mendoza
tosowines@impsat1.com.ar
Toso is the second-largest producer (after Chandon Argentina) of sparkling wine in Argentina, but it is increasingly looking to produce value-for-money still wines for export, from vineyards in Barrancas and other Central Mendoza areas. Improved vineyard practices and cleaner winemaking since 2001 have given Toso's Cabernet Sauvignon, Malbec, and Sauvignon Blanc much-needed personality and depth.

Pedro del Castillo *See* Weinert

Peñaflor
Maipù, Mendoza
Tel: (+54) 11 4394 4722
Argentina's largest wine producer crushes more than 100 million kilograms of grapes annually, 5% of Argentina's total grape production. Peñaflor originated in 1913 in San Juan province, where it still has a winery. Its breakthrough came in 1930 when the company began transporting wine in bulk by tank-train from its Mendoza winery to Buenos Aires for bottling. This allowed wines to arrive in the capital tasting fresher, while saving Peñaflor money and making the wines more competitively priced. Peñaflor controls 2% of Argentina's fine wine

vineyards. The company is co-owned by a New York-based investment bank and the powerful Pulenta family. Its best wines are made through subsidiaries such as Finca Las Moras (*see* above) and Trapiche (*see* below). Peñaflor also owns the Bodegas y Viñedos Andinos group (*see* above). For wines produced directly by Peñaflor, *see* Bright Brothers Argentina (above). Peñaflor's cheaper wines are made for the Argentine market.

Peñalva Frías *See* Lavaque

Piedra Negra *See* J.&F. Lurton Argentina

Pircas Negras *See* La Riojana

Punte del Monte
Ciudad, San Juan
Tel: (+54) 0264 421 7150
This family owned winery produces improving wines from organic vineyards in San Juan province, but is yet to rival its near-neighbour, Fabril Alto Verde.

Pr1mus *See* Salentein

Pura Sangre *See* Domaine St Diego

Q *See* Zuccardi

Ranftl (C63)
Vistaflores, Tunuyán, Mendoza
coarex@arnet.com.ar
Roberto Ranftl is developing a small luxury hotel and guesthouse at Vistaflores for the increasing numbers of wine visitors to this part of the Uco Valley. Ranftl's family also

has Chardonnay, Tocai Friulano, Cabernet Sauvignon, Malbec, Merlot, and Syrah vineyards in the area. In 2002 Ranftl hired an Australian winemaking consultant to make wines at Vistaflores.

RD *See* Tacuil

Ricardo Santos (C36)
Godoy Cruz, Mendoza
rsantos@elsitio.net
Ricardo Santos sold Norton to the Austrian Swarovski family in 1989. He now makes a red with gentle tannins, called El Malbec de Ricardo Santos, from the Finca Las Madras vineyard in Maipù, Central Mendoza.

Roca (C69)
San Rafael, Mendoza
by-roca@satlink.com
The Roca family has four vineyards in and around San Rafael town in Mendoza's San Rafael region, plus a whitewashed stone winery. The best wines for export see stainless steel tanks, with occasional ageing in new oak barrels. The Roca family took full control of the winery only in 1989, having arrived in Argentina in 1912. Old, and sometimes unidentified, vine varieties are being replaced with Cabernet Sauvignon, Malbec, and Sangiovese. Whites made from Chardonnay and Tocai Friulano, and reds from Cabernet Sauvignon, Malbec, and Syrah, provide some of San Rafael's liveliest wines, with fresh fruit flavours to the fore.

Rosell Boher (C17)
Pueyrredon 1212, Chacras de Coria
Tel: (+54) 0261 496 1710

This producer of good-quality, mainly sparkling wine works from a winery in Chacras de Coria, in the Luján de Cuyo department of Central Mendoza.

Ruca Malen *See* Bacchus

Rutini (C23)

Maipù, Mendoza
Tel: (+54) 0261 497 2013
Rutini was known as La Rural until 1994 when the La Rural/Escorihuela Group (*see* above) acquired it. The new owners renovated the winery in Coquimbito, in the Maipù area of Central Mendoza, and modified the vineyards to achieve riper grapes for basic labels including Trumpeter, La Rural, Felipe Rutini, and Destino, and extra ripeness for Apartado (the flagship wine) an oak-aged blend of Cabernet Sauvignon, Merlot, and Malbec.

Rural *See* Rutini

Salentein (C58)

Alto Valle del Uco, Mendoza
www.bodegasalentein.com
Dutch investors created Salentein's spacious gravity-fed winery in the Tupungato area of Mendoza's Uco Valley in 1996. It is surrounded by three vineyards (*fincas*) called La Pampa, El Portillo, and San Pablo. Around 1.5 million bottles are produced annually, using these vineyard names, and other names such as Signos, the basic range for early drinking. The oak-aged Salentein Estate range includes two sound reds, the ripe Malbec and the slightly less-convincing Cabernet Sauvignon. The Merlot is in a class

of its own in terms of the denseness, balance, and flavour profile of its fruit. Winemaker Laureano Gómez trained under Michel Rolland at Alta Vista, and is probably Rolland's most naturally talented wine protégé in Argentina. The Salentein Estate Pr1mus range includes a potent, barrel-fermented dry white Chardonnay and an unfiltered dry red Pinot Noir which has polished, but rather reticent, cherry fruit; it should become more forceful and complex as the vines age.

San Huberto *See* Saúl Menem y Hijos

San Pedro de Yacochuya (A12)

Cafayate, Salta
Tel: (+54) 03868 421233
Arnaldo B. Etchart, his wife, and French winemaker Michel Rolland founded San Pedro de Yacochuya in Salta province's Calchaquíes Valley in 1988. The two men met when Rolland became consultant winemaker to Etchart, in nearby Cafayate, which Señor Etchart and his family once owned. They sold this to Pernod Ricard and concentrated their efforts on San Pedro de Yacochuya. This new venture is a high-profile, high-altitude affair. Both the winery and its fourteen-hectare (thirty-five-acre) vineyard are enclosed by a stone wall at around 2,000 m (6,560 ft) in the mountains at Yacochuya, above Cafayate town. "Yacochuya" is a Quechua Native American word meaning "clear water," after the mountain springs that flow here. The oldest Malbec

vines date from 1915 and the oldest Cabernet Sauvignon from the 1950s. Nearby scrub-land has been cleared in preparation for new vineyards. Wines produced under the San Pedro de Yacochuya label include a dry white Torrontés with a crisp, green grass flavour, and a dry red with soft grape and oak tannins blended from Malbec and smaller percentages of Cabernet Sauvignon and Tannat. A red wine called Yacochuya de Michel Rolland made from 100% Malbec (old vines) combines a generous texture and wild red fruit. This is Rolland's own wine. He provided the fermentation tanks and presses in the Yacochuya winery, while the Etchart family paid for its construction. Other Michel Rolland projects in Argentina include Alta Vista (*see* above), Clos de Los Siete (*see* above) and Trapiche (*see* below).

Santa Ana (C1)

Ciudad, Mendoza
Tel: (+54) 11 4716 8000;
bvsa@bodegas-santa-ana.com.ar
Founded close to Mendoza city in Guaymallén, North Mendoza, in 1891, Argentina's fifth largest winery has a confusing recent history. It changed hands during the 1930s Depression and massively expanded its vineyards in the 1990s, before becoming part of Santa Carolina of Chile (*see* p.178) which, within four years, had sold it to Peñaflor's Bodegas y Viñedos Andinos group. Young vines and changes of ownership mean the only wines consistently worth drinking here are made by flying winemakers who jet

in on behalf of foreign supermarkets to make wines under supermarket own-labels.

Santa Faustina

Rivadavia, Mendoza
wrwines@infovia.com.ar
Santa Faustina is a potentially excellent Mendoza jointventure between Peter Weinert, son of Bernardo Weinert (*see* Weinert, below), and his wife Graciela Reta (*see* Tittarelli, below). Around 6,000 bottles of red are produced annually. Grapes are purchased from quality vineyard areas such as Lunlunta in Central Mendoza for Malbec, and warmer areas such as Junín in East Mendoza, where Bonarda, Tempranillo, and Syrah thrive. Some of the vineyards that Santa Faustina sources from are more than fifty years old and still ploughed using horses to avoid compacting the soil. Reta likes most of the grapes to enter the fermentation vats uncrushed to slow the fermentation and accentuate the fruit. Santa Faustina Syrah captures this variety's elusive wild raspberry character. The chapel in Medrano shown on Santa Faustina's wine label is where Peter and Graciela were married.

Santa Julia *See* Zuccardi

Santa Rita Argentina *See* Doña Paula

Santa Rosa Estate *See* Zuccardi

Santa Silvia *See* Santiago Graffigna

Santiago Graffigna

San Juan
Tel: (+54) 11 4752 7903
This winery in San Juan province is the largest supplier of wine to Argentine supermarkets. Owners Allied Domecq Argentina (*see* above) produce more obviously fruity and better-value wines here than at Balbi (which Allied Domecq also owns) in San Rafael. Seventy per cent of the grapes are bought in from growers, some of whom have supplied them for more than fifty years. To give wines balance, flavour-rich grapes from cooler, higher-altitude sites in the El Pedernal Valley are blended with grapes from the lower-lying, warmer Tulum Valley, which produces more alcohol-rich wines. Graffigna is enjoying considerable success on export markets with its generally excellent-value Graffigna, Santa Silvia, and Santiago Graffigna labels. The winemaking team is young and dynamic, and the wines reflect their approach. Reds are boldly coloured, spicy, aromatic, and juicy. Bonarda, Greco Nero, Syrah, and Tannat are all remarkably consistent. Well-crafted whites from Chardonnay and Pinot Gris have rich tropical-fruit flavours.

Saúl Menem (B2)

Anillaco, La Rioja
bodegasmenem@arnet.com.ar
Former Argentine president Carlos Menem (*see* Introduction to Argentina, p.94) part-owns this winery in La Rioja province. New vineyards have been acquired and

others replanted. The wines have improved since 2001, when foreign consultants came in to advise. Labels include Domaine Don Carlos, and San Huberto. Whites made from Chardonnay and Torrontés, and reds made from Bonarda, Malbec, Merlot, and Syrah are the top performers.

Secreto de los Andes *See* Cavas de Santa María

Sendero Alto (C3)

Guaymallén, Mendoza
Tel: (+54) 02623 494026
Sendero Alto has extensive vineyards around Lavalle, North Mendoza. Martin Fowke, who runs a successful English vineyard called Three Choirs, has helped create an excellent range of good-value wines under the Valle Alto label, including vibrant reds from Bonarda, Malbec, Merlot, and Shiraz, plus clean, refreshing Sauvignon Blanc.

Señor de Robledal *See* Luigi Bosca (Leoncio Arizu)

Séptima (C43)

Luján de Cuyo, Mendoza
www.bodegaseptima.com.ar
The oldest Spanish Cava (sparkling wine) house, Codorníu, founded this vineyard and winery in Agrelo, in Mendoza's Luján de Cuyo area, in 1998. As Séptima's young vineyard ages, more interesting flavours should emerge in its clean, early drinking Malbec, Syrah, and Tempranillo reds. The striking winery was built using drystone walls, a technique first developed

here by the Huarpe Native Americans.

Serie Terra *See* Viniterra

Signos *See* Salentein

Sobre El Río (C59)
Tunuyán, Mendoza
www.weingutvollmer.de
Heinrich Vollmer, a German vineyard owner and fanatical mountaineer, had a near-fatal accident in the Argentine Andes during an earthquake there in June 1983. Local Native American mountain people saved his life by carrying him seventy kilometres (forty-four miles) on their backs. Vollmer has since employed some of these indigenous peoples at his Sobre El Río vineyard and winery, created in the Tunuyán area of Mendoza's Uco Valley from 1987. The German government helped Vollmer establish a solar-powered drip irrigation system. The wines are made for immediate drinking and sell under the Sobre El Río label mainly in Germany.

Sucesión Michel Abel Torino
See Cavas de Santa María

Susana Balbo *See* Vintage

Suter *See* Covisan

Tacuil (A13)
Ciudad, Salta
Fax: (+54) 0387 432 1393
Raúl Dávalos and his family sold Colomé (*see* above) to Donald Hess in 2001, but retained a portion, calling it Tacuil. The Tacuil vineyard

covers nine hectares (twenty-two acres) at 2,365 m (7,757 ft), west of Molinos town in Salta province's Calchaquíes Valley. The wines, under the Viñas de Dávalos and RD labels, can be among South America's most aromatically intense, densely coloured red wines. The RD Malbec is the essence of Malbec, such is its intensity and purity of fruit flavour.

Tapiz (C44)
Luján de Cuyo, Mendoza
Tel: (+54) 0261 4900 202;
tapiz@tapiz.com.ar
California's Kendall-Jackson founded Tapiz in 1996, initially calling it Mariposa Winery (*see also* Calina in Chile, p.51). Chardonnay, Cabernet Sauvignon, Malbec, Merlot, Syrah, and Cabernet Sauvignon/Malbec are produced under the Tapiz label. These wines are produced in a generous, early drinking style. Tapiz Alzada is a juicy red blended from Cabernet Sauvignon, Merlot, and Malbec, showing more elegant oak influence than the Tapiz range and slightly greater capacity for ageing.

Temporada
Luján de Cuyo, Mendoza
Tel: (+54) 0261 498 2330;
domvistalba@infovia.com.ar
Domaine Vistalba (*see* above) produces the Temporada and Altos de Temporada ranges. These include a Chardonnay, plus Cabernet Sauvignon, Malbec, and Merlot reds. They offer reliable quality for fair prices without being as good as Domaine Vistalba's Infinitus or Fabre-Montmayou.

Tenorio *See* Valle de la Puerta

Termidor *See* Peñaflor

Terra *See* Viniterra

Terra Orgánica *See* Zuccardi

Terrazas de los Andes (C51)
Luján de Cuyo, Mendoza
Tel: (+54) 0261 490 9900;
info@terrazasdelosandes.ar
Terrazas is the high-quality, still wine arm of Chandon Argentina (*see* above). It produces more than two million bottles from a renovated winery at Perdriel, in Luján de Cuyo, Mendoza province. Terrazas has steadily improved since its tentative debut in 1996. The idea behind Terrazas is that each grape variety best expresses itself in Chandon's vineyards if the vines are grown on Andes mountain terraces (*terrazas*) at a precise altitude: Cabernet Sauvignon at 980 m (3,214 ft) in Perdriel, Malbec at 1,067 m (3,500 ft) in Vistalba in Luján de Cuyo, and Chardonnay at 1,200 m (3,936 ft) in Tupungato in Mendoza's Uco Valley. The importance of the *terrazas* concept means that the evocative names given to the vineyards by the Native American Huarpe do not appear on the labels. These include Albente ("dawn of the day"), Caicayén ("place of paradise"), Corel ("Andean sand"), and Panco ("river stone"). Terrazas make the point that these names may be quite difficult to pronounce in all their export markets. The basic Terrazas Alto range includes attractive, lightly

wood-aged Cabernet Sauvignon and Malbec reds, with plenty of ripeness and body to the tannins, and Chardonnay wines styled for those who find bone-dry Chardonnay too rasping. The grapes for these wines come from roughly the heights given on the labels, whereas grapes for the Terrazas Reserva range, a more concentrated version of Terrazas Alto, come almost precisely from what Terrazas believe to be the ideal height above sea level for each grape. The top range, called Gran Terrazas, includes Cabernet Sauvignon and Malbec reds sourced from specific blocks within the best Terrazas vineyards. These two reds show powerful fruit texture and soft oak influence. *See also* Cheval des Andes (above).

Terruño 27 *See* Bacchus

Tierra del Fuego *See* J.&F. Lurton Argentina

Tittarelli (C56)

Rivadavia, Mendoza
Tel: (+54) 0261 429 1084;
titvosa@sanmartinmza.com.ar
In 1998, Italian winemaking consultant Alberto Antonini (*see* Altos Las Hormigas, above) began working with Tittarelli's winemaker, Graciela Reta (*see* Santa Faustina, above). The original idea was for Antonini to concentrate on Syrah red wines, but initially he spent most of his time working with Bonarda and Tempranillo, two red grapes he felt had greater potential here. The Tittarelli wines are sold under the

Bodega del Novecientos (Bodega del 900), Finca El Retiro, Finca El Retiro Reserve, and Tittarelli labels. Particularly notable is how the wines from each grape variety bear distinct, absorbing flavours: cherry and mint for Bonarda; wild blackcurrant for Cabernet Sauvignon; light melon for Chardonnay; damson and cinnamon for Malbec; exuberant blackberry and plum for Sangiovese; leather and raspberry for Syrah; strawberry and blackberry for Tempranillo; and pronounced ripe peach and musk for Torrontés whites. The Tittarelli family founded the company in the 1950s, but recent restructuring of its wine and olive oil business by an Argentine food and beverage group saw Alberto Antonini depart as winemaking consultant, and some of the company's oldest vineyards lost.

Trapiche (C21)

Maipù, Mendoza
Tel: (+54) 11 4394 4722;
www.trapichewinery.com
Trapiche is a subsidiary of Peñaflor (*see* above) and Argentina's number one wine exporter, with five million bottles annually. Trapiche was founded in 1883 when a banker, and then Mendoza's provincial governor, Tiburcio Benegas, bought the El Trapiche vineyard in Godoy Cruz on the outskirts of Mendoza city. A mill (*trapiche*) on the property gave the firm its name. Benegas became a key figure in Argentine and South American wine history by introducing European grape varieties and French winemaking techniques. Trapiche now has more than

1,000 ha (2,471 acres) of vineyards across Mendoza province, and a gravity-fed winery in Coquimbito, Central Mendoza. The Astica range is named after the Huarpe Native American word for "flower", and includes a good-value range of red and white wines, much improved since 2002 (Astica is called Falling Star in some markets). Astica Chardonnay shows ripe, red apple flavours, with Tempranillo and Merlot/Malbec blends hinting at wildness. The main Trapiche range includes an unoaked Malbec with classic Argentine Malbec flavours (soft black fruit), plus one of Argentina's more fulsome Cabernet Sauvignons, as well as agreeable Chardonnay and Sauvignon Blanc. The Oak Cask and Fond de Cave ranges usually provide better-value, oak-aged varietal wines than the Medalla range (the wines, particularly the Merlot and Cabernet Sauvignon, tend to fade rather quickly, so catch their fruit young, within three years of the vintage). Trapiche's top red wine, Iscay, is named after an Inca word meaning "two". This is because Iscay is made from two grapes, Malbec and Merlot, and by two winemakers (Bordeaux's Michel Rolland and Argentina's Angél Mendoza, until the latter left Trapiche in 2002) from two cultures (European and South American), holding two winemaking philosophies. Iscay is aged in new French oak barrels, but the debut 1997 vintage was variable and the 1998 suffered from the effects of bad weather caused by El Niño. *See also* Alta Vista, Clos de Los Siete and San Pedro de Yacochuya (Michel Rolland) and Domaine St Diego (Angél Mendoza), all above.

Trivento (C24)
Maipù, Mendoza
www.trivento.com
Chile's Concha y Toro founded this export-oriented venture in 1996. Initially Trivento was called Viña Patagonia, even though Trivento's main vineyard and winery at Russell, in Central Mendoza, are 1,200 km (745 miles) north of

below Los Arboles in Uco Valley, where some top estates source grapes.

Argentina's Patagonian wine region. Trivento's early wines lacked style, but this was probably only to be expected of a new Argentine wine venture carrying Chilean winemaking baggage. Recent releases are more sure-footed, and are characterized by clean, tropical white wines for early drinking and deeply coloured reds with broad, if simple, flavours and a creamy, lactic texture.

Trumpeter *See* Rutini

Urquiza (C2)
Maipù, Mendoza
videurquiza@sinectis.com.ar
A group of businessmen with

backgrounds in Argentine wine founded Urquiza in Guaymallén, North Mendoza. Urquiza is a Basque word meaning "abundance of birch trees", hence the birch symbol on the wine label. The wines are sourced from a variety of vineyard sources, and as we watch the winemaking here find its feet this should be a good source of fruit-driven, modern-style red wines.

Valentín Bianchi (C70)
San Rafael, Mendoza
Tel: (+54) 02627 22046;
informes@vbianchi.com
This quality-oriented, family owned producer owns three well-managed

vineyards (Finca Asti, Finca Doña Elsa, and Finca Las Paredes) and three wineries around San Rafael town. Bianchi is one of the leading producers of sparkling wines in Argentina with two brands, New Age Bloody and New Age White. These seductively styled semi-dry pink and white wines account for one-third of Bianchi's annual wine sales of eight million bottles. Drier-tasting and fully sparkling white wine under the Bianchi Extra Brut label, made from Chardonnay and Pinot Noir, is more refined. Bianchi's still wines are consistently high in quality. Whites made from Chardonnay, Sauvignon Blanc, or a blend of Semillon and Chardonnay, show a balance between tropical fruit and mineral flavours. Reds made from Barbera, Cabernet Sauvignon, Malbec, and Merlot display generous, typical flavours. Other labels include Elsa's Vineyard, Valentín Bianchi Luz, and Famiglia Bianchi. The keys to Bianchi's success have been the quality of the vineyards; excellent vineyard management, including advanced hail protection and sensible yields under the respected agronomist Laura Montero; seeking and then adopting winemaking advice from consultants such as Paul Hobbs, and the steadily increasing cash-flow generated by the New Age wines, which has been reinvested in the vineyards, the winery, and the staff. Bianchi has become almost the perfect prototype Argentine-owned wine producer.

Valle Alto *See* Sendero Alto

Valle de la Puerta (B3)

Chilecito, La Rioja

vdlp@sinectus.com.ar

The owner here sold grapes from his Famatina Valley vineyards in La Rioja Province to the La Riojana cooperative (*see* above) until 2001, when he launched his own, richly promising wines under the good-value "Tenorio" label. A La Rioja estate to watch.

Vasija Secreta *See* La Banda

Vicien *See* Cabernet de los Andes

Vieja Abadía *See* Peñaflor

Villa Atuel (C73)

Ciudad, Mendoza

Tel: (+54) 0261 420 4847

An entrepreneurial Spanish company that also owns a hotel chain in the Caribbean created the Villa Atuel wine brand. Production is based at Villa Atuel in Mendoza's San Rafael region using grapes from vineyards once part of Arizu (*see* above). Early releases of Villa Atuel wines included elegant, subtle Merlot and Syrah reds with direct, occasionally complex, fruit flavours. The winemaking team includes Susana Balbo (*see* Vintage, below) and Alberto Antonini (*see* Altos Las Hormigas and Tittarelli, above).

Villa Seca *See* López López

Villar Cortes *See* Viña Amalia

Viña Amalia *See* Amalia

Viña Fundación de Mendoza (C57)

Santa Rosa, Mendoza

vinicola@elsitio.net

New owners here since 1998 have renovated this company's extensive vineyards and crumbling winery in Santa Rosa, East Mendoza. The wines, called Viña Fundación de Mendoza and (oak-aged) Prestigio should improve as a result.

Viña Patagonia *See* Trivento

Viñas Argentinas (C4)

Lavalle, Mendoza

Tel: (+54) 0261 493 0293

This large North Mendoza-based producer uses the Finca Santa María, Guaymare labels. Another range called Arriero Andes Sur and Arriero Alto Agrelo is named after the "*gaucho arriero,*" the typical Argentine labourer on horseback. The wines offer value for money but flavours can be blurred.

Viñas de Dávalos *See* Tacuil

Viñas de Altura (A14)

Molinos, Salta

www.hesscollection.com

California's Hess Collection Winery owns this estate and nearby Colomé. This site covers 21,000 ha (51,891 acres) in the Cachi area of Salta province's Calchaquíes Valley. Hess is planting test plots of Malbec, Cabernet Sauvignon, Pinot Noir, Merlot, and Syrah vines at what could become the highest commercial vineyard in the world. *See also* Amalaya.

Viñas de Salta *See* La Banda

Viniterra (C14)

Luján de Cuyo, Mendoza

Tel: (+54) 0261 498 5888;

viniterra@infovia.com

Viniterra, based in Luján de Cuyo town, describes itself as a "a young winery with experience." It was founded by Flavio Senetiner and Walter Bressia, respectively the former commercial manager and winemaker at Nieto y Senetiner, which Flavio's father Adriano Senetiner had co-founded (since leaving Nieto y Senetiner Adriano Senetiner has become an investor in Viniterra). The Viniterra wines have improved with each vintage and are characterized by light, simple flavours. Pinot Gris and Viognier provide whites with deep, oily textures while Malbec and Tempranillo reds show bright fruit and ripe tannins. Labels include Bykos (a Greek word for amphora), Jubileus, Omnium (Latin for "for everyone"), Serie Terra, and Viniterra.

Vintage (C45)

Ciudad, Mendoza
Tel: (+54) 0261 424 5994;
admvin@vintagesa.com.ar
Susana Balbo (*see* Bodega Villa Atuel) and her husband Pedro Marchevsky completed their own well-designed winery in Agrelo in 2002. In the 1980s Marchevsky gave up a professorship at Mendoza's leading university to join Catena Zapata, where he worked until early 2003. Marchevsky is one of the most respected people in the Argentine wine business. Susana Balbo has also worked for the Catena Group. She is an experienced winemaker and is much in demand as a winemaking consultant (*see* Villa

Atuel, above). As well as developing their own vineyards, Marchevsky and Balbo also buy in grapes from local growers who they advise on vineyard management. Their Anubis range includes a Chardonnay with plenty of body, and attractively firm, fruit-filled reds made from Bonarda, Cabernet Sauvignon, Malbec, Merlot, and Tempranillo. The Anubis Syrah/Bonarda blend works well, the Syrah giving the leaner Bonarda some richness and complexity. The Brioso ("with vigour") range includes a Bordeaux-style red blend of Cabernet Sauvignon, Merlot, Malbec, and Petit Verdot, which has its firm blackberry tannins (from the Cabernet Sauvignon) softened by redcurrant textures (from the Malbec and Merlot). The Susana Balbo range includes dense Cabernet Sauvignon and Malbec reds with overt oak influences. The Susana Balbo Crios red is a 100% Cabernet Sauvignon aged in new and second-use French oak. The Susana Balbo BenMarco wine is a mouthfilling Malbec with a glycerol richness and sinewy tannins. The Susana Balbo BenMarco VMS (Vineyard Master Selection) red is blended from the best grapes in any given harvest and aged in new oak barrels. The 2000 BenMarco VMS (50% Malbec, with 20% Cabernet Sauvignon, 15% Bonarda, 10% Merlot, and 5% Syrah) has a diverse range of intense fruit flavours. The Vintage winery is an ambitious project run by two infinitely experienced professionals

who strive for excellence in everything they do.

VMS *See* Vintage

Weinert (C10 & D4)

Luján de Cuyo, Mendoza
Tel: (+54) 11 4815 0915;
bodegaweinert@ciudad.com.ar
This ultra-traditional winery was founded in Carrodilla, Central Mendoza in 1975 by Bernardo Weinert, a Brazilian entrepreneur (*see also* Santa Faustina, above). The winery, dating from 1890, was restored and Weinert quickly gained a solid reputation. However, Weinert stores more than 25% of its wines in large, old wooden vats, which can impart characters into the wine increasingly deemed unpalatable by modern palates, which prefer ultra-clean wines. In 1997 the winemaking was revamped and a greater emphasis placed on hygiene. Weinert remains an iconic wine name in Argentina and in foreign markets such as Switzerland, where the taste of wines aged in large older wooden vats is preferred to the vanilla flavours imparted by a shorter period in smaller, new oak barrels. However, to describe Weinert as "indisputably South America's finest wine producer," as one renowned wine critic famously did, is unfortunately no longer valid (if indeed it ever was). Weinert's second-most expensive red wine, Cavas de Weinert, blends Cabernet Sauvignon, Malbec, and Merlot and

tastes like a well-aged red Bordeaux. Beneath Cavas de Weinert in price is the Weinert range, which includes above-average Cabernet Sauvignon, Malbec, and Merlot reds, but disappointing whites lacking freshness or clarity. Weinert's most diverting white is a sweet wine called Cosecha de Otoño ("autumn harvest"). The least-expensive wines include Carrascal and Pedro del Castillo (named after the Spanish conquistador who founded Mendoza City). Miscelánea red is an odd, peppery blend of more than a dozen red and white grapes, some of which are grown a trial vineyard plot. Bernardo Weinert has acquired two vineyards in Patagonia called Baso del Sapo and El Hoyo de Epuyén which lie close to the forty-second parallel. These are two ultra-cool-climate areas where he is hoping to develop grapes more suited to sparkling wine production or cool-climate dry reds from Pinot Noir.

White Label *See* Norton

Y. López (C20)

Maipù, Mendoza
www.bodegaslopez.com.ar
This fourth generation, family owned wine (and olive oil) producer has well-sited, often old, vineyards across Central Mendoza's Maipù department. Y. López's olive oil, called Marilen, (from trees on the estate dating from 1934) is superior to its wines, which show dusty flavours from ageing in old wooden vats.

Yacochuya de Michel Rolland

See San Pedro de Yacochuya

Zorzetto (D5)

Valle Azul, Río Negro
Tel: (+54) 0941 491329/464095
The Zorzetto family left Italy for Argentina after the Second World War and farmed in Santa Fe province until president Perón forced a compulsory purchase of their estate. So, Luis Zorzetto and his wife travelled to Río Negro province where they began another farm. The oldest vineyards date from the 1950s and are organically farmed. The Zorzettos make no wine themselves, but sell their grapes to Humberto Canale.

Zuccardi (C33)

Maipù, Mendoza
Tel: (+54) 0261 427 2027;
agricola@lasa.com.ar
The Zuccardi family produces ten million bottles annually from its vineyards in Fray Luis Beltrán in Central Mendoza and Santa Rosa, East Mendoza. All the vines are trained to overhead pergolas, rather than vertical hedges, and flood irrigation is usual with this system. However, the Zuccardis are developing micro-jet irrigation systems to reduce the amount of water they use and to improve wine quality by minimizing dilution. Organic vineyard management and education programmes for the 400-plus workers here demonstrate the strong environmental and social

commitment of José Alberto Zuccardi, who runs the business for his family. To most foreign observers José Alberto is the most recongizable (and always smiling) face of Argentine wine because he spends so much time travelling to promote Argentina and his wines in equal measure. José Alberto has become one of Argentina's most successful wine exporters, staking his reputation on clean-tasting, value-for-money wines unashamedly styled for contemporary European and American consumers. A new visitor centre opened at the main Zuccardi winery in Fray Luis Beltrán in 2002. The organic Terra Orgánica range provides carefully made, sensibly priced Torrontés, Malbec, and Tempranillo wines. The Santa Julia Fuzion range "fuses" two grape varieties such as Chenin Blanc/Chardonnay and Tempranillo/Malbec. Santa Julia Magna is an attractively peppery, oak-aged, dry red blend of Malbec, Tempranillo, Merlot, and Cabernet Sauvignon with a strong eucalyptus aftertaste. The more complex, oak-influenced Familia Zuccardi Santa Julia Reserva range includes a critically acclaimed Bonarda and Sangiovese blend juxtaposing ripe fruit tannins with firmer oak tannins, as well as consistently ripe Malbec and Tempranillo reds. Other labels include Santa Rosa Estate and Familia Zuccardi.

URUGUAY

uruguay

Uruguay may be the fourth largest wine producer in South America, but its annual output (120 million bottles) is relatively small. A single winery such as Chile's Concha y Toro, or Argentina's Peñaflor, makes more wine in a year. Uruguay's statistical insignificance has put the country low down in South America's wine pecking-order. What's more, some wine commentators still believe that Uruguay is one of the least favourable countries in the New World for wine. They cite the climate, particularly the fact that rain falls here during the summer and is common at harvest.

Uruguay's critics forget that rain also falls in the summer and autumn in Bordeaux and New Zealand, for example, but while wine-growers in those countries might accept that it does occasionally rain at harvest, it only ever falls on their neighbours' vineyards, of course. Rain during the growing season should be seen more positively outside Europe, for irrigation then becomes optional, not the lifeline upon which New World vineyards generally depend. Irrigation can cause problems. It tempts wine-growers to swell the grapes with water to increase yields, which dilutes quality and weakens vines. And irrigated soil becomes saline, which means the wines are more likely to need artificial acidification during winemaking.

Even though summers in Uruguay are frequently hot, there is enough rainfall to enable local vineyards to survive without irrigation. Uruguay is bounded by water on three sides: by the Atlantic in the east, by the wide River Plate in the south, and by the River Uruguay in the west. The word Uruguay even has a watery connotation: it means "river of birds." The tempering effects of water are felt particularly strongly in southwest and south Uruguay, where the majority of Uruguay's vineyards are located.

Rain, plus moist, cooling Atlantic breezes, cause enough humidity to moderate the extreme heat of the strong summer sun. As in Bordeaux and New Zealand, this combination of warmth, humidity, and rainfall causes considerable variation among vintages, especially if the heaviest rain falls near harvest-time. But, by slowing the ripening process, the climate also enables Uruguay to produce dense, richly aromatic wines with naturally crisp textures and subtle, complex flavours.

Uruguay's wine is quite European in style; traditionally made Uruguayan red wines have a firm, rather tannic feel. This may be because many Uruguayan winemakers trained at French universities. Recently, however, the arrival of Bordeaux winemakers such as J.&F. Lurton at Cerro Chapeu and Patrick Valette at Filgueira, as well as the Australian Bright Brothers at Establecimiento Juanicó, British-led teams at Dante Irurtia, and New Zealanders such as Duncan Killiner at Castillo Viejo (Killiner has also consulted to Pizzorno, Varela Zarranz, Ariano, and Plaza Vidiella), has widened Uruguay's winemaking horizons, leading to riper, fruitier, less-tannic red wines, and much cleaner whites. It has also led to improvements in viticulture.

key facts about uruguay

Most vineyards and wineries are found around Montevideo; foreign winemakers are taming the **famously tannic Tannat**; a special vine trellis called the "lyre" is used to combat the humid **Atlantic-influenced climate**; an extended growing season is ideal for aromatic white wines from Sauvignon Blanc and **refined, complex reds**, like Cabernet Franc; **lush, flat terrain** contrasts with Argentina's mountains and deserts.

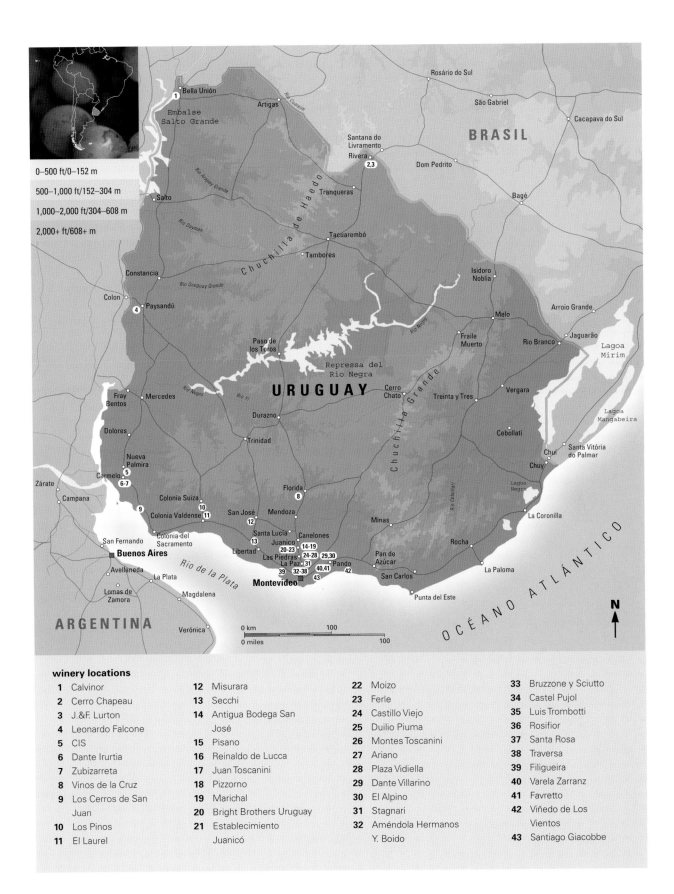

winery locations

1   Calvinor
2   Cerro Chapeau
3   J.&F. Lurton
4   Leonardo Falcone
5   CIS
6   Dante Irurtia
7   Zubizarreta
8   Vinos de la Cruz
9   Los Cerros de San
    Juan
10 Los Pinos
11 El Laurel

12 Misurara
13 Secchi
14 Antigua Bodega San
    José
15 Pisano
16 Reinaldo de Lucca
17 Juan Toscanini
18 Pizzorno
19 Marichal
20 Bright Brothers Uruguay
21 Establecimiento
    Juanicó

22 Moizo
23 Ferle
24 Castillo Viejo
25 Duilio Piuma
26 Montes Toscanini
27 Ariano
28 Plaza Vidiella
29 Dante Villarino
30 El Alpino
31 Stagnari
32 Améndola Hermanos
    Y. Boido

33 Bruzzone y Sciutto
34 Castel Pujol
35 Luis Trombotti
36 Rosifior
37 Santa Rosa
38 Traversa
39 Filigueira
40 Varela Zarranz
41 Favretto
42 Viñedo de Los
    Vientos
43 Santiago Giacobbe

These improvements were much needed. The downside for Uruguay (and Bordeaux) is that humid, maritime climates encourage vines to produce excessively long shoots and too many leaves. The extra foliage in the vine's canopy attracts fungal diseases. So, since the 1980s, some Uruguayan growers have copied a growing technique pioneered in Bordeaux. Vines are trained in a system called "lyre". The the vine canopy is divided in two (making a "V" shape), increasing the surface area of leaves but making it less dense, less humid, and less likely to attract fungal diseases. Sunlight falling into the middle of the "V" falls directly onto the grapes. Although lyre-trained vines have double the amount of shoots and leaves as conventionally trained, hedge-shaped vines, they

below Uruguay has a wealth of old Fords and Chevrolets dating from the 1920s and 1930s. Most – but not all – are still in use.

produce only the same number of grape bunches as the hedge system. The theory is that, with the lyre system, the grapes are of better quality. Producers who have converted all of their vineyards to lyre include Castillo Viejo, Dante Irurtia and Viña Varela Zarranz. Still, only twenty per cent of Uruguay's vines are pruned to the lyre system.

Producers with no lyre-trained vines include Reinaldo De Lucca and Stagnari. They claim that hedge-trained vines are easier to prune and pick than lyre-trained ones, and cheaper to manage. Problems caused by humidity are dealt with by removing leaves around the grape bunches as harvest approaches so that the grapes receive more direct sunlight.

South America's fourth largest wine producer seems to have a new generation of wine-growers committed to showing that Uruguay's statistical

wines of south america

insignificance gives them something to prove. The outstanding quality of the 2002 harvest, by far Uruguay's best in the modern era, has given them the perfect opportunity to bring Uruguayan wines to the wider audience they deserve.

Uruguayan Wine Regions

Uruguay is divided into five wine regions: Central Uruguay; South Uruguay; South West Uruguay; North East Uruguay; and North West Uruguay. These five regions are subdivided as follows: CENTRAL URUGUAY has one official wine subregion, Durazno department, but only 1.5 per cent of Uruguay's vineyards.

SOUTH URUGUAY has four official wine subregions: Canelones, Florida, Montevideo, and San José. Eighty-four per cent of Uruguay's vineyards are located here, and most of these are in Canelones, with the rest found in San José, Montevideo, and Florida.

SOUTH WEST URUGUAY has one official wine subregion, Colonia department, with eight per cent of Uruguay's vineyards.

NORTH EAST URUGUAY has two official wine subregions, Rivera and Tacuarembó departments that contain only 1.5 per cent of Uruguay's vineyards.

NORTH WEST URUGUAY has three official wine subregions, Artigas, Paysandú, and Salto that contain five per cent of Uruguay's vineyards.

Compared to other major wine-producing countries in South America, Uruguay's topography is low-lying and largely featureless. The landslides and flash floods so common in other South American wine-producing countries are unknown here. Rolling plains stretch in all directions. The only significant topographical features are two ridges (cuchillas), jokingly referred to as the "Uruguayan Andes." They never exceed 500 m (1,640 ft) above sea level and seem mere like molehills compared to the mountains of Bolivia or Argentina. The cuchillas run from north to south, dividing the country into three. The most

easterly, the Cuchilla Grande, forms the eastern limit of wine-growing in Uruguay in the important wine-producing department of Canelones.

Almost all of Uruguay's vineyards run in a swathe between twenty-five and seventy-five kilometres (sixteen and forty-seven miles) from the River Plate. This swathe crosses the departments of Colonia, San José, Montevideo, and Canelones. And unlike in Argentina and Chile, where single vineyards can stretch for miles, in Uruguay vineyards average no more than five hectares (twelve acres) in size. Uruguayan vineyards often form part of a smallholding incorporating livestock and other crops, usually fruit or cereals. Leather, meat and wool continue to be more important to the Uruguayan economy than wine is, so visitors are more likely to see cows and sheep than vineyards or even humans (the population is just 3.2 million). Eighty-five per cent of all Uruguay's land is dedicated to agriculture, the highest proportion in the world, but this is of a distinctly non-intensive type. Hormones in animal feed are banned. In the spring, Uruguay's endless pastures are alive with the purple flowers honoured in the title of William Hudson's picaresque nineteenth-century travelogue based on his time in Uruguay, *The Purple Land*.

Uruguay's total vineyard area halved in size between 1950 and 1990. It now totals 9,000 ha (22,240 acres), one-tenth the area of Chile or Bordeaux. Since the late 1980s, a world wine boom has occurred; people are drinking more – and better-quality – wine. Consequently, the Uruguayan government has encouraged vineyard owners to replace poor-quality varieties planted in the nineteenth century with quality vines such as Cabernet Sauvignon, Merlot, and Chardonnay (which are more attractive to foreign wine drinkers). Even so, only sixty per cent of the Uruguayan vineyard contains the kind of grapes the rest of the world wants to drink.

The problem is that, on average, every one of Uruguay's 3.2 million inhabitants consumes nearly one bottle of wine a week. This adds up to forty-five bottles per person per year, or ninety-six bottles out of every one hundred produced in Uruguay. And as Uruguayans would rather drink sweet, grapey jug wines made from the grape varieties the government is trying to eliminate, the wine industry is caught in a catch-22 situation.

The areas of Uruguay producing wines of international standard are:

ARTIGAS DEPARTMENT

Artigas department is one of three official subregions in North West Uruguay. The region's sandy soils produce early drinking wines, but seem to suit sugar-cane better than grape-vines. Bella Unión, the main town in Artigas, is the only point where the Uruguayan, Brazilian, and Argentine borders meet. *See* Calvinor.

CANELONES DEPARTMENT

One of four departments in South Uruguay, Canelones is Uruguay's major wine-growing area, with more than half of the country's best vineyards. These are found on the farm land enveloping Montevideo's suburbs, an area that, by Uruguayan standards, is fairly densely populated. The generally clay-rich soils and warm climate combine to give wines with markedly high levels of alcohol, and crisp, direct fruit characters. Many of the best wines are selected blends from grapes grown in more than one subregion, a technique which evens out irregularities in the grape quality. The main subregions within Canelones are:

ATLÁNTIDA Due east of Montevideo in pine forests close to the South Atlantic. The wines are delicate and intensely aromatic. *See* Luis Trombotti and Viñedo de Los Vientos.

CANELÓN CHICO Well-regarded vineyard area thirty kilometres (nineteen miles) due north of Montevideo. Elegant wines. *See* Améndola Hermanos Y Boido, Juan Toscanini, Pizzorno, and Reinaldo De Lucca.

CANELONES TOWN The major town in Canelones department lies thirty-three kilometres (twenty-two

miles) north of Montevideo. *See* Ferle and Plaza Vidiella.

CAP ARTIGAS Eastern suburb of Montevideo named after José Artigas, who fought against the Spanish in the nineteenth century. *See* Rosifior and Luis Trombotti.

CUATRO PIEDRAS Clay-rich area due north of Montevideo; produces powerfully flavoured wines. *See* Reinaldo De Lucca and Varela Zarranz.

CUCHILLA VERDE Cuchilla Verde is a sloping swathe of fertile land along the Santa Lucia River valley west of Montevideo. Rich wines. *See* Filgueira.

EL COLORADO Well-drained, quality area thirty kilometres (nineteen miles) northeast of Montevideo. *See* Ariano and Reinaldo De Lucca.

EMPALME OLMOS Sandy area inland of Atlántida, east of Montevideo. Under-exploited. *See* Rosifior.

JOAQUÍN SUAREZ Limestone-rich area between Pando

above The sandy beach at the resort of Punte del Este, on the Atlantic coast.

and Montevideo. Elegant wines. *See* Varela Zarranz.

JUANICÓ Vineyards on the well-exposed slopes around the town of Juanicó, between Montevideo and the town of Canelones, can produce harmonious, complex wines. *See* Establecimiento Juanicó, Moizo, and Santa Rosa.

LA PAZ La Paz is sixteen kilometres (ten miles) north of Montevideo. Full-bodied wines. *See* Stagnari.

LAS BRUJAS Dry, gently sloping sandy area near the Santa Lucia River, suited to dry white Sauvignon Blanc. *See* Plaza Vidiella.

LAS PIEDRAS Due north of La Paz, but with more potential. *See* Ariano, Castillo Viejo, Duilio Piuma, and Montes Toscanini.

LAS VIOLETAS Well-to-do suburb of northwest Montevideo. *See* Ariano, Castel Pujol, and Santa Rosa.

LOS CERILLOS Los Cerillos means "the little hills" in Spanish. A well-drained, dry area similar to nearby Las Brujas. *See* Marichal and Plaza Vidiella.

MANGA In the quiet range of hills northeast of Montevideo. *See* Santiago Giacobbe.

PANDO Hilltop town between Joaquín Suarez and Empalme Olmos with great potential. *See* Favretto and Rosifior.

PROGRESO Well-drained, warm area forty kilometres (twenty-five miles) north of Montevideo, producing intense wines. *See* Antigua Bodega San José and Pisano.

SANTA LUCIA Santa Lucia town forms the north-west edge of Canelones department. Warm, well-exposed area for bright, open, refreshing wines. *See* Ariano.

SAUCE Sauce is a small town about thirty kilometres (nineteen miles) northeast of Montevideo on quite open farm land. *See* Dante Villarino and El Alpino.

COLONIA DEPARTMENT

Colonia department is the only official wine subregion of South West Uruguay. Its name means "colony", for this is where the Spanish colonists (in the form of Jesuit priests) planted Uruguay's first vineyards (the Portuguese, who got here first, were not so wine-oriented). Subsequent waves of colonisation by north-central Europeans are reflected in local architectural styles and town names: Colonia Suiza (Swiss Colony), where Los Pinos is based, and Colonia Valdense (named after a Lutheran/Protestant reformer) where El Laurel is based. From Colonia's main town of Colonia del Sacramento, ferry services run across the River Plate to Buenos Aires, the Argentine capital. The only wine producer in the town is the historically significant Los Cerros de San Juan. Its winery is thirty minutes' drive north of Colonia del Sacramento. Even farther north, the Parana and Uruguay Rivers meet at Carmelo to form the River Plate. Here the tiny CIS and the much bigger Dante Irurtia are located. Zubizarreta is a twenty minute drive inland.

DURAZNO DEPARTMENT

Durazno is the only official subregion of Central Uruguay. Summer daytime temperatures are higher here than in any other wine region in Uruguay. Heat is retained by pebbles in the soil, so the grapes stay warm at night, contributing to extra-ripe wines. The dark-skinned Tannat and Cabernet Sauvignon grapes recently planted here by Bruzzone y Sciutto should produce wines of distinction when the vines mature.

FLORIDA DEPARTMENT

One of four official wine subregions of South Uruguay, Florida lies roughly 120 kilometres (seventy-five miles) north of the capital, Montevideo. Hot summers, coupled with deep topsoils over granite plates, create potentially intense wines with crisp, juicy textures. *See* Vinos de La Cruz and Plaza Vidiella.

MONTEVIDEO

Montevideo is Uruguay's capital city. In the 1930s it was one of the wealthiest, trendiest places in South America; now the city's run-down air earns it very bad press from travel writers. However, unlike in Argentina, where public image is everything, Montevideo feels very unselfconscious and very European. Locals still drive old Ford and Chevrolet cars bought sometime between the 1920s and the 1950s, when Uruguay was one of the world's richest countries. The country generated huge profits by selling wool and leather for uniforms during the two World Wars, and beef tinned in the Uruguayan town of Fray Bentos was supplied for Allied army rations (the Uruguayan government remained neutral, at least officially, during both conflicts).

For tourists, Montevideo has excellent sandy beaches, and a selection of museums; its centre is easily traversable by foot. Steaks, wood-fired grills and seafood from the city's seafront market, the Mercado del Puerto, or produce from the countryside served in the city's many restaurants, offer excellent quality and value for money. During the late seventeenth century, European immigrants arrived, and the outskirts of Montevideo were covered with their vineyards. Few of these have survived the expansion of contemporary Montevideo, but Améndola Hermanos Y Boido, Bruzzone y Sciutto, Castel Pujol, Santa Rosa, and Traversa (among others) have wineries or vineyards (or both) in the suburbs.

PAYSANDÚ DEPARTMENT

Paysandú department is one of three official subregions in North West Uruguay. Paysandú's calcium-rich subsoil, below-average rainfall and above-average sun can produce wines rich in alcohol but with enough flavour to remain balanced. The main city, called Paysandú, is Uruguay's second-largest after Montevideo. Leonardo Falcone is based here, while fifteen kilometres (nine miles) north of Paysandú city, at Constancia, are vineyards belonging to Ariano.

RIVERA DEPARTMENT

Rivera department is the only significant official wine subregion of North East Uruguay. It lies on the thirty-second parallel, along Uruguay's northern border with Brazil's Santana de Livramento region (*see* p.183). The deep, red, sandy soils are favoured by timber growers (eucalyptus trees dominate the skyline). Wine producers include Cerro Chapeu and J.&F. Lurton Uruguay.

SALTO DEPARTMENT

Salto, in North West Uruguay, is 400 km (250 miles) northwest of Montevideo, close to the Argentine border. It was here that the revival of Uruguayan wine-growing began in the late nineteenth century, when the pioneer Pascual Harriague brought the first Tannat vines to Uruguay (*see* Uruguayan Grape Varieties, below). Salto's harsh climate (spring frosts, early autumns) and its distance from Montevideo, the main area for local wine sales, mean few vineyards remain today. *See* Stagnari.

SAN JOSÉ DEPARTMENT

San José is one of four official subregions in South Uruguay. Its prevailing dark clay soils mean the wines produced here tend to have a very dense texture. Castillo Viejo's new vineyard, on lighter soil at Mal Abrigo, is an exception. High temperatures during the growing season are tempered by the breezes coming off three local rivers, the Plate, the San José, and the Santa Lucía. This wind influence, plus cold night-time temperatures, gives the wines their powerful aromas. Producers based here include Misurara and Secchi.

TACUAREMBÓ DEPARTMENT

Tacuarembó is an official wine subregion of North East Uruguay but it has no recognized wineries.

Uruguay Wine Label Terms

APELACIÓN DE ORIGEN Denotes a wine that comes from an official Uruguayan wine region.

VARIETAL WINES Must contain eighty-five per cent of the grape variety named on the label.

VC (or *Vino Común*), wine made from lesser-quality grapes, for the domestic market, usually sold in 1-, 1.5-, or 3-litre jugs, hence the term "jug wine".

VCP (or *Vinos de Calidad Preferente*). This translates as "preferred quality wine" or "fine wine." VCP is made only from export-quality grapes and sold only in standard seventy-five centilitre wine bottles, or smaller (no jugs or magnums).

Uruguayan Wine Styles – Introduction

Within Uruguay, slightly sweet, still rosé wines are the most popular styles. These account for more than half of all the wine sold locally, and are usually made using inferior grape varieties. Wines made from superior (*Vitis vinifera*) vines are about ninety per cent. The best of these are made from a grape brought from South West France in the late nineteenth century, the Tannat. Uruguay's dry red Tannat wines are the most powerful examples of this grape variety in the world. Other red grapes suited to Uruguay are also of French origin, including Cabernet Franc, Merlot, Syrah, Cabernet Sauvignon, and Pinot Noir. Italian grapes such as Nebbiolo and Sangiovese also show promise.

Uruguay's best white wines are usually dry and occasionally sparkling. They often release strong, almost overpowering aromas and are generally crisp and full-bodied. Sauvignon Blanc, Chardonnay, and Viognier are the most heavily promoted white wine grapes, but Torrontés, Gewurztraminer, Trebbiano Toscano, Riesling, Semillon, Marsanne, and Sauvignon Gris all ripen extremely well.

Uruguayan Varietal Wine Styles (Blended)

Uruguayan wineries are beginning to get more adventurous about blending grape varieties to create better-balanced, more age-worthy wines. For red wines, Tannat is often used to provide the backbone, while Merlot, Syrah, and Cabernet Sauvignon are used to give complexity and depth. For white wines, the combination of Chardonnay and Viognier is providing some of Uruguay's most complex white wines.

RED BLENDED WINES

Tannat, Uruguay's most important quality variety, is the backbone of the country's best red blends. Its firm structure is softened by the addition of Merlot and a degree of oak-ageing, as blended wines from Bright Brothers Uruguay, Castillo Viejo (Catamayor), Juan Toscanini, Leonardo Falcone (Santa Cecilia), Moizo, Pisano (Primera Viña), Pizzorno (Don Próspero and Why Try Uruguay), Plaza Vidiella (100 Años and Las Brujas), and Reinaldo De Lucca demonstrate. Extra aroma is provided when Cabernet Sauvignon is added to the Tannat/Merlot mix, with Castel Pujol (del Museo), Pisano (Arretxea), and Pizzorno (Don Próspero Reserve) the most notable examples; Establecimiento Juanicó's ambitious Preludio also includes Petit Verdot. Dual-varietal Tannat/Cabernet Franc blends from Castillo Viejo (Corazón de Roble) and Dante Irurtia (Posada del Virrey) work well, combining Tannat's denseness with Cabernet Franc's silky elegance. Both Plaza Vidiella (100 Años and Las Brujas) and El Alpino (J Chiapella Roble) show that Tannat/Cabernet Sauvignon blends need not be overly tannic, while Dante Irurtia (Ca' del Sacramento) opts for Tannat with both Cabernets (Sauvignon and Franc). Blends using Syrah at Ariano (Selección) and Dante Irurtia (Winemaker's Selection), Ruby Cabernet at Viñedo de los Vientos (Eolo Gran Reserva), and Nebbiolo at Dante Irurtia (Dante's Red) show healthy innovation.

WHITE BLENDED WINES

Viognier and Chardonnay are natural bedfellows in Uruguay, with good examples made by Pisano (Primera Viña) and Plaza Vidiella (100 Años and Las Brujas). Dante Irurtia (Winemaker's Selection) also adds Gewurztraminer and Riesling for (respectively) aroma and freshness. Dante Irurtia's large vineyard and wide range of grape varieties provides blending opportunities using Riesling and Trebbiano (Dante's White), Viognier, Roussanne (Posada del Virrey), and, most interesting of all, Semillon, Chardonnay, Sauvignon Blanc, and Marsanne (Ca' del Sacramento).

Uruguayan Varietal Wine Styles (By Grape Variety)

CABERNET FRANC (RED)

Cabernet Franc ripens at the height of the Uruguayan autumn. Such perfect timing means it can produce consistently elegant, floral-toned reds. Its soft tannins make it potentially more approachable than Tannat. The vine tends to overproduce, so yields need reining in. *See* Castillo Viejo, Dante Irurtia, El Alpino, and Pisano.

CABERNET SAUVIGNON (RED)

Cabernet Sauvignon ripens about ten days later than Cabernet Franc in Uruguay; it can be unripe and dilute if autumn rains arrive too soon. The variety ripens earlier if growers reduce yields through strict

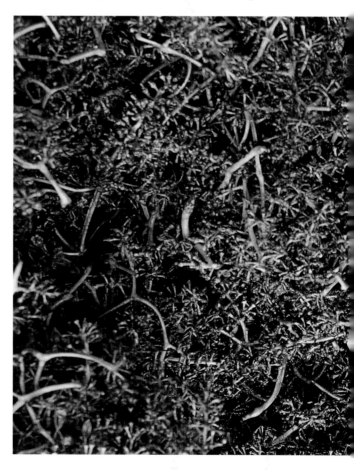

winter pruning. *See* Antigua Bodega San José, Ariano, Bruzzone y Sciutto, Castillo Viejo, Dante Irurtia, El Alpino, Filgueira, Reinaldo De Lucca, Santa Rosa, Stagnari, Varela Zarranz, and Viñedo de Los Vientos.

CHARDONNAY (WHITE)

Chardonnay, though fashionable, has yet to produce great wines, perhaps because it is often planted on clay, which can be too heavy. On limestone, it can produce mineral-rich whites in the style of Burgundy. *See* Ariano, Castillo Viejo, Dante Irurtia, El Alpino, Establecimiento Juanicó, Juan Toscanini, Leonardo Falcone, Moizo, Pizzorno, Plaza Vidiella, and Varela Zarranz.

GEWURZTRAMINER (WHITE)

Gewurztraminer's musk and rose-petal aromas can be very pungent in Uruguay. *See* Viñedo de Los Vientos.

below Bunches of red wine are destemmed before fermentation; otherwise wines may taste vegetal, bitter, and rasping.

MERLOT (RED)

Merlot is Uruguay's chameleon grape, taking on noticeably distinct characters according to which soil type it is grown on. It becomes like fruit cake when grown on sand, like red plums when grown on clay, and like black hedgerow fruit when grown on limestone. *See* Antigua Bodega San José, Ariano, Castillo Viejo, Dante Irurtia, Dante Villarino, Filgueira, Moizo, Montes Toscanini, Reinaldo De Lucca, and Stagnari.

NEBBIOLO (RED)

This northern Italian grape is even more tannic than Tannat, so Dante Irurtia use it as a blending component. *See* also Castel Pujol.

PINOT NOIR (RED)

This Burgundy grape could prosper in Uruguay, especially on limestone, rather than clay, soils while

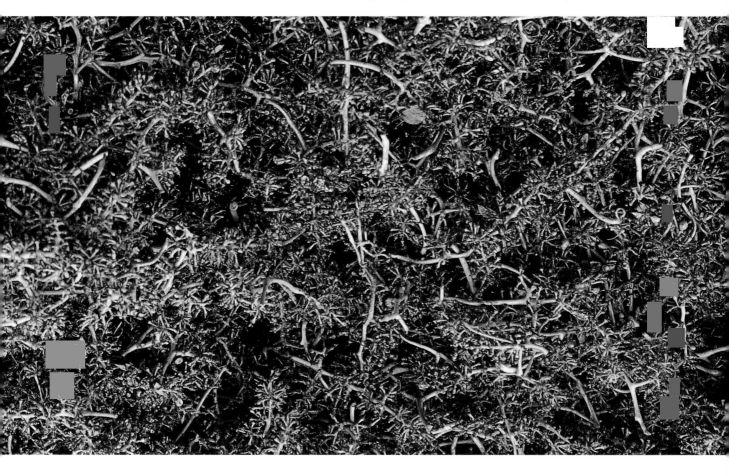

benefiting from the cool, maritime influences. *See* Cerro Chapeu, Dante Irurtia.

SAUVIGNON BLANC (WHITE)

Sauvignon Blanc is an outstanding performer in Uruguay (prompting occasional comparisons with world-beating New Zealand Sauvignon Blanc). Uruguayan Sauvignon Blanc shows less extrovert aromas than its New Zealand equivalent, where it is often likened to cat's pee, but has fuller body than French Sauvignon Blanc (such as the Loire Valley's Sancerre and Pouilly-Fumé wines). *See* Castillo Viejo, Dante Irurtia, Filgueira, Juan Toscanini, Plaza Vidiella, Varela Zarranz.

SYRAH (RED)

Syrah is not widely planted in Uruguay, but it has great potential for aromatic, crimson-coloured wines with bittersweet fruit. Syrah needs a lot of summer and late-autumn heat to ripen fully; it also likes free-draining rather than heavy soils for its full range of flavours to develop successfully. Uruguay's best dry Syrah reds, from Plaza Vidiella and Reinaldo De Lucca, are grown on such soils. *See* also Dante Irurtia.

below An "*asado*" or barbecue in Montevideo's famous Mercado del Puerto. Excellent value, and perfect with a red Tannat wine.

TANNAT (RED)

Tannat is Uruguay's most widely planted, quality grape variety. It became popular after the Uruguayan government organized a wine competition in the 1880s to promote wine-growing among its new European immigrant population. A man called Pascual Harriague won with a Tannat wine, and Uruguayan Tannat was born. Its thick, black skins comfortably resist Uruguay's maritime squalls, at the same time soaking up the summer sun without breaking a sweat. The result is jet-black coloured wine smelling of violets, mulberry, and black-cherry. Even a moderate-quality Tannat is capable of ageing for more than five years in bottle, but generally Uruguayan Tannat wines are best drunk within two to four years of the vintage stated. Some producers are making lighter-style Tannats for earlier drinking, too. *See* Antigua Bodega San José, Ariano, Bruzzone y Sciutto, Castel Pujol, Cerro Chapeu, Dante Irurtia, Dante Villarino, Establecimiento Juanicó, Filgueira, Juan Toscanini, Moizo, Montes Toscanini, Reinaldo de Lucca, Pizzorno, Santa Rosa, Stagnari, Varela Zarranz, and Viñedo de Los Vientos.

TORRONTÉS (WHITE)

Torrontés is renowned in Argentina but little used in Uruguay. *See* Calvinor, and Pisano.

TREBBIANO (WHITE)

This Italian grape (also known as Ugni Blanc) can produce crisp, inoffensive wines if yields are kept extremely low, but even then it has little inherent flavour. For some unknown reason, Trebbiano was one of the "quality" grapes recommended by the Uruguayan authorities after they subsidized the grubbing-up of lesser-quality vines in the 1980s. *See* Pisano.

VIOGNIER (WHITE)

This Rhône grape variety is often blended with Chardonnay to give full white wines with strong, musky aromas. *See* Dante Irurtia, Pisano, Plaza Vidiella.

UGNI BLANC (WHITE)

See Trebbiano, above.

Uruguayan Wine Styles (Other)

DIABETIC WINE
See Vinos de La Cruz.

KOSHER WINE
See Bruzzone y Sciutto.

ORGANIC WINE
Vinos de La Cruz was the only Uruguayan winery with certified organic vineyards in 2002; even then, only part of its holding was officially organic. Reinaldo de Lucca, Viñedo de Los Vientos, and Establecimiento Juanicó all have organic projects in progress. The main obstacles for organic grape-growing in Uruguay are the fungal diseases that thrive here (*see* Introduction, pp.154-155, for how these are being combated).

SPARKLING WINE
Vinos Finos J. Carrau produced Uruguay's first sparkling wines, in the 1930s, but Santa Rosa is now the market leader. *See also* Pizzorno.

VERMOUTH
See Ariano.

Uruguayan Wine Producers – Background
Most of Uruguay's 300-plus wineries are small-scale and privately owned. Many operations incorporate other crops and livestock; subsequently, grape and wine quality often suffers by not being prioritized sufficiently, especially as several crops must be harvested simultaneously. Most Uruguayan wineries have existed for at least three generations, founded usually by Italian and Basque immigrant wine-growers, who left Europe for Uruguay during the 1870s, after Europe's vineyards were devastated by the phylloxera louse, or ruined by (then incurable) fungal diseases such as mildew.

The most commonly used type of fermentation tank in Uruguay is concrete lined with epoxy. This is especially good for red winemaking, as long as the fermenting wine is kept from overheating. The key winemaking trick in Uruguay is to make Tannat wines that taste fruity, rather than tannic.

The Tannat grape comes from South West France, where it is used in Madiran, Irouléguy, and Tursan wines. The name may well derive from the fact that it makes highly tannic wine. Each Tannat grape contains five seeds (pips); most wine grapes have between one and three. During red winemaking the grape seeds, skins, and juice soak together for days, even weeks, while sugar in the grape juice is converted by the fermentation yeast to make alcohol (and thus wine). The alcohol draws the ultra-dry-tasting tannin from the seeds into the wine; this type of tannin can cling unpleasantly to the enamel on our teeth.

To make wines with more fruit and less tannin, winemakers now remove the seeds from the fermentation vats after just a few days. (The grape-skins contain tannins that taste sweet rather than dry, so these are not removed.) Winemakers at Establecimiento Juanicó and other wineries are also using a process called micro-oxygenation to soften the tannins. The technique involves bubbling fine jets of oxygen into the wine vats for a few minutes every day. The oxygen encourages rough-edged, single tannin molecules to form smoother groups of tannin chains. The wines taste smoother, and retain their colour better. This softening does happen naturally over several years as wines age, but micro-oxygenation speeds up the process to a few months. More sensitive winemaking means the best modern Uruguayan Tannat is now generally far more approachable than its French counterparts are.

notable producers

100 Años

See Plaza Vidiella

Abuelo Domingo

See Leonardo Falcone

Administración Nacional de Combustibles, Alcohol y Portland (ANCAP)

ANCAP was the former owner of Establecimiento Juanicó (*see* below), as well as the powerful Uruguayan government monopoly for both alcohol and fuel. Hence, some Uruguayan petrol stations still bear the ANCAP logo.

Améndola Hermanos Y. Boido (32)

Camino de los Tropas 3192, Montevideo

Tel: (+598) 02 222 2107;

delcabildo@info-red.com

This small producer has vineyards in both Canelón Chico, in Canelones department, and next to the company's winery in nearby Montevideo. The winery belongs to the Améndola brothers, while wines are made by partner and co-founder Eduardo Boido, who is a professor of winemaking. A dry Semillon-based white called "YvY" shows encouraging texture, but Tannat-based red blends, and Cabernet Sauvignon and Merlot single-varietal reds, labelled under the names Antiguas Bodegas del Cabildo 1811, show more clarity.

ANCAP *See* Administración Nacional de Combustibles, Alcohol y Portland

Antigua Bodega San José (14)

Progreso, Canelones

Tel: (+598) 02 369 0166;

mseijas@adinet.com.uy

Antigua Bodega San José produces complex, concentrated, and natural-tasting red and rosé wines (but no whites) in Progreso, in Canelones department. The owners, (trading as Tessa – A. Ltda), thirty-something Gustavo Seijas and his sister, Graciela, buy grapes from family growers in Canelones department. The Seijas decide how the vines are pruned, in order to control yields, and when to pluck leaves from around the grape bunches in the run-up to harvest (the ultimate aim is to achieve extra ripeness). The San José winery after which the wines are named dates from 1880. Once owned by monks, it is one of Uruguay's most spacious and beautiful cellars: neat rows of concrete vats, oak beams, and wooden floors feature. The wines include: a deep, berry-rich, Cabernet Sauvignon red, one of the best in Uruguay in terms of its tannic richness and clarity; a broad, succulent Merlot red (with a rosé version made from juice run off early from the fermenting Merlot vats); and a thick, but digestible Tannat, which shows an appealing nose of wild fruit and eucalyptus.

Antiguas Bodegas del Cabildo 1811 *See* Améndola Hermanos Y. Boido

Ariano (27)

Las Piedras, Canelones

Tel: (+598) 02 364 5290;

www.arianohermanos.com

This family run business has huge potential and produces above-average, clean, mainly red wines for fair prices under the Ariano and Don Adelio Ariano labels. The Arianos have five vineyards located 370 km (230 miles) apart at opposite ends of Uruguay: at Constancia in Paysandú in North West Uruguay, and in Canelones department in South Uruguay. The Canelones vineyards are near the family winery in Las Piedras. Wines under the Ariano brand see little or no oak-ageing, and include early drinking red wines made from Cabernet Sauvignon, Merlot, or Tannat, with attractive red-fruit flavours. Ariano Selección is a subtle, complex red blended from Tannat, Syrah, and Cabernet Franc. The more concentrated Don Adelio Ariano range is oak-aged and includes a sound dry white Chardonnay and an even better Tannat in which the oak influence adds to, rather than dominates, the wine. In keeping with their Italian origins, the Ariano family also produces Vermouth (in both rosso and bianco versions).

Arretxea

See Pisano

Bodegas del Plata

Bodegas del Plata was created as an export arm by a group of Uruguayan producers, but its Costas del Plata and Río de la Plata wines no longer exist. For a similar but more successful group, *see* Sunybell, below.

Bright Brothers Uruguay (20)

Tel: (+351) 219 583192
www.brightbrothers.pt
The Australian Bright Brothers produce a range of reliable, value-for-money wines at Establecimiento Juanicó winery. *See also* Bright Brothers Argentina (p.124) and Bright Brothers Chile (p.51).

Bruzzone y Sciutto (33)

Punte de Rieles, Montevideo
Tel: (+598) 02 514 5722;
bys@adinet.com.uy
This large, Montevideo-based producer has a huge winery west of Uruguay's international airport and two distinct vineyards: one near the Montevideo winery, planted from 1888 by Italian immigrants Bruzzone and Sciutto; and another on warmer, better-drained ground at El Carmen in Durazno department, purchased in 1997. New vineyards, plus big improvements in winemaking from 2002, should make this a producer to follow for Cabernet Sauvignon and Tannat. The main brand is Bruzzone y Sciutto. The top label, Padre Barreto, is oak-aged. The winery also produces Uruguay's only kosher wine.

Calvinor (Viñedos y Bodegas Bella Unión) (1)

Bella Unión, Artigas
Tel: (+598) 02 507 3023;
calvinor@multi.com.uy
This large-scale, but uninspiring, producer is based at Bella Unión, Artigas department. Local sugar-cane growers looking to develop other crops founded it in 1975.

Carlos Montes Reserva

See Montes Toscanini

Casa Filgueira

See Filgueira

Casa Luntro

See J.&F. Lurton Uruguay

Casco Noble

See Ferle

Casilla Dorada

See J.&F. Lurton Uruguay

Castel Pujol (34)

Montevideo
Tel: (+598) 02 320 0238;
www.castelpujol.com
Part of Vinos Finos J. Carrau SA and producer of the Castel Pujol, Castel Pujol Reserve, and Castel Pujol del Museo ranges. Castel Pujol's red wines, particularly those made from Tannat, seem to be more consistent than its whites.

Castillo Viejo (24)

Las Piedras, Canelones
Tel: (+598) 02 369 1855;
castilloviejo@castilloviejo.com
Castillo Viejo produces Uruguay's most commercially successful fine wine (*i.e.*, made under the VCP designation), the export brand, Catamayor. The arrival here from 1996 of internationally trained "flying winemakers" (from Australia and New Zealand via Britain) catalysed export sales. Castillo Viejo's owners, the Etcheverry family, laid the foundations for the arrival of the flying winemakers from 1986, by visiting Europe and importing better-quality grape varieties. The family has two vineyards in San José department. The newest, at Mal Abrigo ("place of bad shelter") is being developed with French investors. It will bear grapes, including Syrah, from 2004. Mal Abrigo is on an unusually rocky site, so room is made for new vines by blasting the rock with dynamite. Castillo Viejo's winery is at Las Piedras, Canelones department. The basic Catamayor wine range consists of: Chardonnay made in a rich Californian, rather than lean French, style; vibrant dry Sauvignon Blanc, one of Uruguay's best; Cabernet Franc, Cabernet Sauvignon, Merlot, Merlot/Tannat, and Tannat red wines with direct, appealing flavours (the Tannat is the only one that might age for more than two or three years, though). The Catamayor Corazón de Roble ("heart of oak") range includes oak-influenced Chardonnay and Tannat/Cabernet Franc. The even better Catamayor Vieja Parcela Reserva ("old-vine reserve selection") range includes: a dry white Sauvignon Blanc, fermented in barrel but aged in stainless steel tanks to prevent the oak from becoming too dominant; and Castillo Viejo's best wine, the Cabernet Franc, which has floral aromas of violets, along with, fruity damson and plum flavours, and a smooth texture.

Catamayor

See Castillo Viejo.

Cerro Chapeu (2)

Rivera

Tel: (+598) 02 320 0238;

www.carrauwines@st.com.uy

Vinos Finos J. Carrau SA, which owns Castel Pujol in South Uruguay, established Cerro Chapeu at Rivera, North East Uruguay, on the Brazilian border among bowler-hat shaped hills (called "Cerro Chapeu") in 1976. The vineyards are claimed to be the highest in Uruguay at 300 m (984 ft) above sea level. However, the climate is subtropical, rather than Alpine. A futuristic, hexagonal-shaped and gravity-fed modern winery has been cut into the hills. Wines produced here lack a little intensity and polish, but are steadily improving. They include: Cerro Chapeu, a range of basic red and white varietals in which the red wines show best; the Cerro Chapeu Colección of oak-aged varietals, including Pinot Noir; Cerro Chapeu Gran Tradición 1752, a blend of 50% Tannat, 30% Cabernet Sauvignon, and 20% Cabernet Franc, aged in French oak with fairly balanced fruit and oak flavours; and Amat, the top French-oak aged red wine made from the best Tannat. Within Uruguay, Amat is considered to be one of the country's top red wines. *See also* J.&F. Lurton Uruguay, below.

Chateau Fond de Cave

See Santa Rosa

Cien Años

See Plaza Vidiella

CIS (5)

Cerro Carmelo, Colonia

Tel: (+598) 542 3358

This small, family-owned winery owns five hectares (12.4 acres) of vineyards close to those of Dante Irurtia at Carmelo, in Colonia department. The winery's Vinos CIS brand comprises Cabernet Sauvignon, Merlot, and Tannat red wines made in a crisp, light French style. The wines are much improved since 2002.

Costas del Plata

See Bodegas del Plata

Cresta Roja

See Reinaldo De Lucca

Cuatro Piedras

See Varela Zarranz

Cuna de Piedra

See Los Cerros de San Juan

Dante Irurtia (6)

Cerro Carmelo, Colonia

Tel: (+598) 02 900 4019;

info@irurtia.com

Dante Irurtia owns the largest single vineyard in Uruguay, which covers 340 ha (840 acres) at Carmelo, in the Colonia department. Flying winemakers working with European wine importers have made Dante Irurtia's wines better-balanced, cleaner and easier drinking since 2001. In particular, where oak is used, its influence is becoming subtler. The wines are: Dante Irurtia Ca' del Sacramento, which, in its dry white form, is a tropical fruit-tasting blend of Semillon, Chardonnay, Sauvignon Blanc, and Marsanne, and, in its red form, is a crisp, Bordeaux-style blend of Cabernet Franc, Cabernet Sauvignon, Malbec, and Merlot; Dante Irurtia Dante's Red, an interesting pairing of Tannat and Nebbiolo, and Dante Irurtia Dante's White, a dry, neutral blend of Riesling and Trebbiano; Dante Irurtia Cosecha Particular ("Special Harvest"), a range of single-varietal wines of which the dry white Sauvignon Blanc and the red Tannat show best; Dante Irurtia Novello, a range for immediate drinking; Dante Irurtia Winemaker's Selection, which in its red form is a bubblegum-scented blend of Tannat and Syrah, and in its white form is a musky blend of Viognier, Chardonnay, Riesling, and Gewurztraminer; Dante Irurtia Posada del Virrey, the most interesting range on Dante Irurtia's list, which includes a rich white blend of the Rhône grapes Viognier and Roussanne, a light Pinot Noir lacking texture, a more substantial Tannat with some ripe tannins (and some unripe ones), and an improving red blend of Tannat and Cabernet Franc; and, finally, Dante Irurtia Reserva del Virrey, a more concentrated version of the Dante Irurtia Posada del Virrey range.

Dante Villarino (29)

Sauce, Canelones

Tel: (+598) 03 902095

This emerging producer possesses well-sited (and well-farmed)

right Checking a Tannat for its characteristic aroma of violets, mulberry, and black-cherry.

vineyards on hills near Sauce in Canelones department. During winemaking, the grape destemming machine is placed directly above the red wine fermentation vats. This process allows more berries to go into the vat whole, rather than crushed, producing a notably cleaner and more vibrant style of red wines. Of these, Merlot and Tannat show the greatest potential clarity.

De Lucca
See by Reinaldo de Lucca

Don Adelio Ariano
See Ariano

Don Balvino
See Montes Toscanini

Don Luis
See Los Cerros de San Juan

Don Pascual
See Establecimiento Juanicó

Don Próspero
See Pizzorno

Don Santiago
See Santiago Giacobbe

Duilio Piuma (25)
Las Piedras, Canelones
Tel: (+598) 02 364 5960;
dpiuma@montevideo.com.uy
This small producer in Las Piedras, Canelones department, produces simple, fruity wines under the Piuma, Piuma My Personal, and Santa Clara labels.

El Alpino (30)

Sauce, Canelones
Tel: (+598) 02 940437;
kchiap@internet.com.uy

This small winery owned by the Chiappella family farms good vineyards in Sauce, Canelones department. Karina Chiappella, who is in her twenties, took over from her father in 2001, and already her wines show clear aromas and elegant, refreshing fruit, thanks to winemaking techniques inspired by California, where she studied. The wines sell under the J. Chiappella and J. Chiappella Roble (when the wines are oak-aged) labels. Unoaked varietal red wines made from Cabernet Franc, Cabernet Sauvignon, and Tannat are lively, ripe, and expressive. The oak-aged dry white Chardonnay and the red blend of Tannat and Cabernet Sauvignon show clean, harmonious flavours.

El Laurel (11)

Camino Las Toscas
Colonia Valdense, Colonia
Tel: (+598) 55 88944

This charming producer of pleasant wine for local consumption is based among bucolic, rolling farmland at Colonia Valdense, in Colonia department.

Establecimiento Juanicó (21)

Juanicó, Canelones
Tel: (+598) 02 902 8888;
www.juanico.com

Juanicó is the dominant producer of fine wine with the VCP designation in the Uruguayan market, and has a 25% share of fine wine sales. Its vineyards in the Juanicó subregion of Canelones department are the largest in Uruguay. Juanicó's owners, the influential Deicas family, are moving towards organic management. The winery's underground barrel cellars date from the 1840s, while the modernized winemaking area above looks like a UFO, and was built by the French to make brandy. After the end of the Second World War, these cellars were used by the Uruguayan government to produce brandy under ANCAP, the Administración Nacional de Combustibles, Alcohol y Portland. Uruguay had been one of the major lenders of money to France to help the country to defeat the Nazis, and after the war ended France repaid part of its war debt to Uruguay with the Juanicó vineyards, and gave Uruguay the right to call its brandy Cognac. Uruguay is the only non-French country in the world with this right. (The British repaid their war debt by giving Uruguay public utilities such as water, electricity, telephone service and the railways, which the British had built between the World Wars). Juanicó produces wines under the Juanicó and Familia Deicas labels. These value-for-money, clean, easy drinking wines are gaining recognition in demanding foreign markets. Juanicó's Don Pascual range is named after Pascual Harriague, who brought the Tannat grape to Uruguay from France in the nineteenth century. The Don Pascual wines are approachable, rather than blockbuster, styles, with Tannat and Chardonnay the most consistent. Juanicó's top red wine is Preludio ("Prelude"). This is an unfiltered wine blended from up to five grape varieties, including Cabernet Sauvignon, Merlot, Petit Verdot, and Tannat. It is sold under individual batch or lot numbers and combines flavours of ripe fruit with vanilla-rich oak from barrel-ageing. The oak flavours in Preludio need a couple of years to settle down once the wine has been bottled. *See also* Bright Brothers Uruguay, above.

Estancia del Rey Rosado

See Zubizarreta

Euzkodeya Rosado

See Zubizarreta

Faisan

See Traversa

Favretto (41)

Pando, Canelones
Tel: (+598) 02 293 9317;
favredra@adinet.com.uy

This medium-quality producer of the Favretto and Viños Hogareño wines is based in Pando in Canelones department. Beef and vegetables (mainly carrots, plus Swiss chard, beetroots, and leeks) are also farmed.

Ferle (23)

Canelones
Tel: (+598) 332 4722;
ferleltda@hotmail.com

This family owned producer has vineyards immediately west of Canelones town. Ferle's medium-quality red wines, made from Merlot and Tannat, are better than the whites. Wines labelled Casco Noble are oak-aged (*casco* means "oak cask").

Fiesta de San Juan

See Los Cerros de San Juan

Filgueira (39)

Cuchilla Verde, Canelones
Tel: (+598) 2336 6868;
vybfilgueria@netgate.com.uy
Filgueira's vineyards and winery are in Cuchilla Verde, Canelones department. Since 1999, teams from France have managed the winery. The wines, under the Casa Filgueira and Filgueira Roble (when oak-aged) labels, are more consistent and richer as a result. Reds from Cabernet Sauvignon, Merlot, and Tannat show unusually sweet tannins, while whites from Sauvignon Blanc and Sauvignon Gris are full-bodied and direct. Filgueira is one of the most-improved Uruguayan wineries in recent years.

Fond de Cave

See Santa Rosa

Gianni Secchi

See Secchi

Gota de Flor

See Leonardo Falcone

INAVI

Las Piedras, Canelones
Tel: (+598) 236 43486;
inavi@adinet.com.uy
INAVI stands for Instituto Nacional de Vitivinicultura (the National Wine Institute of Uruguay). It controls wine production in Uruguay, and levies tax on each bottle produced. Thus, the INAVI stamp appears on all wine labels.

J.&F. Lurton Uruguay (3)

Tel: (+33) 05 57 55 12 12;
jflurton@jflurton.com
This joint venture between the Bordeaux-based Lurton brothers and Vinos Finos J. Carrau SA was established in 1998 to produce the Casa Luntro and Casilla Dorada brands. The wines are made at the Cerro Chapeu winery in Rivera. While perfectly drinkable, these are the Lurton brothers' least convincing wines in their South American portfolio (*see also* J.&F. Lurton Argentina, p.135 and J.&F. Lurton Chile, p.66).

J. Chiappella

See El Alpino

Juan Marichal (19)

See Marichal

Juan Toscanini (17)

Canelón Chico
Tel: (+598) 02 368 9696;
www.toscaniniwines.com
This emerging producer is based in Canelón Chico in Canelones department. Its wines are commendably clean but rather light. They include decent Sauvignon Blanc under the Toscanini label, oak-aged Chardonnay under the Toscanini Roble label, and oak-aged Tannat under the Toscanini Roble Best Selection label. Juan Toscanini is distinct from Montes Toscanini (Toscanini Hnos), below.

Jubileum

See Los Cerros de San Juan

Las Brujas

See Plaza Vidiella

Leonardo Falcone (4)

Paysandú
Tel: (+598) 72 27718;
lfalcone@adinet.com.uy
Falcone is the leading producer in Paysandú department, North West Uruguay. It owns three well-sited vineyards and two well-maintained wineries around Paysandú town. The wines are: Gota de Flor, decent dry rosé Tannat made by running off pink juice from the red wine tanks early in fermentation (hence "*gota de flor*," which means "flower drop"); Leonardo Falcone, Chardonnay with some barrel-ageing, with faint but clear fruit flavours; Santa Cecilia, simple, fruity, early-drinking Tannat and Merlot; and Abuelo Domingo, a range of two dry red wines including a Cabernet Sauvignon from young but potentially interesting vines, and a Tannat, made from much older vines, the thick fruit of which is made more elegant by the addition of about 20% old-vine Merlot. The Falcone wines sell effortlessly in the domestic market (including in the winery's shop), but are of export quality.

Los Cerros de San Juan (9)

Los Cerros de San Juan, Colonia
Tel: (+598) 02 481 7200;
www.LosCerrosdeSanJuan.com.uy
This is one of Uruguay's most historic wine producers. Its winery is said to be the oldest in Uruguay,

dating from 1872. The winery, and the company's vineyards, are located midway between the port of Colonia del Sacramento and the town of Carmelo in Colonia department. Until 2001, the wines produced were extremely disappointing, given the location and the age of some of the vineyards. Labels used include: Cuna de Piedra ("cradle of stones"), a premium oak-aged range; Don Luis, a Tempranillo; Fiesta de San Juan; Jubileum, a special-release Tannat; Los Cerros de San Juan; Mignon, an unoaked Merlot; a red, white, and rosé line called Mil Botellas; Sensual, an off-dry white blend of Gewurztraminer and Riesling; Sol Rosado, a dry rosé Tannat; and Soleado, a fortified sweet wine made from Riesling. This estate also breeds beef cattle and Quarter Horses.

Los Pinos (10)

Colonia Suiza, Colonia
Tel: (+598) 55 45286
Pine trees (*pinos*) surround this whitewashed winery in Colonia Suiza in Colonia department. Los Pinos was founded in 1923 by Italians but is now run by Basque immigrants. Old vines and a non-interventionist winemaking approach contribute to some characterful wines.

Luis Trombotti (35)

Cap Artigas, Canelones
Tel: (+598) 288 3701
This family owned vineyard and winery, located in Montevideo's Cap Artigas suburb, produces medium-quality wines from vines which are located within seven kilometres (five miles) of the South Atlantic at Atlántida, Canelones department.

Marichal

Los Cerillos, Canelones
Tel: (+598) 33 24926;
bmarichal@adinet.com.uy
Marichal's vineyards at Los Cerillos in Canelones department are exposed to the wind, so the vines can dry quickly after rainfall, which reduces the risk of disease and dilution. In 2002, light, scented wines were produced under the Juan Marichal and Marichal Reserve/Colección brands.

Mignon

See Los Cerros de San Juan

Mil Botellas

See Los Cerros de San Juan

Misurara (12)

San José
Tel: (+598) 034262
This family owned winery has Sicilian origins and is based in San José department. The winery contains metal fermentation tanks originally designed to make beer. Misurara produces light, fresh wines of medium quality.

left Sorting a catch of shellfish near Altántida.

Moizo (22)

Juanicó, Canelones
Tel: (+598) 33 59686;
www.moizohnos.com

In 1856, the Moizo family left Piedmont, Italy, for Uruguay. Six generations later, they are producing clean, above-average wines with good character from vineyards around Juanicó, in Canelones department. Their Moizo Hermanos range includes: Chardonnay in both oak-aged and unoaked forms (with the unoaked version showing greater harmony prior to the 2001 vintage and the oak-aged version gaining in elegance from 2002); reds from Merlot (one of Uruguay's most Bordeaux-like, with fruit cake flavours and agreeably firm tannin), and Tannat. A Merlot/Tannat blend tastes somewhat green (both grape varieties are fermented together, even though they ripen in the vineyard at different times) but this is more a reflection of the high yield of grapes than any deficiency in the winemaking. Moizo is a small producer to follow.

Montes Toscanini (Toscanini Hnos) (26)

Las Piedras, Canelones
Tel: (+598) 236 44320;
eleeme@info-red.com

Montes Toscanini's winery is at Las Piedras in Canelones department, but its wines are made from grapes sourced from contracted growers elsewhere in Canelones department. The wines can lack consistency, but at their best they show distinct, appealing flavours. They sell as:

Don Balvino, for basic quality; Carlos Montes Reserva, a Tannat that combines lively fruit and solid oak flavours; and Montes Toscanini Reserva Familiar, which includes a concentrated but unoaked Merlot. Montes Toscanini is distinct from Juan Toscanini (*see* above).

Noble Bocoy

See Santiago Giacobbe

Padre Barreto

See Bruzzone y Sciutto

Piedra del Toro

See Rosifior

Pisano (15)

Progreso, Canelones
Tel: (+598) 02 368 9077;
www.pisanowines.com

The Pisano family produce Uruguay's most complex range of wines. Yet just ten years ago, the Pisanos produced bulk wine for the local market. The brothers, Daniel, Eduardo, and Gustavo Pisano, who live around the family winery in Progreso in Canelones department, sparked the quality revolution here. They decided that, as well as improving their knowledge of winemaking, they would have to improve the quality of their grapes. They opted for lower grape yields to get more flavour, and later harvesting dates to get more ripeness. Grapes are sourced from Pisano's two estate vineyards and from local grape growers within Canelones. The winery is tiny but crammed with dozens of small, white-washed concrete vats. These

vats enable the brothers to vinify separately the different grape varieties grown on different soil types (clay or limestone), allowing potentially complex blends to be assembled later on. The Pisanos say: "We produce flavourful, long-lasting wines with distinctive Uruguayan character, oriented to the high-quality niche of the market." And it's not boasting, it's true. A key winemaking influence here from the middle of the 1990s was Danish consultant Hans Vinding-Diers of Noemí, in Argentina (*see* p.139), who describes the Pisanos as "extremely good pupils, who were very quick to learn." The wines are: Arretxea, a structured, intense, appetizing, barrel-aged blend of Cabernet Sauvignon, Merlot, and Tannat (one-third each), which is one of Uruguay's most age-worthy, genuinely complex wines; Polo Sur ("South Pole"), a soft-textured but serious red with ripe flavours and strong oak influence, produced exclusively for the UK; Primera Viña, an unoaked, lighter style range produced for the USA, which includes dry rosé Cabernet Franc, ripe but not overripe Cabernet Sauvignon, a warm, inviting Merlot/Tannat blend, a distinctive, delicate, Tannat exhibiting hedgerow fruit, and three very individual dry white wines, including an aromatic Torrontés Riojano, which is whole-bunch pressed to avoid bitterness, a straw-coloured Trebbiano Toscano from old vines, and a mineral-rich Viognier/Chardonnay, first produced in 2001 (3,000 bottles) which is dense, despite being made from young vines; and RPF (Reserva Personal de la Familia), a barrel-aged range of red and white wines. The RPF single-varietal red wines, a Cabernet Sauvignon, a Merlot, and a Tannat, all show dense, complex fruit flavours supported by, rather than dominated by, the oak (a Pinot Noir is less successful in this respect). The RPF Chardonnay has rich oak flavours, reminiscent of good-quality white Rioja from Spain. Pisano is emblematic about all that is best about Uruguay: a small, family-owned vineyard and winery prepared to sacrifice quantity for quality.

Piuma
See Duilio Piuma

Pizzorno (18)
Canelón Chico, Canelones
Tel: (+598) 8368 2220;
apizzorno@info-red.com
The Pizzorno family run the oldest winery in the small town of Canelón Chico in Canelones department. Fortunately, the Pizzornos are not slaves to their own history, and produce modern, fruity, and increasingly attractive wines in both still and sparkling forms. Their main brand is called Don Próspero. Since 1997, this range has consistently improved, and it now rivals any in Uruguay for deftness of fruit. Two Chardonnays (one oak-aged, the other unoaked) show balance. Tannat is made in two styles: a medium-bodied, cherry scented wine fermented from uncrushed

grapes (to obtain fruit rather than tannin); and a deeper, tar-scented wine fermented from crushed grapes. The Don Próspero Reserve red (debut vintage 2000, 3,000 bottles) blends Cabernet Sauvignon, Merlot, and Tannat (all three from crushed grapes and barrel-aged) with younger-vine Tannat (whole berry fermentation, unoaked) to complex effect. The Don Próspero Tannat/ Merlot blend has more ripeness than the single-varietal Cabernet Sauvignon. Pizzorno also makes a lighter Tannat/Merlot blend for the UK market called "Why Try Uruguay?" Its refreshing cherry fruit should tempt more wine drinkers into trying Uruguayan wine. Pizzorno's inventive winemaking augurs well for the future of Uruguayan wine.

Plaza Vidiella (28)
Canelones
Tel: (+598) 33 20307;
www.plazavidiella.com
This quality oriented, family owned producer has well-equipped cellars in the centre of Canelones town, at the very heart of Uruguay's main wine-growing area. Well-managed estate vineyards cover several distinct sites in Canelones at Las Brujas and Los Cerillos, as well as one at the town of Mendoza, where Canelones department borders Florida. These provide intriguing options for creative blending, and, since the 2000 vintage, have been increasingly well exploited. Basic quality wines are sold locally in

bag-in-box as Vino Cotidiano ("daily wine"). The export ranges, 100 Años and Las Brujas ("the witches"), include: rich, scented Chardonnay containing a little Viognier, which gives the wine a twist of peach-skin flavour in the aftertaste; an appealing, clean-tasting and subtle Syrah made from vines planted in 1991; a distinctive Sauvignon Blanc with the rich texture one would expect of this grape variety in Uruguay; and elegant, increasingly complex red blends made from Tannat/Merlot and Tannat/ Cabernet Sauvignon.

Polo Sur
See Pisano

Preludio
See Establecimiento Juanicó

Primera Viña
See Pisano

Reinaldo De Lucca (16)
El Colorado, Canelones
Tel: (+598) 2367 8076;
reideluca@adinet.com.uy
Reinaldo de Lucca is Uruguay's most garrulous, idiosyncratic, even brilliant, winemaker. He became trilingual in order to gain degrees and doctorates in grape-growing and winemaking from France, the USA and Uruguay. He owns four small vineyards at Cuatro Piedras, El Colorado (near his winery), and Canelón Chico in Canelones department. Low yields of grapes per vine, eco-friendly wine-growing, and non-interventionist winemaking

contribute to a distinctive range. He is "a man who dares", prepared to take risks. The wines sell as: Cresta Roja, for basic quality; and De Lucca, which includes concentrated varietal white wines made from Marsanne or Sauvignon Blanc, bright, berry scented, single-varietal reds made from Cabernet Sauvignon, Merlot, Syrah, and Tannat, and a sumptuous Merlot/Tannat red blend. A British Master of Wine once described a De Lucca Cabernet Sauvignon as "not typical of the grape variety", which, far from offending De Lucca, pleased him enormously. He wants his wines to be distinctive rather than typical, and he undoubtedly achieves his aim.

Río de la Plata
See Bodegas del Plata

Rosifior (36)
Cap Artigas, Canelones
Tel: (+598) 288 4105;
rosifiorltda@hotmail.com
Rosifior's winery in Montevideo's Cap Artigas suburb belongs to the De Maio brothers. They produce clean, basic dry rosé Merlot, crisp Sauvignon Blanc, and cherry scented Tannat/Cabernet Sauvignon red wines under the "Piedra del Toro" label from vineyards at Empalme Olmos and Pando in Canelones department.

RPF (Reserva Personal de la Familia)
See Pisano

Santa Cecilia
See Leonardo Falcone

Santa Clara
See Duilio Piuma

Santa Rosa (37)
Ruta 5, Canelones
Tel: (+598) 02 320 9921/23;
srosaventas@netgate.com.uy
Santa Rosa is one of Uruguay's most-historic and most-respected wine producers, known for its "Fond de Cave" sparkling wines. These have more than 80% of the local market share for sparkling wines. The Santa Rosa winery at Colón, on the outskirts of Montevideo, is a cross between something one might find in France's Champagne region and a winery in Communist-era Eastern Europe. Massive underground cellars can hold 300,000 bottles of the Fond de Cave sparklers, which are made in the same way as Champagne (using the "traditional method" of secondary fermentation in the bottle). Meanwhile, above-ground, the high, greying brick warehouses could come from Bulgaria. Santa Rosa's vineyards are in the Juanicó and Las Violetas subregions of Canelones department. The company's still wines are sold as: Château Fond de Cave, a basic range of clean, early drinking wines; Santa Rosa, of which the best are the oak-aged Cabernet Sauvignon and Tannat wines suffixed "del Museo;" and Vinos de Punte del Este, named after the popular Uruguayan Atlantic beach resort of Punte del Este, where Santa Rosa sells much of its wine.

Santiago Giacobbe (43)
Montevideo
Tel: (+598) 02 223200;
sgiaco@adinet.com.uy
Producer of somewhat simple but pleasant-tasting wines under the Don Santiago and Noble Bocoy labels, from vineyards at Manga in Canelones department.

Secchi (13)
San José
Tel: (+598) 0345 2987
This above-average producer in San José department is concentrating sales of its pleasant wines under the Gianni Secchi brand in the Uruguayan market.

Selección Zubizarreta
See Zubizarreta

Sensual
See Los Cerros de San Juan

Soleado
See Los Cerros de San Juan

Sol Rosado
See Los Cerros de San Juan

Stagnari (31)
La Paz, Canelones
Tel: (+598) 02 362 2137;
lapuebla@adinet.com.uy
Stagnari is one of Uruguay's largest wine exporters, and it has a reputation for producing rich-tasting wines. The grapes for these come from vineyards in Salto, in North West Uruguay, and from La Paz in Canelones in South Uruguay, where Stagnari is based. Pascual Harriague, who was one of the pioneers of

Uruguayan wine-growing, planted Stagnari's vineyard in Salto back in the 1870s. It is claimed that Harriague brought the first Tannat grapevines to Uruguay (some people still refer to Tannat as "Harriague"). Tannat remains, as does Harriague. He died in France in 1894, but was buried in Salto.

Sunybell

Montevideo
Tel: (+598) 02 322 9003;
sunybell@hotmail.com
Sunybell is an association of thirteen wine-growing families from Canelones department, including Favretto, Luis Trombotti, Moizo, Montes Toscanini, and Rosifior. As well as making their own wines, these families collectively produce the concentrated, if rather coarse, Silver River brand (Silver River replaced a wine called Del Mar Dulce, or "of the soft sea"). Collectively, the Sunybell growers account for 6% of Uruguayan wine production, and, with such a large amount of grapes and wine to select from, they should be more strongly representative of Uruguay's undoubted potential.

Sust

See Vinos Finos J. Carrau SA

Tessa – A. Ltda

See Antigua Bodega San José

Toscanini

See Juan Toscanini and Montes Toscanini (Toscanini Hnos)

Traversa (38)

Montevideo
Tel: (+598) 02 220035;
www.traversahnos.com.uy
Traversa is a large, Montevideo-based producer making uncomplicated wines for early drinking, from both estate and purchased South Uruguay grapes. The winery is one of the most modern in Uruguay. Traversa's best wines are sold under their own name, while a cheaper range bears the Faisan ("pheasant") label.

Trombotti

See Luis Trombotti

Varela Zarranz (40)

Juaquín Suarez, Canelones
Tel: (+598) 02 364 4587;
www.varelazarranz.com
Uruguay's fourth largest wine producer is also one of its most adaptable and forward-thinking. The winery is hidden behind a colonnade of century-old olive trees at Joaquín Suarez in Canelones department. There are two vineyards: one, at Cuatro Piedras, is on heavy, iron-rich soil which gives dense, powerful wines with mineral-rich aromas; the other vineyard, around the Joaquín Suarez winery, is nearer the South Atlantic ocean. Wines from the latter taste more elegant as a result of their proximity to the modifying influence of the ocean. The wines are sold as Cuatro Piedras (or VUDU for the domestic market). The best wines for export bear the Varela Zarranz or Varela Zarranz Roble (when oak-aged) labels. Since 2000, these wines

have been made with help from winemaking consultants from France and New Zealand, but to their extreme credit, the owners here are keen to retain a strong Uruguayan character in their wines. The Tannat is one of Uruguay's richest and most complex, dominated by classic black cherry flavours with truffle and forest fruit; the Merlot is a juicy mix of plum and cherry; the Cabernet Sauvignon has vibrant colour and energetic structure; the Chardonnay has some elegance but rather more flavour; the Sauvignon Blanc is crisp, and typically dense for Uruguay. As the vineyard management here improves along with the winemaking, this estate could become one of Uruguay's best.

Vieja Calera

See Zubizarreta

Viña del Sur

See Améndola Hermanos Y. Boido

Viña Santa Rosa

See Santa Rosa

Viñas de Aitona

See Zubizarreta

Viñedo de Los Vientos (42)

Atlántida, Canelones
Tel: (+598) 037 21662;
vvientos@adinet.com.uy
The "Vineyard of the Winds" is based five kilometres (three miles) from the South Atlantic at Atlántida in Canelones department. Benign sea breezes can dry the vines, and thus concentrate the juice in the grapes, producing wines of complex

aromas and vibrant fruit character. However, winds coming off the sea when it is stormy have blown the winery roof off more than once. Owner Pablo Fallabrino works with a wide range of grape varieties, and practices sustainable wine-growing. The basic range under the Viñedo de Los Vientos label includes: a Cabernet Sauvignon with the depth and clarity one hopes for from France, and Tannat with a strong tannic backbone. The oak-aged Viñedo de Los Vientos Eolo Gran Reserva is a red blend of around 80% Tannat (100% oak-aged) and 20% Ruby Cabernet, which combines red and black fruit in equal measure. A delicious dry white wine, Viñedo de Los Vientos Summertime, is made from Gewurztraminer.

Viñedos y Bodegas Bella Unión

See Calvinor

Vino Cotidiano

See Plaza Vidiella

Vinos Cis

See CIS

Vinos de La Cruz (8)

La Cruz, Florida
Tel: (+598) 350 2115;
www.vinosdelacruz.com
Vinos de La Cruz is the most isolated winery in Uruguay. It was created as the agricultural town of La Cruz in La Florida department in 1877. At that time, Uruguay was undergoing profound social change. Itinerant peasants on horses (*gauchos*) were reined in as land was divided up into enclosures for a new wave of European immigrants. The town of

La Cruz ("The Cross") became a sanctuary for the displaced. Now privately owned, Vinos de La Cruz is the only winery in Uruguay with certified organic (*ecológico*) vineyards and wines approved for diabetics (it also produces eggs, polo ponies, dairy calves, and timber). Wine quality has improved dramatically from 2000, but is not yet reliable enough. The winery has changed little since its creation, and older wooden vats are still sometimes used, giving the wines undesirable flavours. However, the winery's vaulted roof, wrought-iron columns, and granite wine vats are extremely picturesque, and reflect the Basque traditions of the Arocena family who own Vinos de La Cruz. The best white wine, green-hued and green-tasting, is made from the Arriloba grape, while the best reds come from Tannat and Malbec rather than the insubstantial Pinot Noir.

Vinos de Punte del Este

See Santa Rosa

Vinos Finos J. Carrau SA

Montevideo
Tel: (+598) 02 320 0238;
www.carrauwines@st.com.uy
The Carrau family celebrated 250 years of winegrowing in 2002, having planted their first vines in Spain in 1752. In the 1930s, they planted vines at Las Violetas, Canelones department (South Uruguay), producing "Sust", Uruguay's first sparkling wines. The Las Violetas vineyards, and the winery at nearby Colón, are known as Castel Pujol (*see* above).

The other, younger side of the Carrau business, Cerro Chapeu (*see* above), is located in Rivera, North Uruguay. Castel Pujol and Cerro Chapeu have a deserved reputation within Uruguay for leading the industry. Now they have some welcome competition from a new generation of Uruguayan producers, which should contribute to raising the standards across the country.

Viños Hogareño

See Favretto

VUDU

See Varela Zarranz

YvY

See Améndola Hermanos Y. Boido

Zubizarreta (7)

Carmelo, Colonia
Tel: (+598) 542 5160;
pzubiza@adinet.com.uy
This family winery with Basque origins, based in Carmelo in the Colonia department, produces the following, improving brands: Estancia del Rey Rosado, a dry rosé wine made from Merlot; Euzkodeya Rosado, a dry rosé made from Cabernet Sauvignon; Selección Zubizarreta, the basic range of still, varietal red and white wines, plus sparkling Muscat in white and rosé forms; Vieja Calera ("old kiln"), a decent red wine made from Merlot; and Viñas de Aitona ("aitona" is the Basque word for "grandfather"), a premium range of varietal red wines including light Cabernet Sauvignon and more substantial Tannat wines.

bolivia

Everyone knows that Bolivia produces coca leaf, the key raw material for cocaine. Yet few know that Bolivia produces wine. In fact, Bolivia's vineyards have the world's highest average altitude, nearly 2,700 m (8,900 ft). The Andes splits in two, like a wishbone, across the country. Vineyards lie in the spurs of the westerly of the two ranges, the Cordillera Occidental. Visitors to Bolivia are advised to prepare against altitude sickness even before entering the country.

Bolivia's high-altitude vineyards (the highest vineyards in Europe, for comparison, are in Italy's Valle d'Aosta, at 1,300 m/4,264 ft) receive stronger sunlight than those nearer sea level, where the sun's rays have farther to travel. This makes ripening dark-skinned grape varieties such as Carignan and Grenache, which thrive in Mediterranean climates, easier. The resulting wines can develop deep colours, intense aromas and soft, mouth-filling textures.

However, the strong sunlight means that white grapes and Bordeaux varieties such as Cabernet Sauvignon, Merlot, and Cabernet Franc, which prefer cooler conditions, can taste "baked." Another possible negative effect of altitude may be "atypical ageing flavour," which is linked to ultra-violet (UV) light radiation from the sun. Grapes need sunlight to ripen, but in high-altitude conditions, UV levels increase. The grapes protect themselves by producing certain

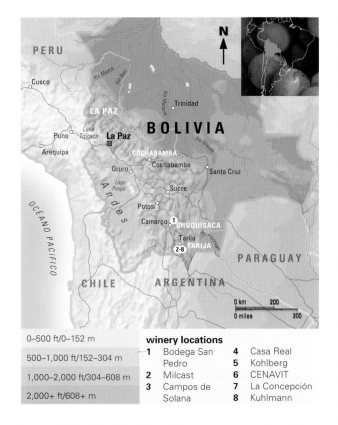

compounds in their pulp and extra pigments in their skins. These extra pigments may create unusual flavours in the wine, but they are only evident once the wine has been in bottle for many years. But, as most Bolivian wines produced today are designed to be drunk soon after bottling, this potential problem may not be much of an issue. Also, global warming means that UV radiation levels have increased even at sea level. So, if atypical ageing flavour exists, it may be a global phenomenon rather than one linked only to altitude.

More positively, scientists suspect that moderate consumption of high-altitude wines may reduce the risk of heart disease. The "anti-sunburn" compounds formed in grapes grown under high-UV light conditions probably contain above-average levels of substances that help circulate blood around the body. What's more, Bolivia is losing its negative reputation over cocaine after a recent USA-backed "dignity plan" removed ninety per cent of the country's coca fields. Despite limited production, Bolivia's wine producers would like us to think that the country is on the verge of establishing a more positive reputation, one for producing wines with life-enhancing properties.

Bolivian Wine Regions

Four of Bolivia's nine provinces have vineyards: La Paz, Cochabamba, Chuquisaca, and Tarija. Vineyards in La Paz and Cochabamba are used mainly for Singani, Bolivian brandy (*see* below). Only half of Bolivia's 4,000 hectares (10,000 acres) of vines are used to produce wine, making Bolivia's wine vineyards fifty times smaller than those of Chile and Argentina.

CHUQUISACA PROVINCE

Chuquisaca is bounded to the east by Santa Cruz, Bolivia's largest province, and by Paraguay. To the south is Tarija, Bolivia's only significant wine province. To the north is Cochabamba province; and to the west is Potosí, the highest city on earth, where Spanish conquistadors once mined the world's largest-ever

left Adobe houses made from dark, desert earth contrast with the intense Bolivian sky.

deposits of silver. The silver brought from these mines back to Europe played an important part in changing the world from a barter economy to a banking-based one. For Chuquisaca's wine-growers, Potosí's legacy is effluent-ridden irrigation water for, although the silver has gone, tin is now mined (Bolivia is the world's fifth largest producer). The Río Grande and Río Chico, which flow from Potosí, are the two main rivers irrigating Camargo, Chuquisaca's main wine subregion. Vineyards are boxed between the Río Grande and the Río Pilaya hills at 2,400 m (7,900 ft). Chuquisaca's main producer is Bodega San Pedro.

TARIJA

Tarija province, in the extreme southeast of Bolivia, is the heartland of Bolivian wine, and, in 1807, it became the first Bolivian region to declare independence from Spain. The rest of the country had to wait eighteen years for the "liberator," Simón Bolívar, to free it from colonial rule and give his name to the new republic. Tarija's vineyards are located in valleys to the south of Tarija town, which dates from 1574 and lies on the Guadalquivir River. This river, and its tributary the Camacho, provide irrigation for fruit as well as vineyards. Otherwise the landscape is barren, with small trees such as the *churqui*, with its sharp needles, and the needle-less *chañar* the only obstacles for the goats and sheep that roam freely.

Tarija's wines are generally light, for immediate drinking. This is partly because most vines are young (twenty years old or younger) but also because of Tarija's light, sandy soils. These attract nematodes, so the vines are grafted onto resistant rootstocks (*see also* Casablanca Valley in Chile, p.25). Around 6.5 million bottles of wine are produced each year in Tarija, most consumed locally. A further 6.5 million bottles are smuggled in across Tarija's border with Argentina each year. The Argentine wine is cheaper than the wine produced locally from grapes farmed by the peasants who control eighty-five per cent of Tarija's vineyards.

Bolivia's geography and corruption culture means that smuggling is nearly impossible to stop, so the future of many of Tarija's vineyard smallholdings looks bleak. Tarija's larger wine producers are finding it less of a problem to survive, because they sell to major supermarkets where smuggled wine is not accepted. These producers are Campos de Solana, Casa Real, Kohlberg, Kuhlmann, La Concepción, and Milcast.

Bolivian Wine Label Terms

VINO DE ALTURA Means "high-altitude wine;" the term has only semi-official significance on Bolivian wine labels.

Bolivian Wine Styles – Introduction

Bolivians probably spend more time discussing the relative merits of soya beans, coffee, cotton, corn, sugar cane, rice, potatoes, timber, and coca, all of which are much more significant crops than wine for Bolivia's economy. Beer and locally produced Singani brandy (*see* below) are easily the nation's most popular drinks. Nevertheless, Bolivians are switching (slowly) from drinking whiskey with their meals to drinking wine; wine consumption averages two bottles per person per year. Most wine is red and most is sold in Tetrapak cartons and is of the most basic standard. Bolivia's best wineries centre around Tarija and produce light-textured wines that are rich in alcohol and soft fruit.

key facts about bolivia

Bolivian wines are starting to gain **international recognition**, not least for their **"high altitude"** status; most Bolivian wines come from around the town of Tarija in the southeast of the country; grapes like **Carignan and Grenache** seem to cope best with the high altitude and the intense **UV light** this entails; Bolivia's **geographic isolation** and limited production make exporting difficult; smuggling from Argentina is also a threat to local growers.

Bolivian Wine Styles (By Grape Variety)

CABERNET SAUVIGNON (RED)

The best Bolivian Cabernet Sauvignons combine classic blackcurrant and cedar flavours with Bordeaux-like elegance. *See* La Concepción, Milcast, Campos de Solana, and CENAVIT.

CARIGNAN (RED)

This earthy, some would say coarse, Mediterranean grape is capable of producing enjoyable wines in Bolivia. It thrives in the heat and is known locally as Cariñena. *See* CENAVIT.

CHARDONNAY (WHITE)

Chardonnay produces acceptable, but unexciting, wine in Bolivia, as winemakers work out how best to style their white wines. *See* La Concepción.

FRENCH COLOMBARD (WHITE)

French Colombard produces crisp wines, light on flavour but useful for blending. *See* Campos de Solana.

GRENACHE OR GARNACHA (RED)

This Mediterranean grape thrives in Bolivia, where it is called Garnacha. The wines have high alcohol levels (up to fifteen per cent) and jammy flavours. *See* CENAVIT.

MALBEC (RED)

This Bordeaux grape produces reasonable wine in Bolivia's hot climate, with a deep colour and a soft texture. *See* Campos de Solana.

MERLOT (RED)

An early ripening Bordeaux grape, Merlot produces high-alcohol wines with low levels of fruit in Bolivia, but expect better-balanced wines as the (mainly young) vines mature.

MUSCAT (WHITE)

Known locally as Moscatel, Muscat is the main grape in Singani brandy (*see* below) but it can produce appealing wine. *See* Campos de Solana and Kuhlmann.

RIESLING (WHITE)

Riesling produces wines of freshness and balance in Bolivia, although German scientists believe it is prone to atypical ageing flavour (*see* p.176). *See* Campos de Solana and La Concepción.

above Salt flats, the remnants of ancient lakes, at Uyuni in the Bolivian Altiplano, where saltpans are five metres (16.4 ft) or more.

SAUVIGNON BLANC (WHITE)

Sauvignon Blanc's characteristic gooseberry aromas tend to become rather subdued in Bolivia's hot daytime temperatures. *See* La Concepción.

Bolivian Wine Styles (Other)

RED WINE BLENDS

As Bolivia tailors its best wines to foreign tastes, expect more Bordeaux-style and Mediterranean-style blends (from more than one grape variety) to emerge. *See* Campos de Solana (Vino Fino Tinto) and Bodega San Pedro (Grand Cru).

FORTIFIED WINES

Bolivia's hot climate is well suited to fortified styles. Bodega San Pedro makes one of the few examples.

Bolivia's Other Drinks

SINGANI BRANDY

Singani is a clear brandy distilled from white Muscat wine. Unlike Chilean or Peruvian Pisco, Singani is distilled twice (not once). Singani originated in Potosí province after the Spanish conquest. *See* Bodega San Pedro, Casa Real, Kuhlmann, and La Concepción.

notable producers

Aranjuez

See Milcast

Bodega San Pedro (1)

Buch Esquina Panamá, La Paz (office)
Tel: (+591) 02 223 344
Bodega San Pedro, one of Bolivia's oldest wine companies, was founded in 1925. It is the only producer of note in Camargo, in Chuquisaca province. Its red wines include a grainy Cabernet Sauvignon for early drinking and a more substantial, fruity blend of several dark-skinned varieties. San Pedro produces Bolivia's only sparkling wines, which get their fizz from injected carbon

dioxide, rather than from a secondary fermentation in bottle (as with Champagne). San Pedro's best wine is a fortified red made in the style of port, with a baked, prune-like taste and about 20% alcohol. Bodega San Pedro's Singani brandies are called San Pedro de Oro, San Pedro de Plata, and Cinteño.

Campos de Solana (3)

Tarija town, Tarija province
Tel: (+591) 04 664 8481;
csolana@cosett.com.bo
Campos de Solana ("Sunny Fields") was founded in 2000 to produce wines for Singani producer Casa

Real (*see* below). Its winery is the most modern in Bolivia. Rather lean Cabernet Sauvignon and Malbec reds are made, as well as neutral dry French Colombard and Riesling whites. These wines should improve once Campos de Solana gains more winemaking experience. An off-dry white Moscatel (French Muscat) is richer, with more appealing flavours than the dry whites have. The most interesting wine, for its dried-fruit and leather flavours, is Vino Fino Tinto, a blend made from Cereza, Criolla, and other varieties brought to South America by the Spanish. Campos de Solana should be an important part of Tarija's wine future.

Casa Real (4)

Tarija town, Tarija province
Tel: (+591) 04 664 8481
Casa Real is owned by three brothers and is known in Bolivia for its Singani brandies: Casa Real Mezclador, Casa Real Primera Clase, Casa Real Gran Singani, and Casa Real Aniversario. These are distilled in traditional gas-fired pot-stills. Casa Real produces wine under the Campos de Solana label (*see* above).

CENAVIT (6)

La Concepción, Tarija
Tel: (+591) 04 613 2014
CENAVIT stands for Centro Nacional de Vitivinícola ("National Wine Research Centre"). It was set up with help from the Spanish government to find which grape varieties work best in Bolivia. CENAVIT's small

left Shoes from the market in the Plaza Luis de Fuentes, Tarija's main square.

vineyard is at Pampa Colorada, near Tarija town. The wines sell under the Vinos de Altura, Pampa Colorada label. CENAVIT's Cabernet Sauvignon is more elegant and balanced than any made in Bolivia so far, and develops blackcurrant and cedar flavours with time in bottle. CENAVIT's Carignan has a striking ruby colour and attractive Mediterranean fruit; its Grenache is rich, succulent, warm, and inviting. Impressive sparkling wine with clear fruit and fine bubbles is made using the same traditional winemaking method and grape varieties as Spanish Cava. CENAVIT must be the only wine research facility in the world that is producing its country's most impressive range of wines.

Cinteño

See Bodega San Pedro

Kohlberg (5)

Tarija town, Tarija province
Tel: (+591) 04 663 6366
The first vines planted around Tarija town were brought by Spanish priests during the sixteenth century. However, Tarija was only taken seriously as a wine producer in the modern era, from 1973, after the Kohlberg family developed vineyards. Tarija's terrain is uneven, but the reddish, sandy soil is light and easily manageable for planting vines. Kohlberg markets its wines enthusiastically to the local market; almost every bus stop, park bench, and café awning around Tarija's main square is emblazoned with its name. Its most balanced red wines come

from hot-climate grapes such as Carignan and Grenache; they are best drunk slightly chilled.

Kuhlmann (8)

Tarija town, Tarija province
kuhlmann@cosett.com.bo
The Kuhlmann family settled in Tarija in 1973 (the same year as the Kohlbergs, above). They distil Tres Estrellas, a Singani brandy, and are developing a luxury resort on the outskirts of the town.

La Concepción (7)

La Concepción, Tarija
Tel: (+591) 04 613 2008;
rujero@olivo.tja.entelnet.bo
La Concepción, based near Tarija town, has nearly 10% of the Bolivian wine market. The highest and coolest of La Concepción's three vineyards at Chaguaya, sixty kilometres (thirty-seven miles) south of Tarija town, reaches 2,100 m (7,888 ft). It grows Sauvignon Blanc and Cabernet Sauvignon. Half an hour's drive from the winery, the Huayrihuana vineyard was planted from 1984. The La Compañia vineyard, next to the winery, was first planted by missionary Jesuits and contains vines more than 200 years old. These are trained up trees, just as the Ancient Greeks grew vines 8,000 years ago. Fortunately, La Concepción's wines are modern Californian rather than Ancient Greek in style, which makes them unique in Bolivia. The basic wines are labelled Viñas de Castilla. The "Concepción" range of single varietals includes Sauvignon Blanc, Riesling, Cabernet

Sauvignon, Merlot, and (best of all in terms of clarity of fruit flavour), Syrah. The top line, Concepción Cepas de Altura, includes oak-influenced Cabernet Sauvignon, the most forceful oak-aged example of this variety in Bolivia, and an appealing Chardonnay. La Concepción's Singani brandies account for around 15% of the local market.

Milcast (2)

Tarija town, Tarija province
milcast@olivo.tja.entelnet.bo
Milcast's winery was built from 1976 in the Aranjuez suburb of Tarija town. The wines are sold under the Aranjuez label, mainly for Bolivian supermarket selections. The range includes probably the best-value Cabernet Sauvignon in Bolivia, a wine with simple texture, but enough cedar and wild-fruit flavours to prompt comparisons with Bordeaux.

Rujero Colección Privada

See La Concepción

San Pedro de Oro

See Bodega San Pedro

San Pedro de Plata

See Bodega San Pedro

Tres Estrellas

See Kuhlmann

Viñas de Castilla

See La Concepción

Vinos de Altura, Pampa Colorada

See CENAVIT

brazil

Mention Brazil, and wine is probably not the drink that instantly springs to mind. Coffee and cachaça, yes; wine, no. But actually, Brazil is South America's third-largest wine producer, after Argentina and Chile. And Brazil not only drinks almost all the wine the country produces, around 300 million bottles annually, but also, to satisfy the high demand, imports wine in bulk from other South American countries (notably Uruguay).

Brazil is South America's most populous country, with 150 million people. Average annual per capita wine consumption is more than two bottles, but, as most Brazilians can't afford wine, the wealthier classes are the main consumers. The wealthy live mostly in the southern half of Brazil, around São Paolo and Rio de Janeiro, and in Brazil's main wine-producing, coastal states of Rio Grande do Sul, Minas Gerais, and Bahia.

Brazil did export wines to Europe and the USA in the 1990s, but then failed to participate in certain world trade agreements, so these markets have been lost. As wine consumption becomes increasingly popular within Brazil, the country's 600-odd wine producers are concentrating on the local market. Don't visit Brazil expecting wines made to suit international palates; in most cases you will be disappointed.

Brazil's hot, humid climate encourages fungal diseases in vines. Vines of European origin (Chardonnay, Merlot, and the like) are particularly susceptible to fungal diseases, while those of American origin are rarely affected by fungus. Sadly, wines made with American vines produce grapes with an odd "foxy" odour. A compromise is to plant "hybrids", vine crossings produced by cross-pollination of European and American vines. Hybrids dominate Brazil's vineyards. The wines produced are of decent quality, albeit with a hint of "foxiness". However, trade laws forbid wines made from hybrid vines entering Europe – another reason why Brazil's wine industry is likely to remain inward-looking.

German researchers have recently developed hybrids that make wines which taste more like those from European vines; these could thrive in Brazil, remaining disease-free, while producing wine with the flavours international palates demand. It may be a decade before they are planted, however, and if successful there would need to be a change in European law before they could be sold in the EU.

Brazil's best wines are sparkling – conveniently appropriate for the country's samba and carnival image. Most of the sparklers are made from Muscat grapes, in the style of Italy's Asti. Brazil's suitability for sparkling wine and its potentially huge domestic wine market have encouraged foreign drinks companies such as Bacardi-Martini (*see* De Lantier) and

left The Amazon River, named after that legendary female race, flows through Peru, Colombia, and Brazil on its way to the Atlantic.

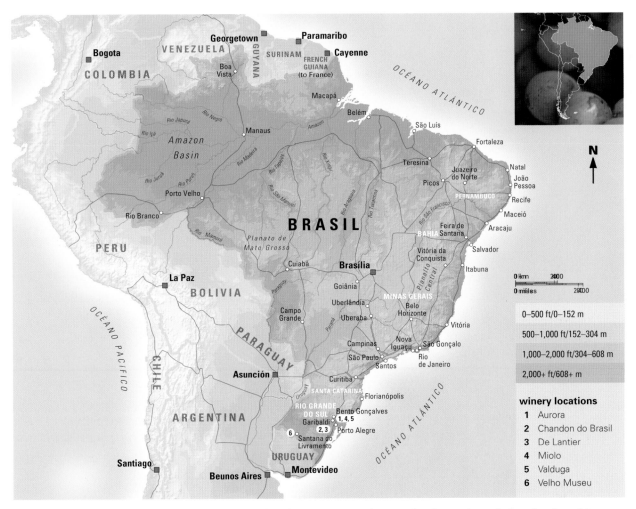

Champagne producer Moët & Chandon (*see* Chandon do Brasil) to establish Brazilian wine operations.

Brazil's most northerly vineyards are in the states of Bahia and Pernambuco along the Vale do São Francisco. Proximity to the Equator means that five crops of grapes can be harvested every two years if vines are pruned and irrigated with quantity, rather than quality, in mind. Miolo owns Syrah/Shiraz vineyards here, and also sells some of its Muscat grapes to Chandon do Brasil for sparkling wines.

Farther south, vineyards are being developed in the state of Minas Gerais by coffee producers keen to diversify. Vineyards along the Peixe River in the state of Santa Catarina are predominantly planted with hybrid or table grapes, leaving the state of Rio Grande do Sul with ninety per cent of Brazil's "fine" wine vineyards, around 30,000 ha (74,130 acres). Most are in the verdant Serra Gaúcha hills around the towns of Garibaldi and Bento Gonçalves.

A wine tourist route called the Vale dos Vinhedos is attracting significant numbers of Europeans and North Americans. Wine producers are very welcoming; they often serve very good food and need no encouragement to party (take note, Bordeaux and California). Rio Grande do Sul's least-accessible vineyards are farther south, near the town of Santana do Livramento, on the border with Uruguay's Rivera region (*see* pp.158–159).

Aurora (1)

Bento Gonçalves

Tel: (+55) 54 455 2000;

aurora@vinicolaaurora.com.br

This huge wine cooperative is the most-visited wine attraction in Brazil. Each year, more than 100,000 visitors make their way through the cooperative's cellars in Bento Gonçalves. Winemaking here improved greatly in the mid-1990s, when foreign consultants from the UK, Australia, and New Zealand were taken on board to advise local winemakers. Hygiene was improved, and the styles of wines that Aurora produced were modernized. However, the winemakers were not quite so successful in persuading all of the local growers to pick their grapes later (and thus riper). As the cooperative has more than 1,300 member/growers, who own a (very small) average of one hectare (2.5 acres) each, implementing a coherent policy on picking dates is extremely difficult. When the grapes arrive at the cooperative, keeping the best (*i.e.*, the ripest) separate from the others is problematic, as the decisions about quality and ripeness are usually made as the trucks bearing the grapes turn up at the weigh station. All things considered, Aurora's Chardonnays are clean, balanced wines with plenty of body and a distinctive, somewhat "oily" texture. Red wines made from Merlot and Cabernet Sauvignon are capable of being aged in bottle with decent results for about one to three years. The sparkling wines are made in the light, fresh style of Italian *spumantes,* and are extremely popular with Aurora's bus-loads of visitors, but they seem to lack the balance of Aurora's best still wines.

below A Brazil nut pod is the size of a human head and can hold two or three dozen nuts.

Chandon do Brasil (2)

Garibaldi

chandon@redesul.com.br

Champagne producer Moët & Chandon's Brazilian outpost makes sparkling wines to a very high standard (*see also* Chandon Argentina, p.127). Champagne gets its sparkle when a still wine is given a second fermentation in a sealed bottle. However, Chandon's Brazilian sparkling wines are given their fizz in a slightly different manner. They are put through a second fermentation in large sealed tanks before being bottled using pressure pumps. This "tank method" of making sparkling wine generally gives the wine slightly bigger bubbles than the traditional bottle-fermentation method used in Champagne does. Chandon do Brasil's classic sparkler, Chandon Brut, has a green-gold colour, subtle, fresh bread aromas, and an uplifting, clean aftertaste. It is suitable for drinking on its own. Despite its dried fig and apricot sweetness, the slightly sweeter Chandon Demi-Sec tastes remarkably fresh. The appealing, sweet-tasting and slightly pink Passion is made from Muscat grapes purchased from Miolo's vineyards in the equatorial Vale de São Francisco. The top sparkling wine, a dry white called Excellence, is made from Pinot Noir and Chardonnay grapes that are grown in Chandon do Brasil's own vineyards in Rio Grande do Sul's Serra Gaúcha hills. Refreshing citrus and crystallized-fruit flavours combine in a serious, full-bodied, elegant wine. A newly developed sparkling red wine, called Chandon Rouge, is aimed at younger, female drinkers. It is full of slightly sweet strawberry and cherry fruit. Chandon's French winemaker, Philippe Mevel, grew up on a cattle and potato farm in Brittany, and came to South America when Moët & Chandon offered him a chance of doing his military service there. "You'd be thought of as mad in France if you tried to make a sparkling red Champagne, but people here are always ready to try something new. Brazil is a great place to make sparkling wine," he says. The quality of his sparkling wines is liquid proof.

De Lantier (3)

Garibaldi
Tel: (+55) 054 462 1566
De Lantier is part of the Bacardi-Martini empire and produces vermouths (which are hugely popular in Brazil) and wine. The best wines the company produces are sparkling, and are sold under the De Gréville label. Grapes are purchased from growers in Rio Grande do Sul. Weed killers are not used on the vineyards, which encourages weeds and flowers to grow between the vines. The vegetation between the vines soaks up the quite heavy rainfall that often falls around harvest in this region, thus preventing the grapes from becoming too dilute. De Lantier's unoaked Chardonnay shows clear citrus flavours, but red wines made from Merlot,

Cabernet Franc, and Cabernet Sauvignon are more consistent, leaving pleasant aftertastes of red fruit.

Miolo (4)

Vale dos Vinhedos
Tel: (+54) 459 1233;
miolo@miolo.com.br
The Miolo family left Italy in the late nineteenth century and settled in Brazil to grow wine grapes. In 1990, the family built their own winery in Bento Gonçalves. The Miolo's vineyards stretch from the Vale de São Francisco in Pernambuco in the north, to Bagé, near the border with Uruguay, in the south. The wines are continually improving in quality, with the still wines, especially the reds, more consistent than either still whites or sparkling wines (some of Miolo's grapes are sold to Chandon do Brasil, *see* above). A dry white wine blended from Riesling, Chardonnay, Sauvignon Blanc, and Semillon shows appealing freshness and body. A Syrah called TerraNova, the grapes for which come from the hot Vale de São Francisco vineyards, shows a thick, heavy texture and firm, spicy fruit. Miolo is one of Brazil's fastest-growing, and most-improved, wineries of recent years.

Valduga (5)

Linha Leopoldina, Vale dos Vinhedos
Tel: (+54) 453 3122;
valduga@casavalduga.com.br
The Valduga family have two wineries and two vineyards around

Garibaldi in the Serra Gaúcha hills. From the outside, the newer winery looks like a cross between Colditz and Disneyland, but don't let appearances put you off. The inside is finished with stained glass and wood, and has the most up-to-date visitor and wine-tasting facilities in Brazil, including a restaurant and extensive accommodation for tourists. Valduga's still wines are among Brazil's best, with white wines made from Chardonnay and red wines made from Cabernet Franc and Merlot particularly noteworthy. Valduga's sparkling wines, made from Pinot Noir and Chardonnay, show plenty of body, with a crisp, "oily" feel more suited to drinking with food than on their own.

Velho Museu (6)

Caixas do Sul
Tel: (+54) 212 1377;
velhomuseu@velho.com.br
Jean-Louis Carrau owns this newly developed organic vineyard and winery near Santana do Livramento on the Uruguyan border (Carrau's brothers run the Cerro Chapeu vineyards on the Uruguayan side of the border, *see* p.166). Velho Museu's rather oaky Cabernet Sauvignon/Merlot red blend will gain in colour and complexity as the vines, which are still young, age. The pick of the wines so far are two lightly aromatic dry whites, one made from Gewurztraminer, the other a creamy Semillon.

peru

Spain's conquest of the Americas involved the defeat of two empires: the Aztecs of Mexico (by Hernán Cortés) and the Incas of Peru (by Francisco Pizarro). Peru's Inca trail, via the town of Cusco, leads to Machu Picchu, South America's most dramatic archaeological site, and one of its most important tourist draws. While the Incas and Aztecs chose human sacrifice to honour their gods, the Spanish used bread and wine to celebrate their god via the sacrament of the Eucharist.

To this end, the Spanish planted vineyards in Peru, from around 1550. Peru gained South America's first cultivated vineyards and became Spain's bridgehead and organizational centre in South America. Wine-growing spread south from Peru, through Bolivia, and into Argentina, then from Mendoza west across the Andes, into Chile.

Peru's wine industry is a shadow of its former self. Peru has around 10,000 ha (24,700 acres) of vines, only twenty-five per cent of the area grown under the Spanish. Most vineyards lie close to the Pacific coast. Table grapes dominate vineyards around Ancash and Trujillo, north of the capital city, Lima. South of Lima, around Arequipa, Moquegua, and as far south

below Lack of money for investment, and low labour costs, mean there is little incentive to switch from hand-picking to expensive machinery.

as Tacna on the (disputed) border with Chile, grapes are largely used for Pisco, Peru's national drink. Pisco takes its name from the run-down port of Pisco, 235 km (146 miles) south of Lima, and has been produced in Peru since about 1651. Pisco exports took off 200 years later, during the California Gold Rush, as supply ships on their way north from Cape Horn would stop in Pisco to take on stocks of the spirit destined for the miners.

Although Peru's coastal vineyards benefit from cooling Pacific breezes, wine producers endure harsh natural conditions for wine production. Coastal sea mist (*garúa*) encourages mildew, and the vines need to be sprayed regularly with sulphur dust to prevent fungal diseases. Rainfall is virtually non-existent, but underground aquifers, or rivers flowing from higher ground inland, provide water for irrigation. Uncultivated areas around some vineyards have turned into desert, and warm winters mean that vines never properly rest during winter (dormancy is necessary for vine longevity).

Peru's wine producers must also endure continuing political instability and corruption. The legacy left by early 1970s land redistribution programmes broke up many of Peru's largest wine estates. The quality of Peru's wines is generally poor, with basic winemaking faults such as oxidation and dirtiness a frequent feature despite strong foreign (usually French) winemaking influence. An undemanding local market and only sporadic export sales mean there is little incentive to invest. Visit Peru for the Inca trail, but don't go just for the wine.

Peruvian Producers

OCUCAJE

Eight brothers from the Rubini family own the Ocucaje winery, some thirty-six kilometres (twenty-two miles) south of Ica, not far from the Pacific. Ocucaje is a desert oasis. It lost its vineyards to land reforms in the 1970s, so the wines, and its better-than-average Pisco, are made from purchased grapes. Fortified wines in the style of port and sherry show oxidized, but not unpleasant, flavours of old varnish and tar.

SANTIAGO QUEIROLO

Peru's shabby side-streets are best navigated by local taxi (agree the fare before you get in); you'll need to hire one to visit Santiago Queirolo. Wine is dispensed in bulk, bottle, and Tetrapak from behind a wooden counter to throngs of eager customers. The vineyards are located in the Cañete Valley, midway between Lima and Ica. A wide range of grapes is planted, including Malbec, Merlot, and Barbera for red wines, Santiago Queirolo's most palatable. Aromatic Piscos are also produced. Wholesome Peruvian meals are available from the winery's El Bolivariano restaurant.

TABERNERO

Tabernero owns four vineyards within a fifteen-minute drive of its winery in the Chincha Valley, 200 km (124 miles) south of Lima. Cabernet Sauvignon, Malbec (here called Malbeck), Chardonnay and Chenin Blanc (called Pineau de la Loire) are usually harvested by the final week in March. Blended red wines from Malbec and Merlot show ripe fruit buried under musty tones, while the Pisco shows a hint of rawness.

TACAMA

Tacama is Peru's only winery with an international reputation. Its pink, fortress-like winery is eight kilometres (five miles) northeast of the town of Ica, 300 km (186 miles) south of Lima along the Pan-American Highway. Tacama's owners, the Olaechea family, hire French winemakers from the old school of winemaking, so the wines show dusty rusticity. Cabernet Sauvignon and Merlot reds display cleaner flavours than Sauvignon Blanc whites. Sparkling whites from Chenin Blanc show a degree of freshness.

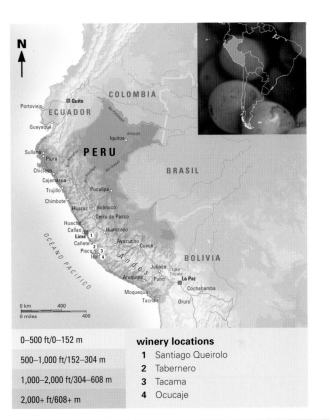

0–500 ft/0–152 m	**winery locations**
500–1,000 ft/152–304 m	1 Santiago Queirolo
1,000–2,000 ft/304–608 m	2 Tabernero
2,000+ ft/608+ m	3 Tacama
	4 Ocucaje

notable producers

El Bolivariano
Pueblo Libre, Lima
Tel: (+511) 463 6333
Santiago Queirolo's winery restaurant serves up wholesome Peruvian dishes.

Ocucaje (4)
Carretera Panamericana, Ica province;
Tel: (+511) 034 408013
Fortified wines and decent Pisco are made from purchased grapes. The winery is owned by the Rubini brothers.

Santiago Queirolo (1)
Calle San Martín 1072
Pueblo Libre, Lima
Tel: (+511) 463 1008

Red wines, or the aromatic Pisco, are the best bets at this winery midway between Lima and Ica; it is popular with the local market.

Tabernero (2)
Chicha Alta, Ica
Tel: (+511) 034 261602
This winery south of Lima makes a range of red and white wines, as well as a Pisco.

Tacama (3)
Ica town, Ica province
Tel: (+51) 34 228394;
tacamai@terra.com.pe
The Oleacha family hire French winemakers and make red, white, and sparkling wines.

venezuela

The first South American travel guide I ever used advised: "Venezuelan wine is truly disgusting and dangerous. It should be avoided at all costs. Do not upset your friends by taking any home as presents." This advice may well be worth heeding for the significant number of "Venezuelan" wines made from imported grape juice (and perhaps other, less appealing – or, indeed, safe – ingredients). However, the advice should be ignored regarding Venezuela's one serious producer of estate wines, Bodegas Pomar.

Pomar is owned by Empresas Polar, a huge food and drink conglomerate whose main beer brand accounts for at least eighty per cent of Venezuela's total beer market (Venezuela has the highest per capita beer consumption in Latin America). Pomar's whitewashed winery is in the cattle town of Carora in the western Venezuelan state of Lara. Carora is a short drive from Barquisimeto airport, which is a forty minute flight from the Venezuelan capital, Caracas.

Pomar's wine project began in the 1980s when French investors and the University of Barquisimeto planted wine grapes to see if they would grow successfully in Venezuela. The country's tropical climate is more suited to table grape production, but Empresas Polar invested in the project, along with a partner, the French cognac producer Martell. The name "Pomar" (a conjuction of Polar and Martell) was eventually chosen for the wine. Today, the winery and vineyards are solely owned by Empresas Polar.

The Pomar winery has extensive barrel cellars and well-equipped winemaking and visitor facilities. Most visitors are Venezuelan, but foreign visitors connected with the country's oil business are increasing. Venezuela is the largest foreign supplier of oil to the USA, and the main oilfields at Lake Maracaibo are less than two hours' drive west of the winery. Pomar's

vineyards, at Altagracia, some twenty-four kilometres (fifteen miles) from the winery, endure desert conditions on arid foothills. Drip irrigation, rather than the more traditional flood irrigation, is used. The drip system allows vineyard managers to starve the vine of water to encourage winter dormancy, something which is difficult here because winters are warm.

Pomar's still white wines, made from Sauvignon Blanc and Chenin Blanc, show lush, fat flavours and mature quickly in bottle. These varieties are also used for increasingly good sparkling wines, made in a rich, apple-cider style with plenty of body. Red wines made from Bordeaux and Mediterranean varieties, including Merlot, Syrah, Grenache, and Tempranillo, are less successful than the whites. They lack colour, last only a few months in bottle, and are best enjoyed as the base material for sangría and Lambrusco-style blends,

above Vines which have been deliberately deprived of irrigation lose their leaves causing their grapes to shrivel and concentrate in the sun.

both of which are popular in Venezuela. Pomar is experimenting with growing vines on cooler, more mountainous sites to try to increase colour intensity in its red wines. Although Pomar's wines generally age quickly, for sheer originality, you are more likely to impress, rather than upset, your friends by bringing them home a bottle or two. Just make sure you drink it soon after landing.

Bodegas Pomar (1)
Caracas, Venezuela
Tel: (+58) 212 202 8906;
www.empresas-polar.com
Martell (Cognac) is a partner in this well-equipped winery, which has extensive cellars, as well as facilities for visitors. Red, white, and sparkling wines are made to a good standard.

index

Page numbers in *italic* refer to the illustrations